[redacted]

TOP SECRE

FIELD TEAM VICTOR 8
SPECIAL OPERATIONS

D1303873

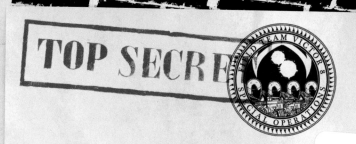

V-Wars
Crimson Queen

written by: JONATHAN MABERRY
art by: ALAN ROBINSON
colors by: JAY FOTOS
lettering by: ROBBIE ROBBINS
series editor: DAVID HEDGECOCK

[redacted]

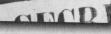

TOP SECRET

FIELD TEAM VICTOR 8 SPECIAL OPERATIONS

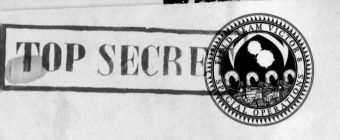

cover by: RYAN BROWN

collection edits by:
JUSTIN EISINGER & ALONZO SIMON

collection design: ROBBIE ROBBINS

PERSONAL and CONFIDENTIAL

LEVEL III CLEARANCE REQUIRED

- CDC confirmation pending.
- Melting Arctic ice possible origin point for release of the I1V1 virus.
- Virus triggering dormant genes from junk DNA, genes that once created vampires.
- Infection rates currently low but reports from major populations worldwide continue to come in.
- Without methods of containment, looking at a global pandemic of epic proportions.
- Characteristics of transformation vary and appear regionally based.Common theme appears to be unnatural and unstoppable hunger.

They are here.

They hide among us.

They hunt us.

They feed on us.

They ARE us.

.... end transmission

ISBN: 978-1-63140-063-6

17 16 15 14 1 2 3 4

IDW®
www.IDWPUBLISHING.com
IDW founded by Ted Adams, Alex Garner, Kris Oprisko, and Robbie Robbins

Ted Adams, CEO & Publisher
Greg Goldstein, President & COO
Robbie Robbins, EVP/Sr. Graphic Artist
Chris Ryall, Chief Creative Officer/Editor-in-Chief
Matthew Ruzicka, CPA, Chief Financial Officer
Alan Payne, VP of Sales
Dirk Wood, VP of Marketing
Lorelei Bunjes, VP of Digital Services
Jeff Webber, VP of Digital Publishing & Business Development

Facebook: **facebook.com/idwpublishing**
Twitter: **@idwpublishing**
YouTube: **youtube.com/idwpublishing**
Instagram: **instagram.com/idwpublishing**
deviantART: **idwpublishing.deviantart.com**
Pinterest: **pinterest.com/idwpublishing/idw-staff-faves**

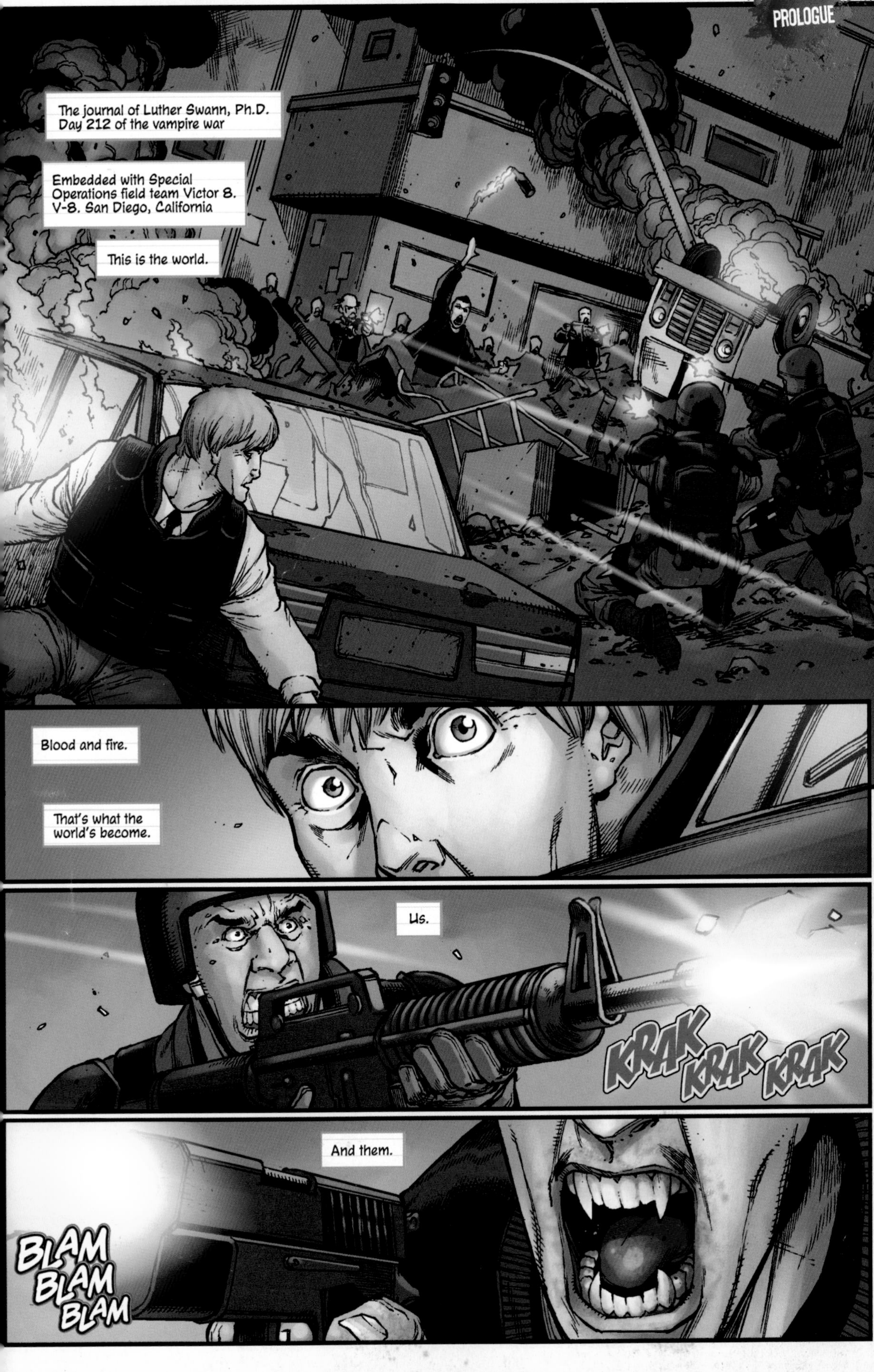
The journal of Luther Swann, Ph.D.
Day 212 of the vampire war
Embedded with Special Operations field team Victor 8. V-8. San Diego, California
This is the world.
Blood and fire.
That's what the world's become.
Us.
KRAK KRAK KRAK
And them.
BLAM BLAM BLAM

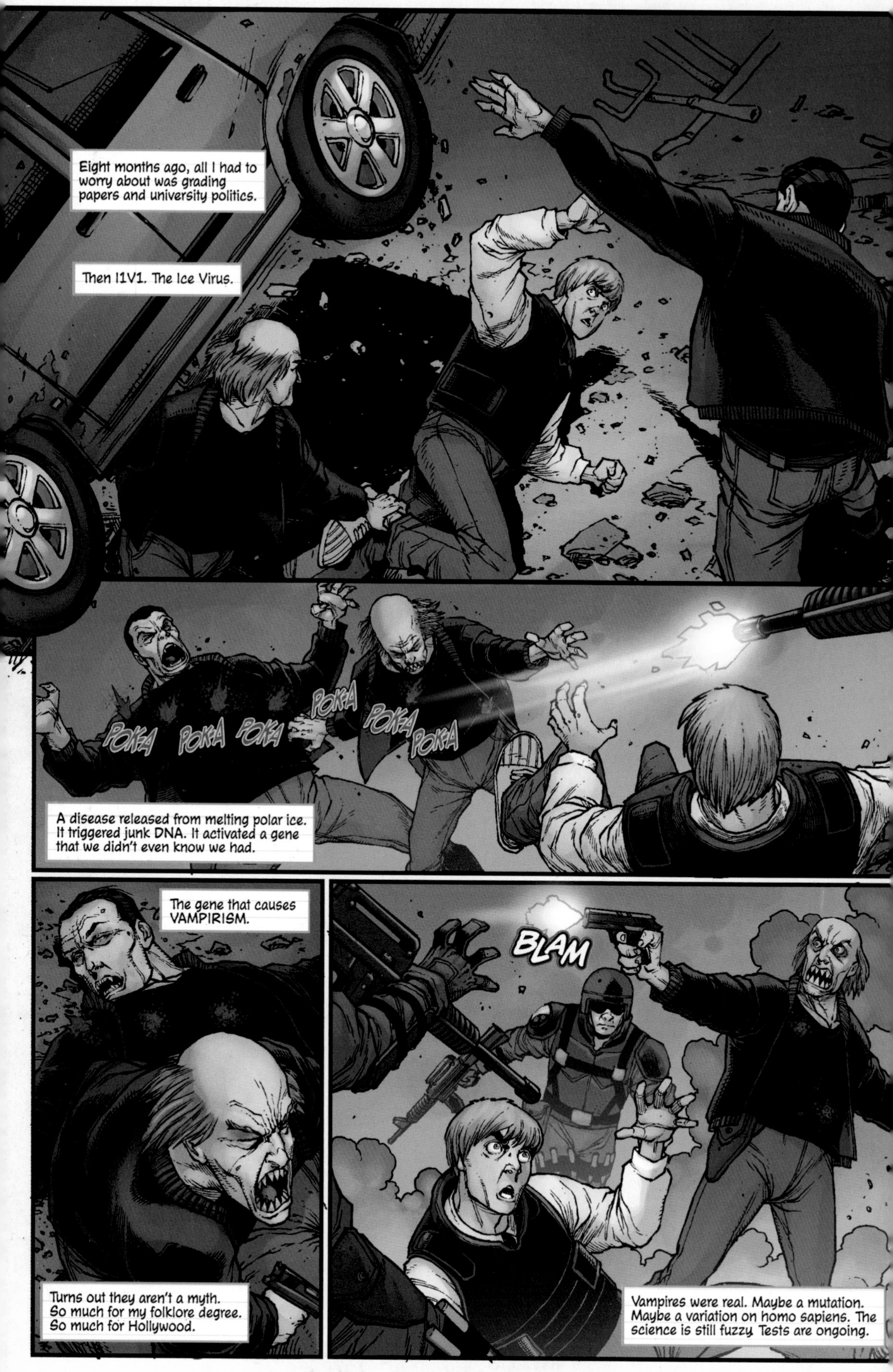
Eight months ago, all I had to worry about was grading papers and university politics.
Then I1V1. The Ice Virus.
POKA POKA POKA POKA POKA POKA
A disease released from melting polar ice. It triggered junk DNA. It activated a gene that we didn't even know we had.
The gene that causes VAMPIRISM.
Turns out they aren't a myth. So much for my folklore degree. So much for Hollywood.
BLAM
Vampires were real. Maybe a mutation. Maybe a variation on homo sapiens. The science is still fuzzy. Tests are ongoing.

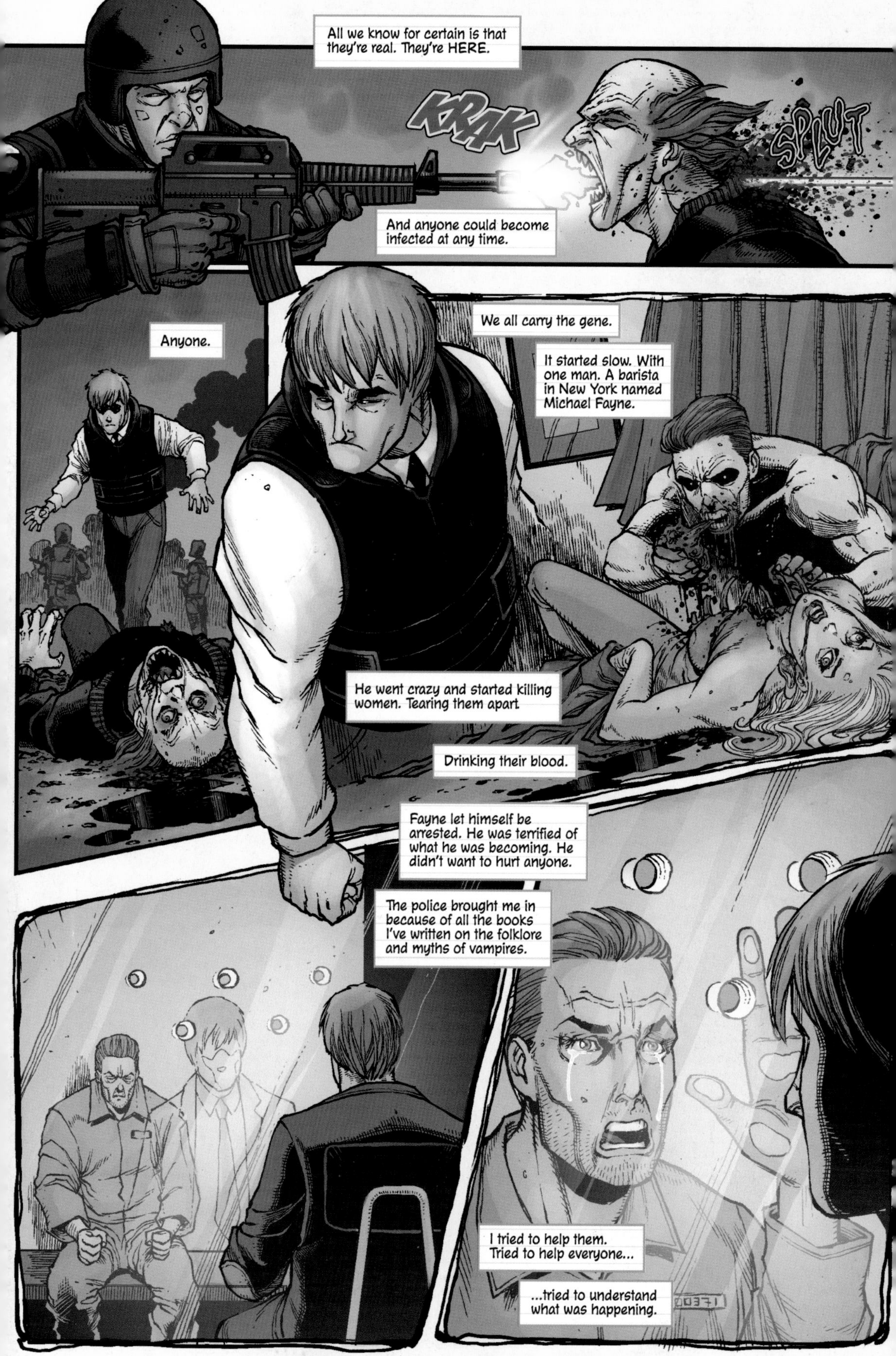
All we know for certain is that they're real. They're HERE.
KRAK
SPLUT
And anyone could become infected at any time.
Anyone.
We all carry the gene.
It started slow. With one man. A barista in New York named Michael Fayne.
He went crazy and started killing women. Tearing them apart
Drinking their blood.
Fayne let himself be arrested. He was terrified of what he was becoming. He didn't want to hurt anyone.
The police brought me in because of all the books I've written on the folklore and myths of vampires.
I tried to help them. Tried to help everyone...
...tried to understand what was happening.

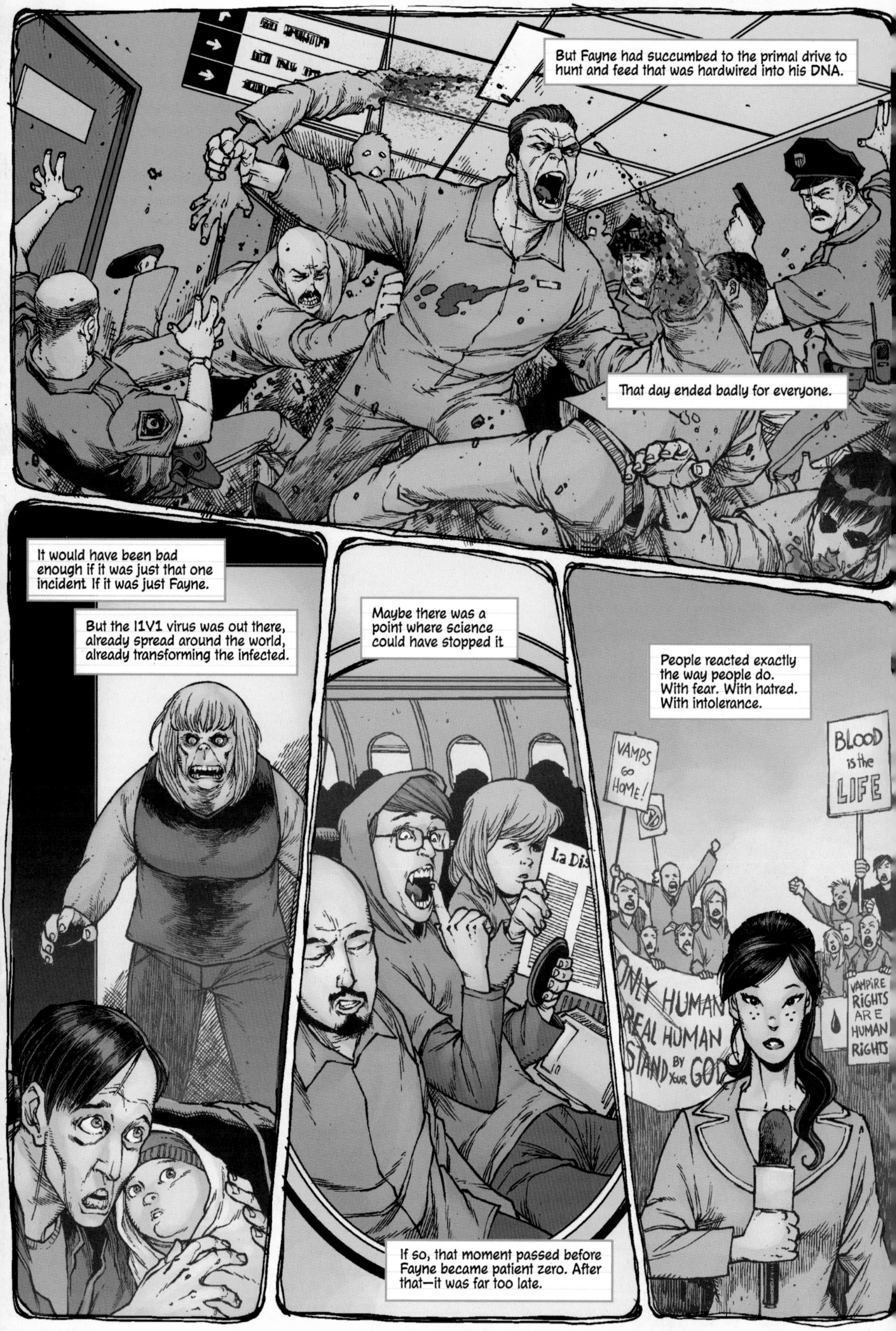
But Fayne had succumbed to the primal drive to hunt and feed that was hardwired into his DNA.
That day ended badly for everyone.
It would have been bad enough if it was just that one incident. If it was just Fayne.
But the I1V1 virus was out there, already spread around the world, already transforming the infected.
Maybe there was a point where science could have stopped it.
If so, that moment passed before Fayne became patient zero. After that—it was far too late.
People reacted exactly the way people do. With fear. With hatred. With intolerance.
VAMPS GO HOME!
BLOOD is the LIFE
VAMPIRE RIGHTS ARE HUMAN RIGHTS

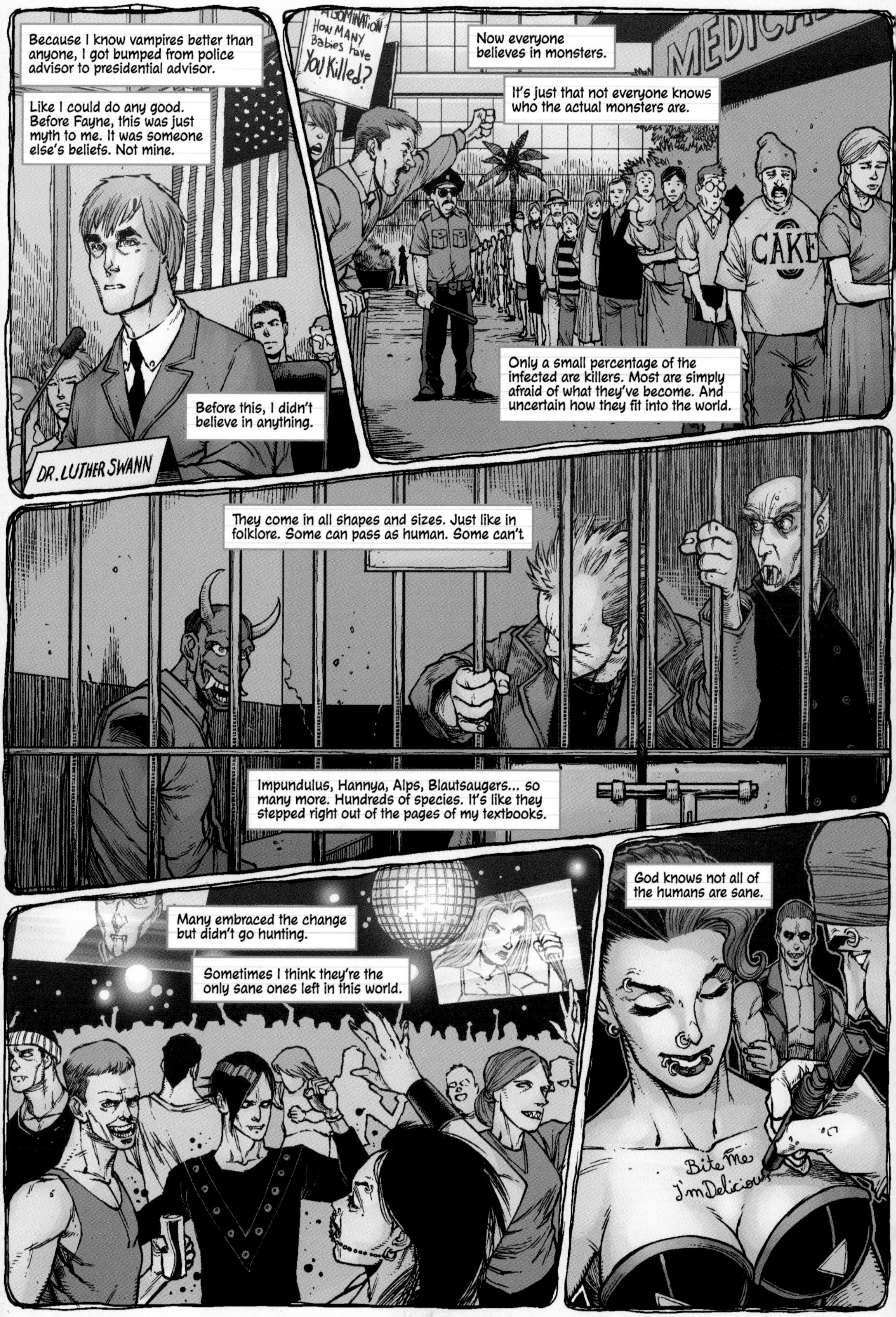
Because I know vampires better than anyone, I got bumped from police advisor to presidential advisor.
Like I could do any good. Before Fayne, this was just myth to me. It was someone else's beliefs. Not mine.
Before this, I didn't believe in anything.
DR. LUTHER SWANN
ABOMINATION How MANY Babies have YOU Killed?
Now everyone believes in monsters.
It's just that not everyone knows who the actual monsters are.
CAKE
Only a small percentage of the infected are killers. Most are simply afraid of what they've become. And uncertain how they fit into the world.
They come in all shapes and sizes. Just like in folklore. Some can pass as human. Some can't.
Impundulus, Hannya, Alps, Blautsaugers... so many more. Hundreds of species. It's like they stepped right out of the pages of my textbooks.
Many embraced the change but didn't go hunting.
Sometimes I think they're the only sane ones left in this world.
God knows not all of the humans are sane.
Bite Me I'm Delicious

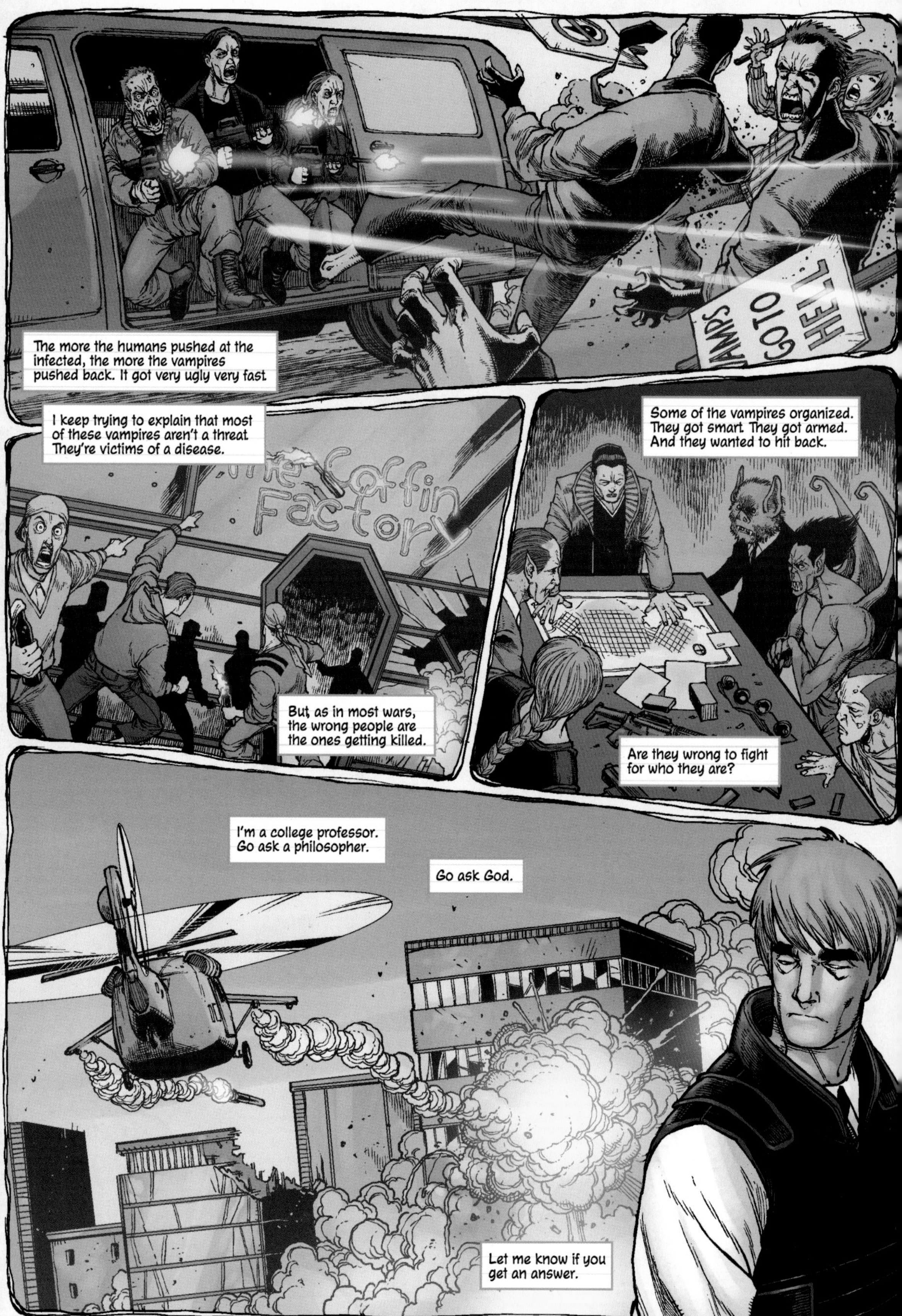
The more the humans pushed at the infected, the more the vampires pushed back. It got very ugly very fast.
VAMPS GO TO HELL
I keep trying to explain that most of these vampires aren't a threat. They're victims of a disease.
The Coffin Factory
But, as in most wars, the wrong people are the ones getting killed.
Some of the vampires organized. They got smart. They got armed. And they wanted to hit back.
Are they wrong to fight for who they are?
I'm a college professor. Go ask a philosopher.
Go ask God.
Let me know if you get an answer.

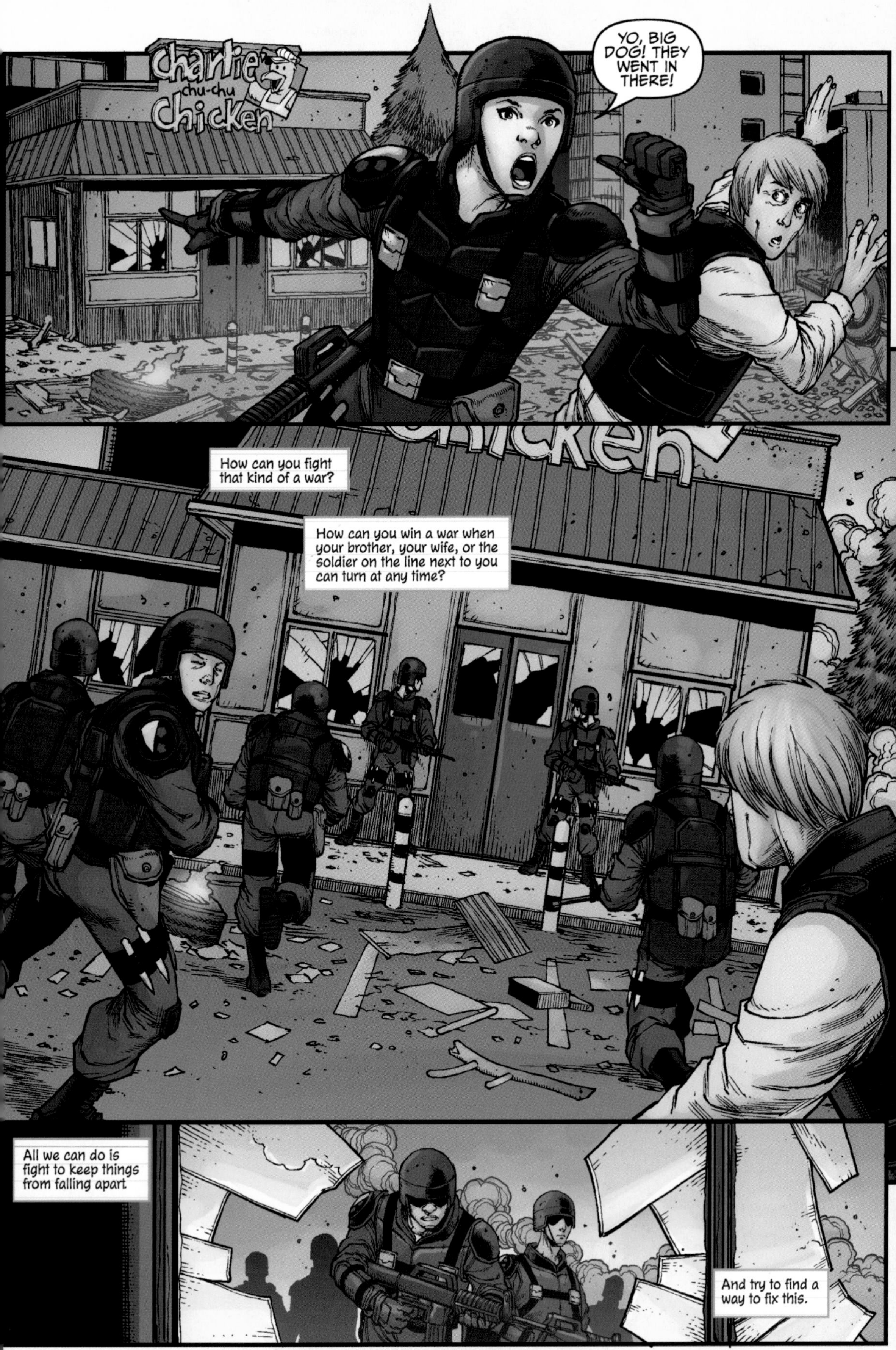
Charlie chu-chu Chicken
YO, BIG DOG! THEY WENT IN THERE!
Chicken
How can you fight that kind of a war?
How can you win a war when your brother, your wife, or the soldier on the line next to you can turn at any time?
All we can do is fight to keep things from falling apart
And try to find a way to fix this.

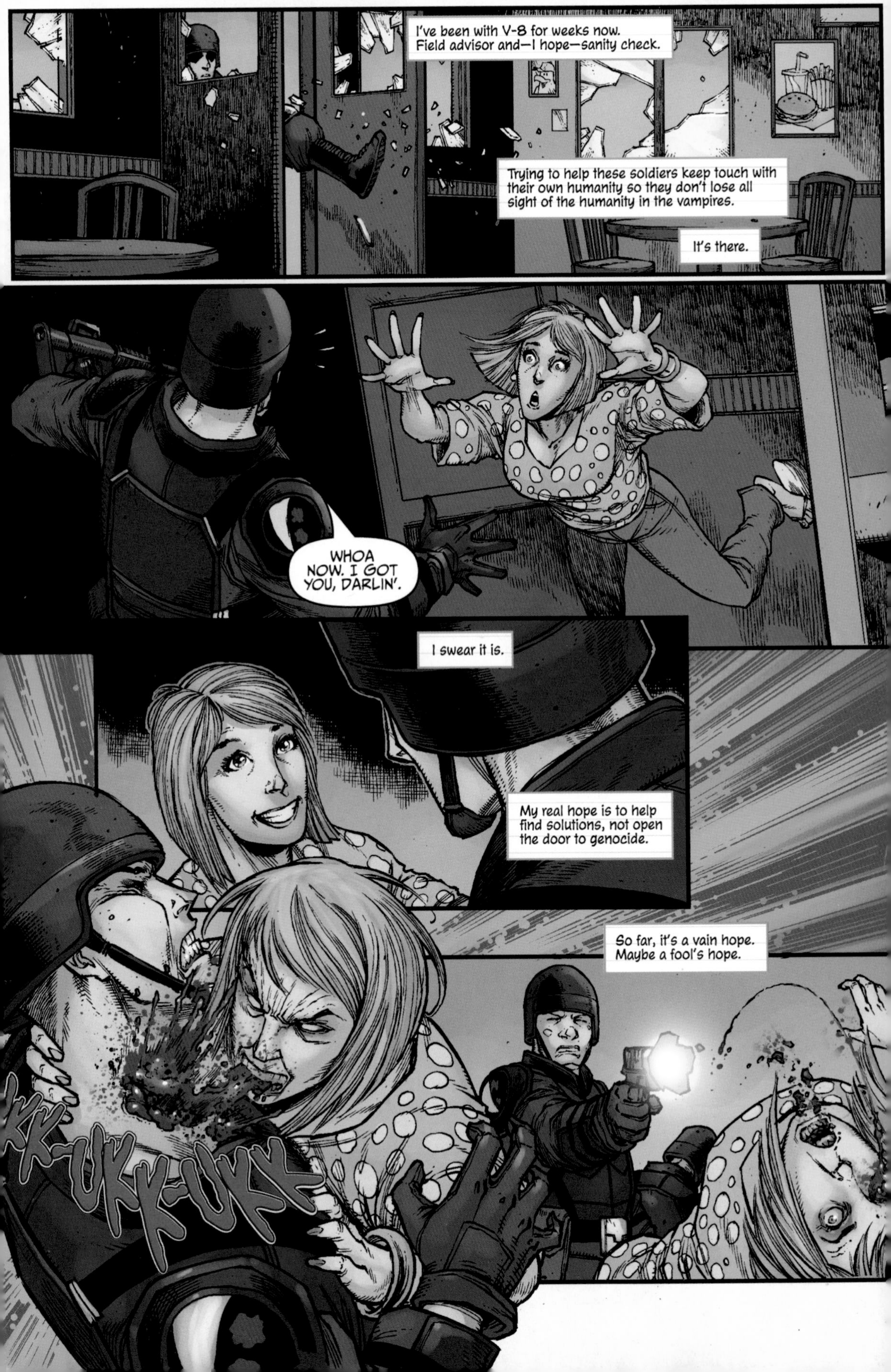
I've been with V-8 for weeks now.
Field advisor and—I hope—sanity check.
Trying to help these soldiers keep touch with their own humanity so they don't lose all sight of the humanity in the vampires.
It's there.
WHOA NOW. I GOT YOU, DARLIN'.
I swear it is.
My real hope is to help find solutions, not open the door to genocide.
So far, it's a vain hope. Maybe a fool's hope.
KK-UKK-UKK

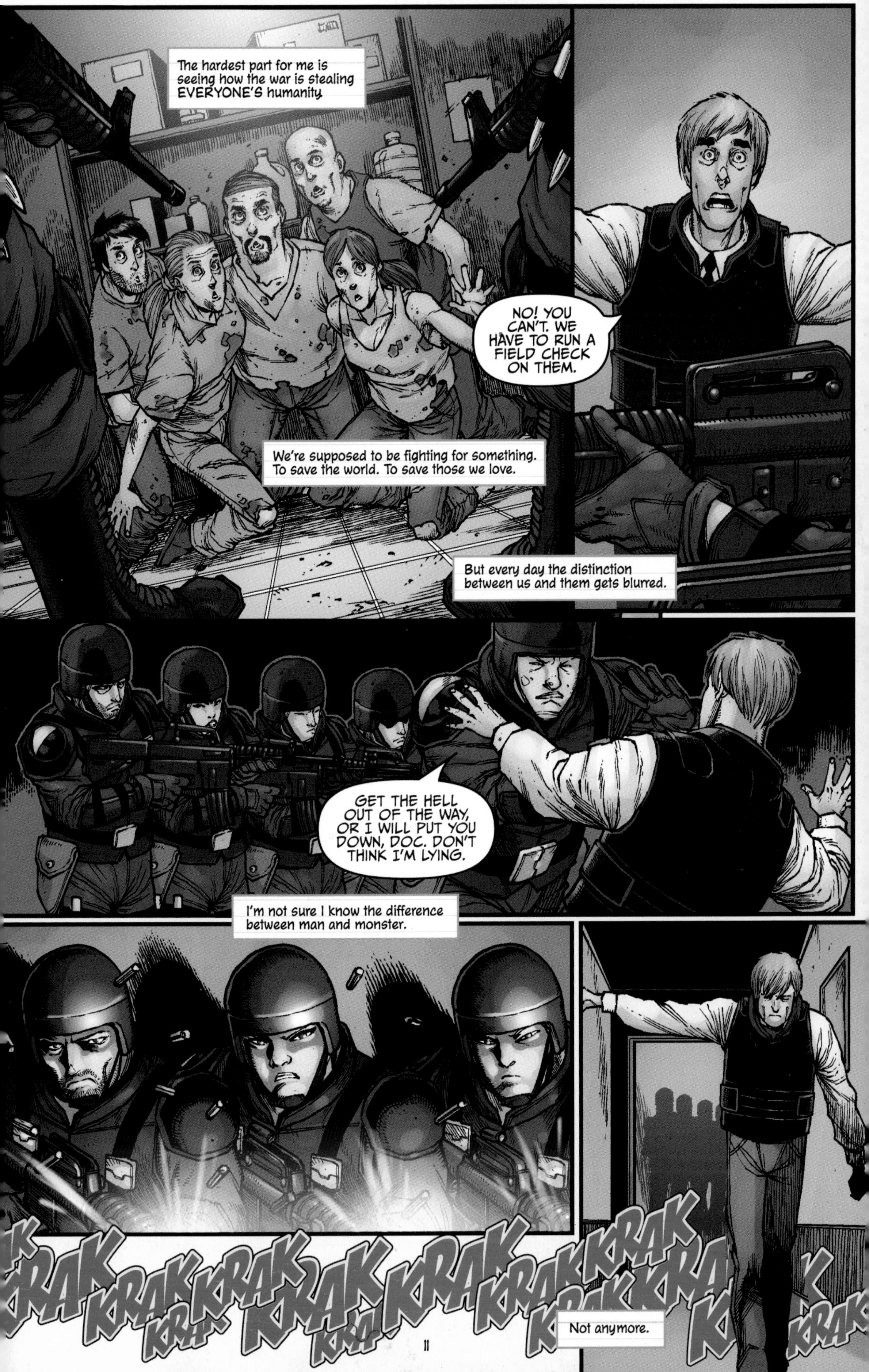
The hardest part for me is seeing how the war is stealing EVERYONE'S humanity.
NO! YOU CAN'T. WE HAVE TO RUN A FIELD CHECK ON THEM.
We're supposed to be fighting for something. To save the world. To save those we love.
But every day the distinction between us and them gets blurred.
GET THE HELL OUT OF THE WAY, OR I WILL PUT YOU DOWN, DOC. DON'T THINK I'M LYING.
I'm not sure I know the difference between man and monster.
KRAK KRAK KRAK KRAK KRAK KRAK KRAK KRAK KRAK KRAK
Not anymore.

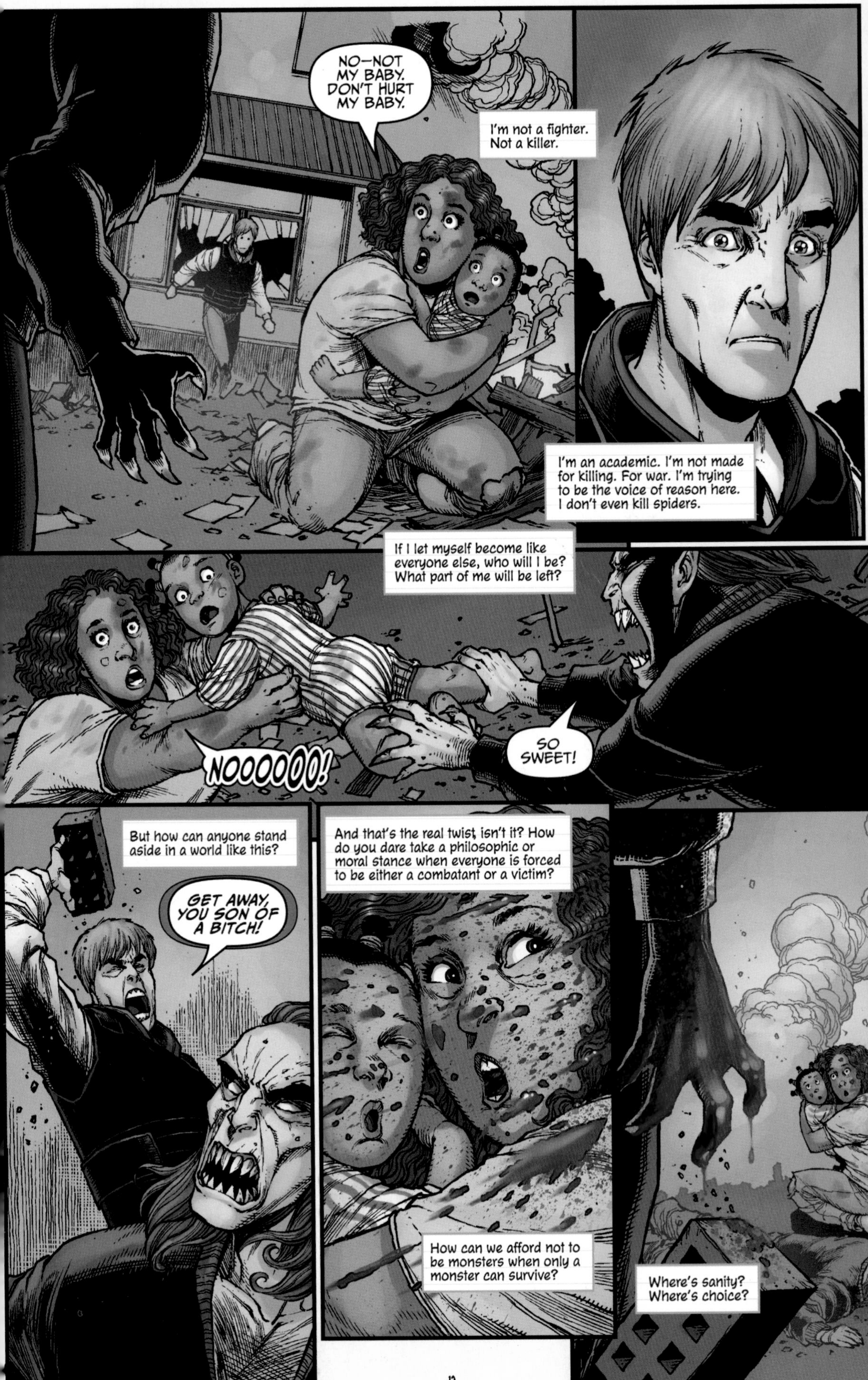

NO—NOT MY BABY. DON'T HURT MY BABY.
I'm not a fighter. Not a killer.
I'm an academic. I'm not made for killing. For war. I'm trying to be the voice of reason here. I don't even kill spiders.
If I let myself become like everyone else, who will I be? What part of me will be left?
NOOOOOO!
SO SWEET!
But how can anyone stand aside in a world like this?
GET AWAY, YOU SON OF A BITCH!
And that's the real twist, isn't it? How do you dare take a philosophic or moral stance when everyone is forced to be either a combatant or a victim?
How can we afford not to be monsters when only a monster can survive?
Where's sanity? Where's choice?

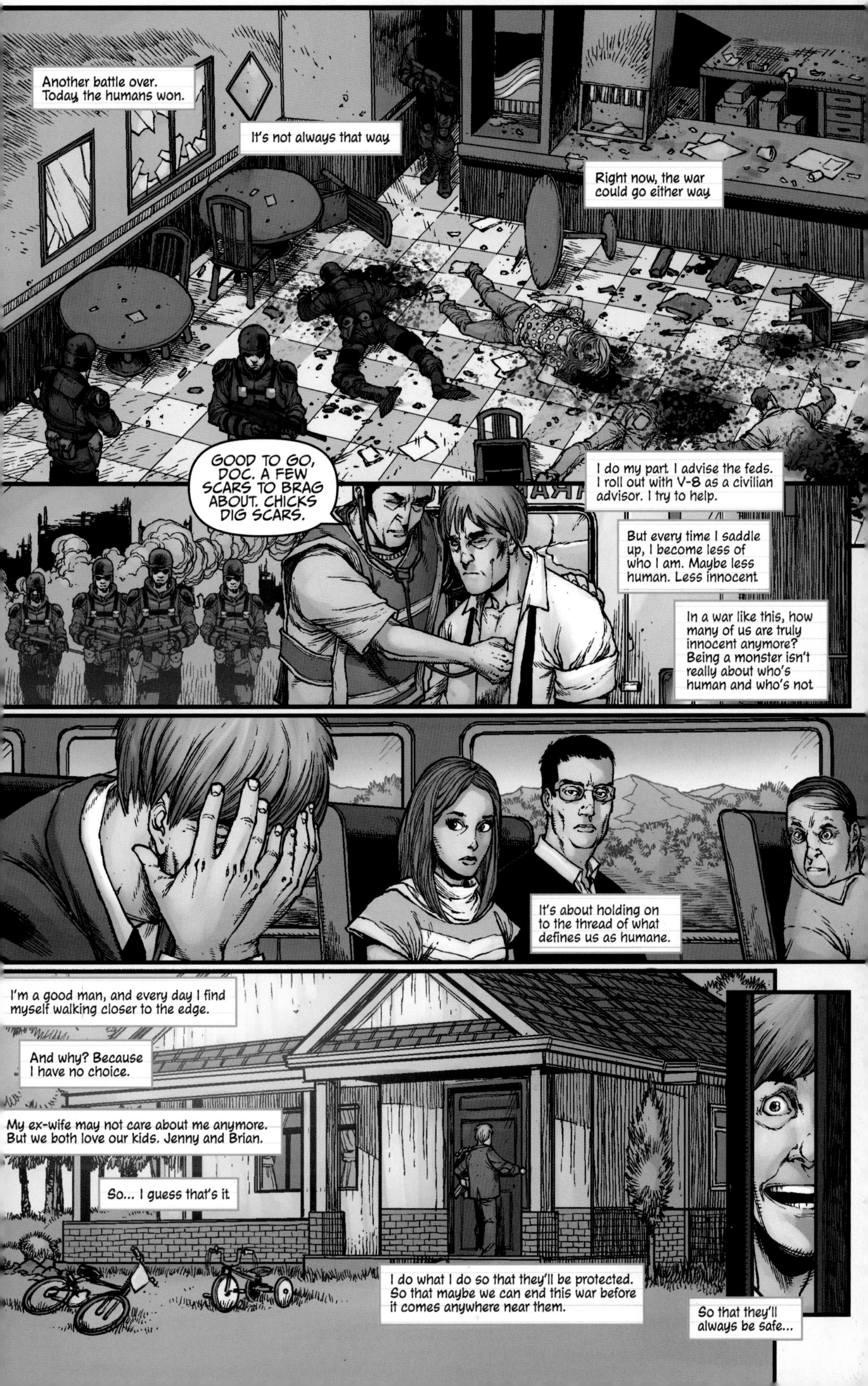

Another battle over.
Today the humans won.
It's not always that way
Right now, the war
could go either way
GOOD TO GO, DOC. A FEW SCARS TO BRAG ABOUT. CHICKS DIG SCARS.
I do my part. I advise the feds. I roll out with V-8 as a civilian advisor. I try to help.
But every time I saddle up, I become less of who I am. Maybe less human. Less innocent.
In a war like this, how many of us are truly innocent anymore? Being a monster isn't really about who's human and who's not
It's about holding on to the thread of what defines us as humane.
I'm a good man, and every day I find myself walking closer to the edge.
And why? Because I have no choice.
My ex-wife may not care about me anymore. But we both love our kids. Jenny and Brian.
So... I guess that's it
I do what I do so that they'll be protected. So that maybe we can end this war before it comes anywhere near them.
So that they'll always be safe...

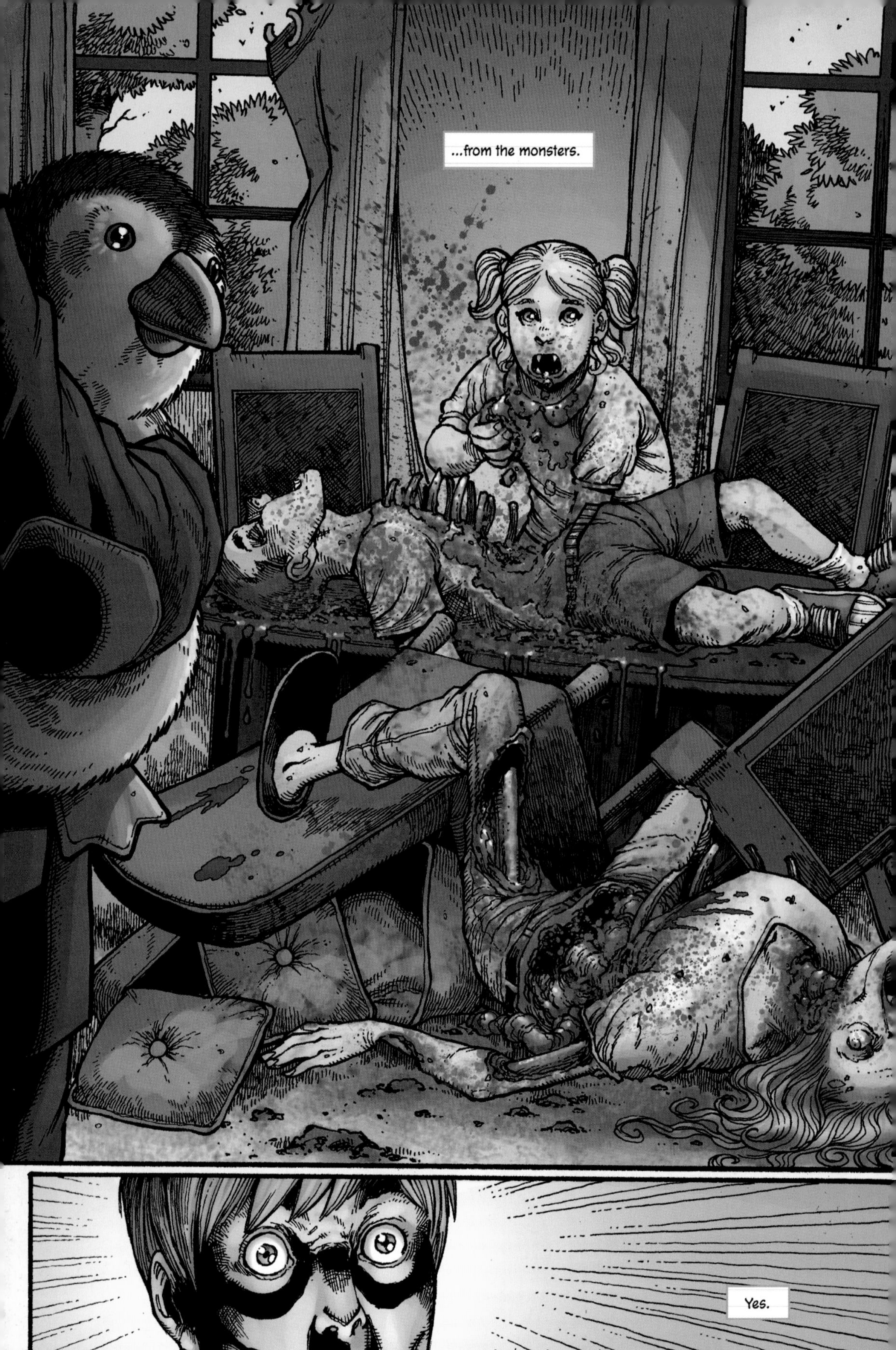
...from the monsters.

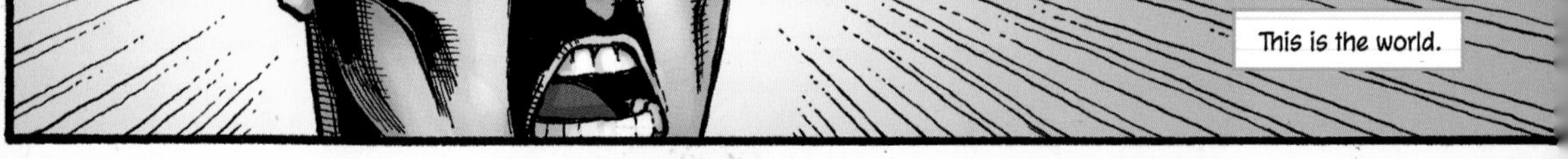
Yes.
This is the world.

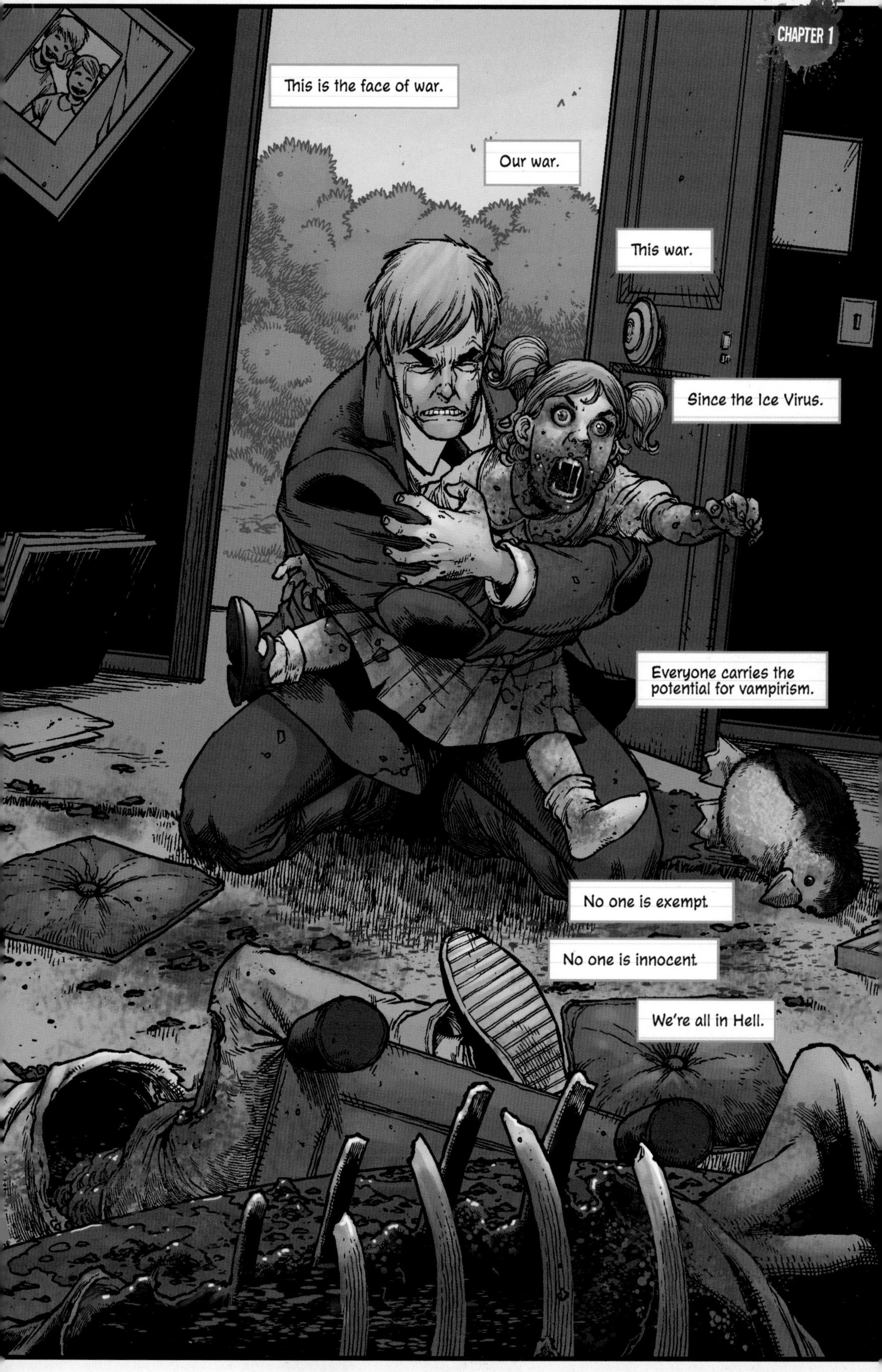
This is the face of war.
Our war.
This war.
Since the Ice Virus.
Everyone carries the potential for vampirism.
No one is exempt.
No one is innocent.
We're all in Hell.

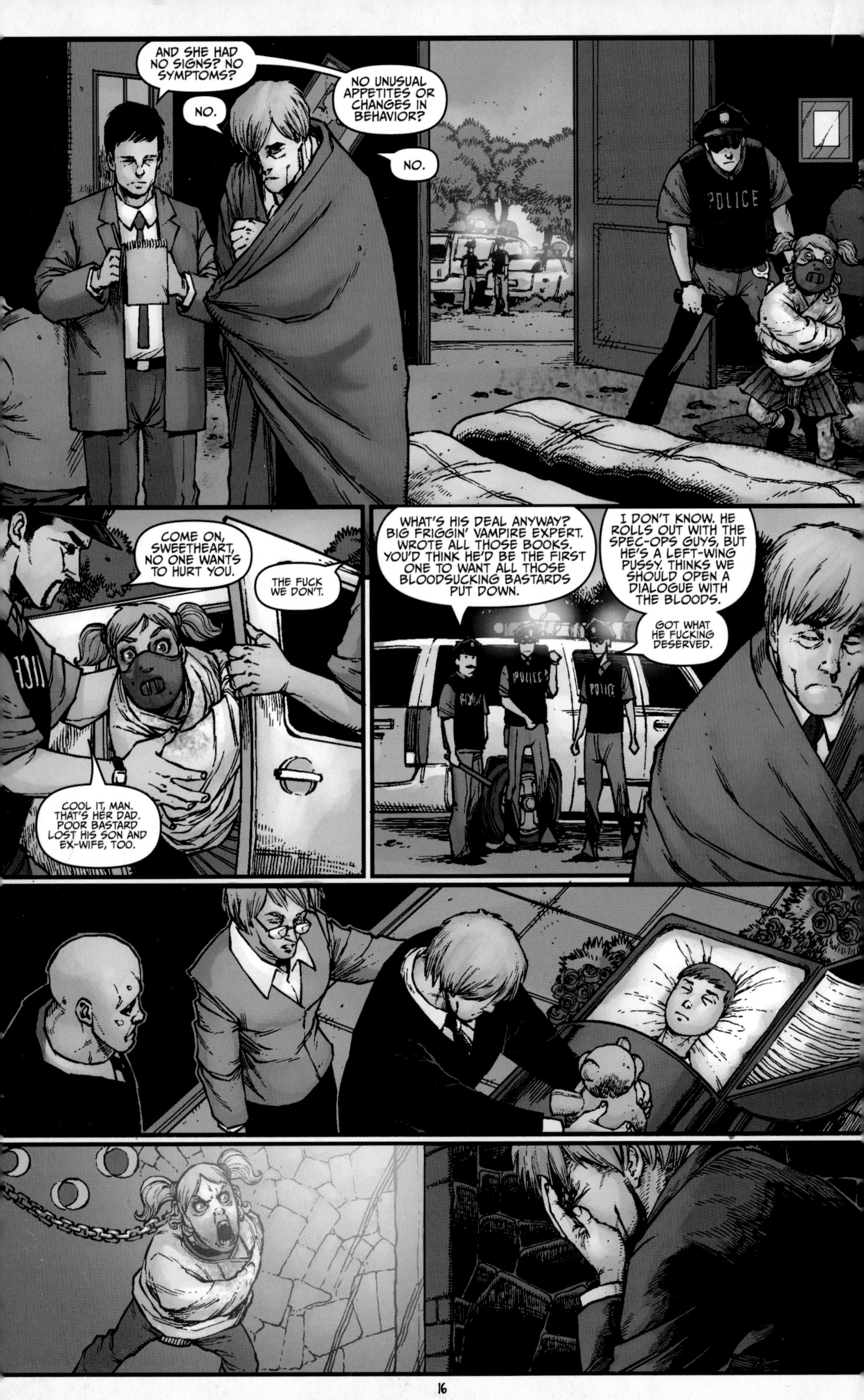
AND SHE HAD NO SIGNS? NO SYMPTOMS?
NO.
NO UNUSUAL APPETITES OR CHANGES IN BEHAVIOR?
NO.
POLICE
COME ON, SWEETHEART, NO ONE WANT'S TO HURT YOU.
THE FUCK WE DON'T.
COOL IT, MAN. THAT'S HER DAD. POOR BASTARD LOST HIS SON AND EX-WIFE, TOO.
WHAT'S HIS DEAL ANYWAY? BIG FRIGGIN' VAMPIRE EXPERT. WROTE ALL THOSE BOOKS. YOU'D THINK HE'D BE THE FIRST ONE TO WANT ALL THOSE BLOODSUCKING BASTARDS PUT DOWN.
I DON'T KNOW. HE ROLLS OUT WITH THE SPEC-OPS GUYS, BUT HE'S A LEFT-WING PUSSY. THINKS WE SHOULD OPEN A DIALOGUE WITH THE BLOODS.
GOT WHAT HE FUCKING DESERVED.
POLICE
POLICE

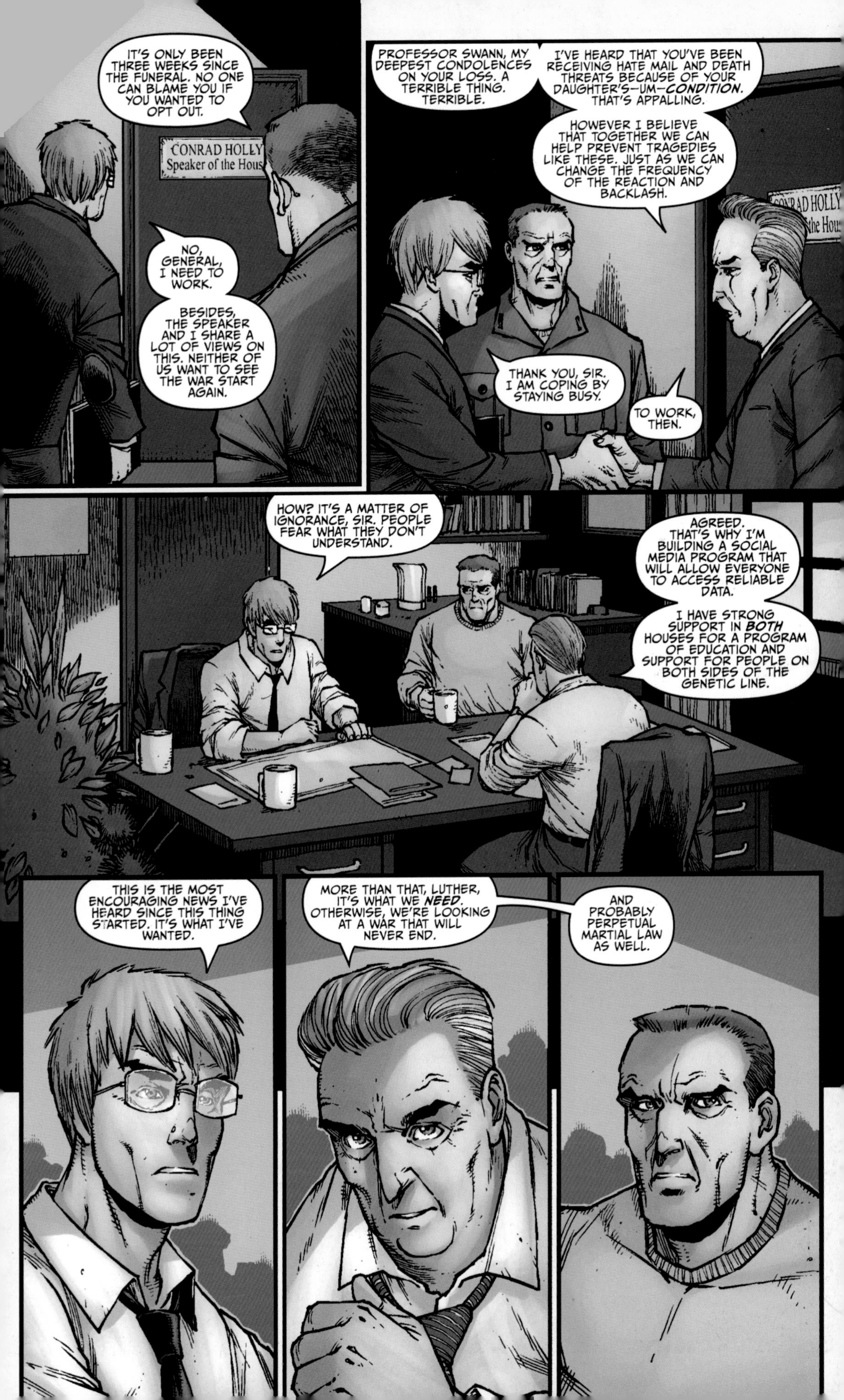
IT'S ONLY BEEN THREE WEEKS SINCE THE FUNERAL. NO ONE CAN BLAME YOU IF YOU WANTED TO OPT OUT.
CONRAD HOLLY Speaker of the Hous
NO, GENERAL, I NEED TO WORK.
BESIDES, THE SPEAKER AND I SHARE A LOT OF VIEWS ON THIS. NEITHER OF US WANT TO SEE THE WAR START AGAIN.
PROFESSOR SWANN, MY DEEPEST CONDOLENCES ON YOUR LOSS. A TERRIBLE THING. TERRIBLE.
I'VE HEARD THAT YOU'VE BEEN RECEIVING HATE MAIL AND DEATH THREATS BECAUSE OF YOUR DAUGHTER'S—UM—*CONDITION*. THAT'S APPALLING.
HOWEVER I BELIEVE THAT TOGETHER WE CAN HELP PREVENT TRAGEDIES LIKE THESE. JUST AS WE CAN CHANGE THE FREQUENCY OF THE REACTION AND BACKLASH.
THANK YOU, SIR. I AM COPING BY STAYING BUSY.
TO WORK, THEN.
HOW? IT'S A MATTER OF IGNORANCE, SIR. PEOPLE FEAR WHAT THEY DON'T UNDERSTAND.
AGREED. THAT'S WHY I'M BUILDING A SOCIAL MEDIA PROGRAM THAT WILL ALLOW EVERYONE TO ACCESS RELIABLE DATA.
I HAVE STRONG SUPPORT IN ***BOTH*** HOUSES FOR A PROGRAM OF EDUCATION AND SUPPORT FOR PEOPLE ON BOTH SIDES OF THE GENETIC LINE.
THIS IS THE MOST ENCOURAGING NEWS I'VE HEARD SINCE THIS THING STARTED. IT'S WHAT I'VE WANTED.
MORE THAN THAT, LUTHER, IT'S WHAT WE ***NEED***. OTHERWISE, WE'RE LOOKING AT A WAR THAT WILL NEVER END.
AND PROBABLY PERPETUAL MARTIAL LAW AS WELL.

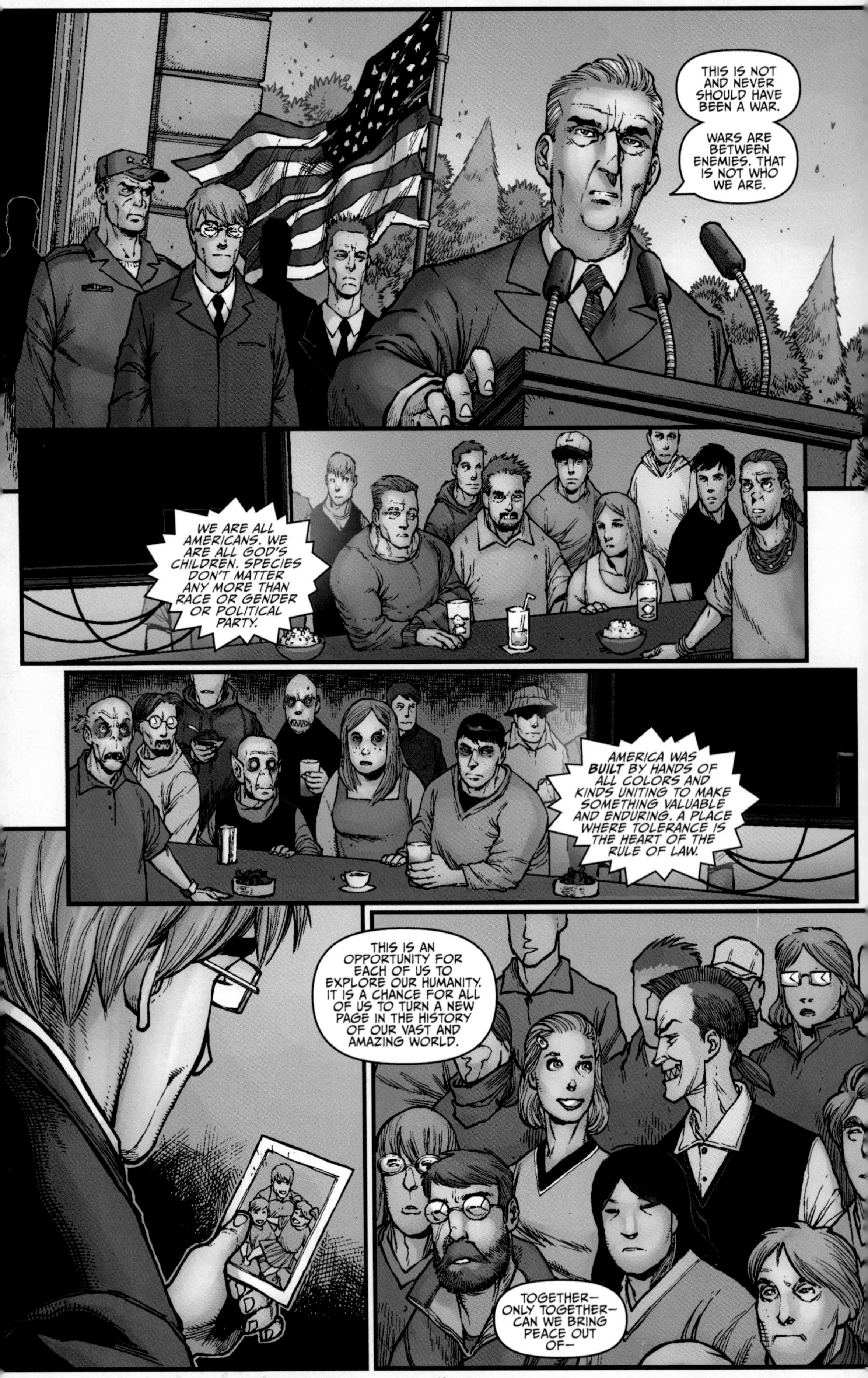

CHAPTER 1

THIS IS NOT AND NEVER SHOULD HAVE BEEN A WAR.
WARS ARE BETWEEN ENEMIES. THAT IS NOT WHO WE ARE.
WE ARE ALL AMERICANS. WE ARE ALL GOD'S CHILDREN. SPECIES DON'T MATTER ANY MORE THAN RACE OR GENDER OR POLITICAL PARTY.
AMERICA WAS BUILT BY HANDS OF ALL COLORS AND KINDS UNITING TO MAKE SOMETHING VALUABLE AND ENDURING. A PLACE WHERE TOLERANCE IS THE HEART OF THE RULE OF LAW.
THIS IS AN OPPORTUNITY FOR EACH OF US TO EXPLORE OUR HUMANITY. IT IS A CHANCE FOR ALL OF US TO TURN A NEW PAGE IN THE HISTORY OF OUR VAST AND AMAZING WORLD.
TOGETHER— ONLY TOGETHER— CAN WE BRING PEACE OUT OF—

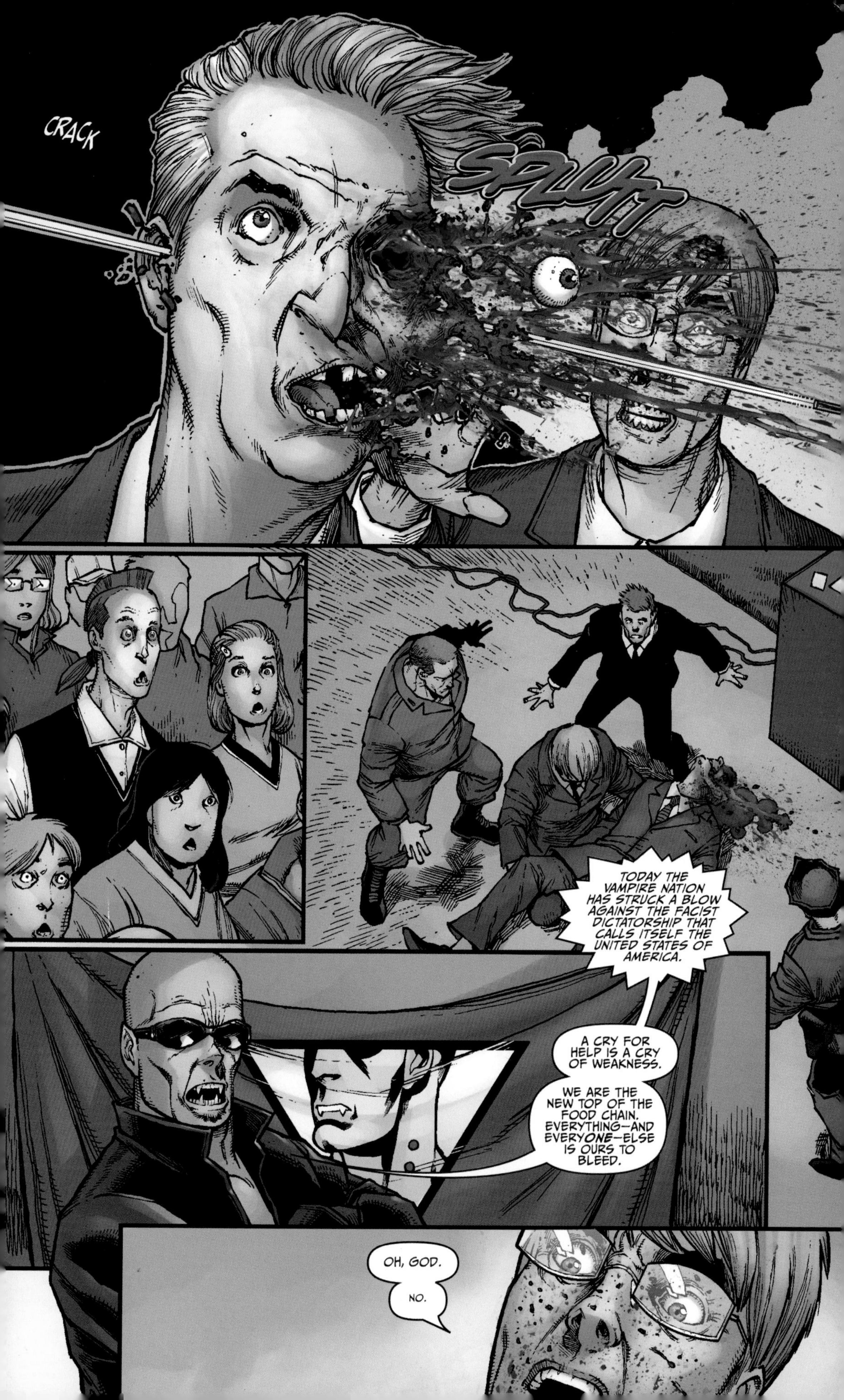
CRACK
SPLUTT
TODAY THE VAMPIRE NATION HAS STRUCK A BLOW AGAINST THE FACIST DICTATORSHIP THAT CALLS ITSELF THE UNITED STATES OF AMERICA.
A CRY FOR HELP IS A CRY OF WEAKNESS.
WE ARE THE NEW TOP OF THE FOOD CHAIN. EVERYTHING—AND EVERYONE—ELSE IS OURS TO BLEED.
OH, GOD.
NO.

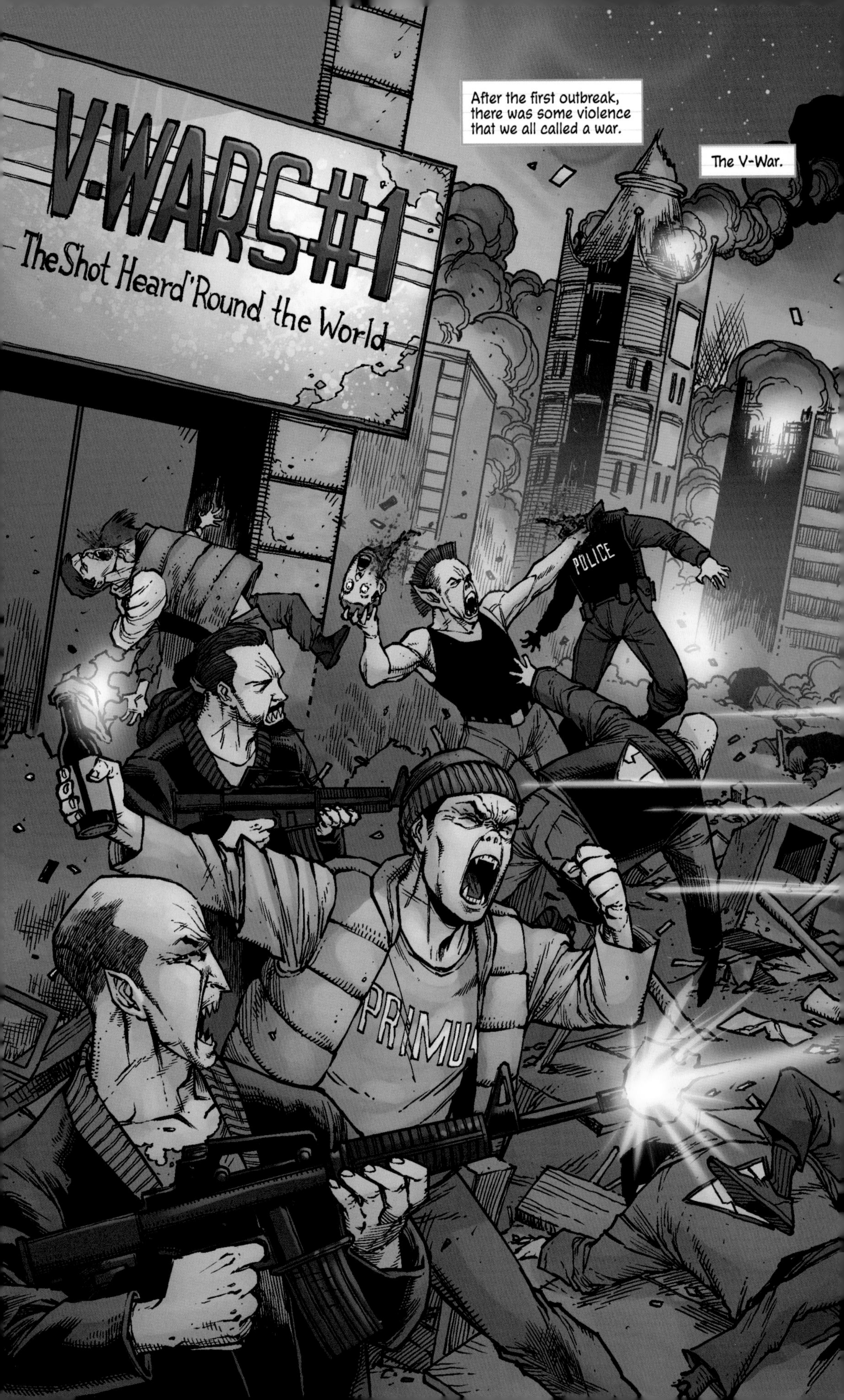
V-WARS #1
The Shot Heard 'Round the World
After the first outbreak, there was some violence that we all called a war.
The V-War.
POLICE
PRIMUA

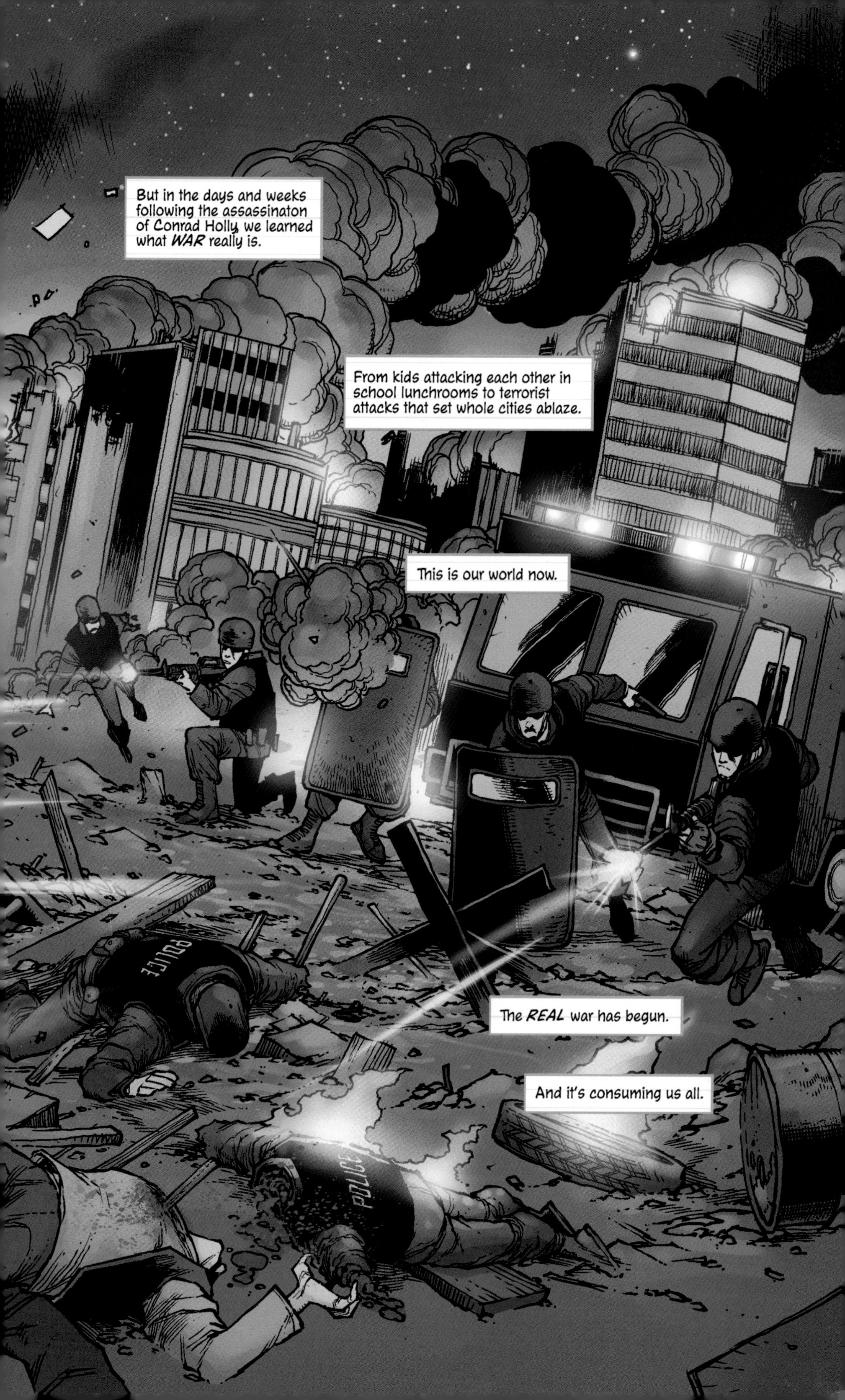
But in the days and weeks following the assassinaton of Conrad Holly we learned what WAR really is.
From kids attacking each other in school lunchrooms to terrorist attacks that set whole cities ablaze.
This is our world now.
POLICE
The REAL war has begun.
And it's consuming us all.
POLICE

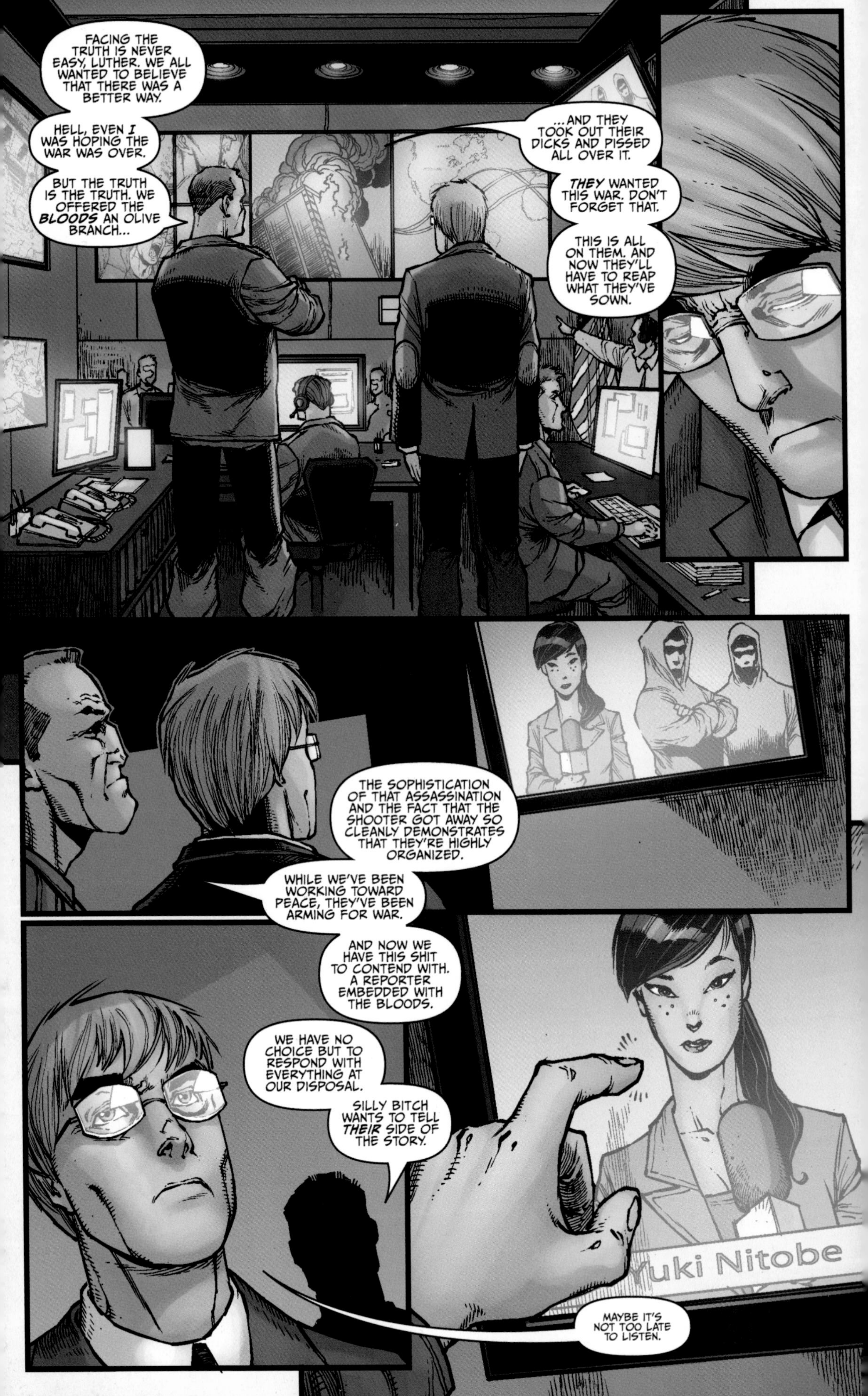
FACING THE TRUTH IS NEVER EASY, LUTHER. WE ALL WANTED TO BELIEVE THAT THERE WAS A BETTER WAY.
HELL, EVEN I WAS HOPING THE WAR WAS OVER.
BUT THE TRUTH IS THE TRUTH. WE OFFERED THE BLOODS AN OLIVE BRANCH...
...AND THEY TOOK OUT THEIR DICKS AND PISSED ALL OVER IT.
THEY WANTED THIS WAR. DON'T FORGET THAT.
THIS IS ALL ON THEM. AND NOW THEY'LL HAVE TO REAP WHAT THEY'VE SOWN.
THE SOPHISTICATION OF THAT ASSASSINATION AND THE FACT THAT THE SHOOTER GOT AWAY SO CLEANLY DEMONSTRATES THAT THEY'RE HIGHLY ORGANIZED.
WHILE WE'VE BEEN WORKING TOWARD PEACE, THEY'VE BEEN ARMING FOR WAR.
AND NOW WE HAVE THIS SHIT TO CONTEND WITH. A REPORTER EMBEDDED WITH THE BLOODS.
WE HAVE NO CHOICE BUT TO RESPOND WITH EVERYTHING AT OUR DISPOSAL.
SILLY BITCH WANTS TO TELL THEIR SIDE OF THE STORY.
Yuki Nitobe
MAYBE IT'S NOT TOO LATE TO LISTEN.

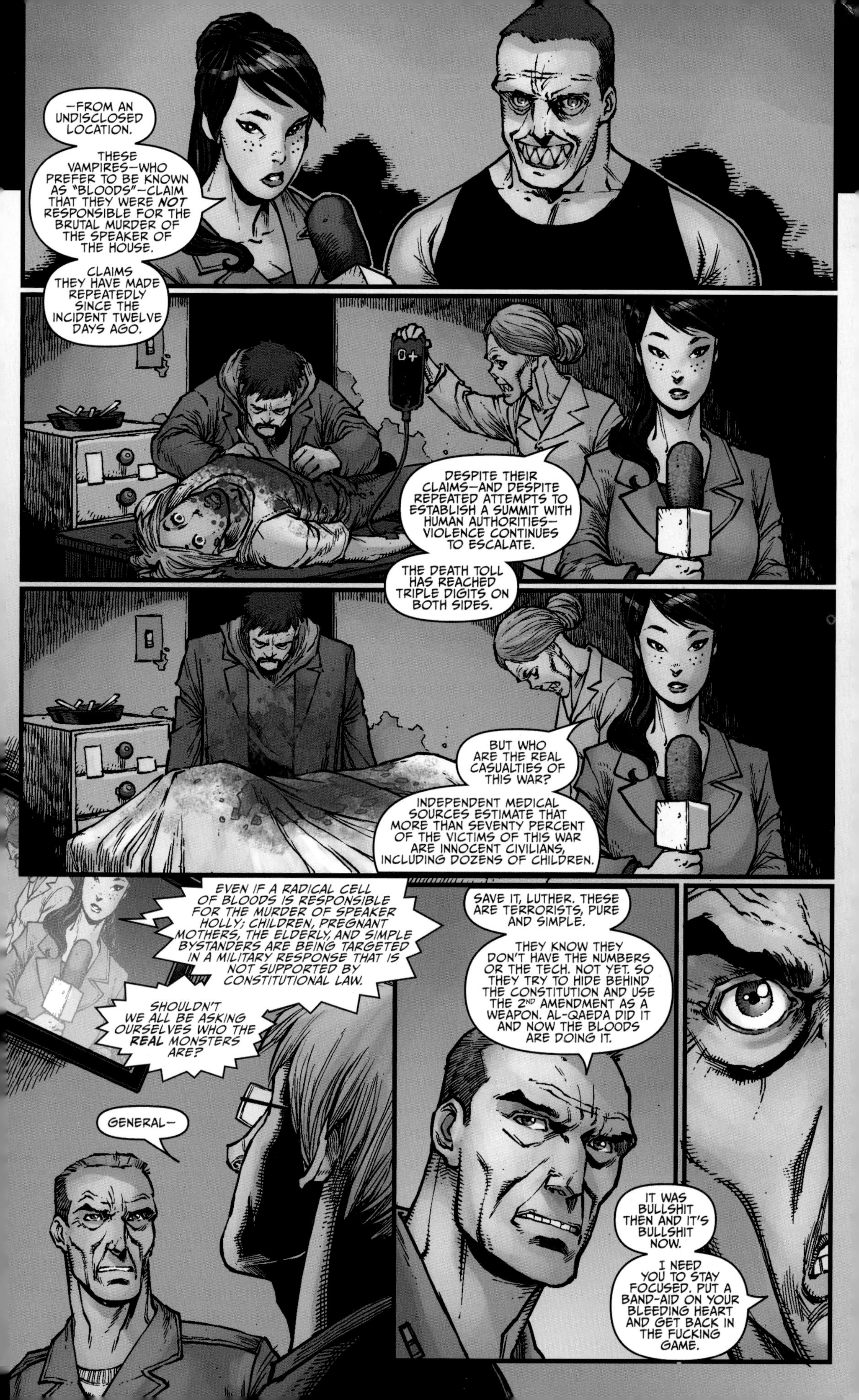

—FROM AN UNDISCLOSED LOCATION.
THESE VAMPIRES—WHO PREFER TO BE KNOWN AS "BLOODS"—CLAIM THAT THEY WERE NOT RESPONSIBLE FOR THE BRUTAL MURDER OF THE SPEAKER OF THE HOUSE.
CLAIMS THEY HAVE MADE REPEATEDLY SINCE THE INCIDENT TWELVE DAYS AGO.
O+
DESPITE THEIR CLAIMS—AND DESPITE REPEATED ATTEMPTS TO ESTABLISH A SUMMIT WITH HUMAN AUTHORITIES—VIOLENCE CONTINUES TO ESCALATE.
THE DEATH TOLL HAS REACHED TRIPLE DIGITS ON BOTH SIDES.
BUT WHO ARE THE REAL CASUALTIES OF THIS WAR?
INDEPENDENT MEDICAL SOURCES ESTIMATE THAT MORE THAN SEVENTY PERCENT OF THE VICTIMS OF THIS WAR ARE INNOCENT CIVILIANS, INCLUDING DOZENS OF CHILDREN.
EVEN IF A RADICAL CELL OF BLOODS IS RESPONSIBLE FOR THE MURDER OF SPEAKER HOLLY; CHILDREN, PREGNANT MOTHERS, THE ELDERLY, AND SIMPLE BYSTANDERS ARE BEING TARGETED IN A MILITARY RESPONSE THAT IS NOT SUPPORTED BY CONSTITUTIONAL LAW.
SHOULDN'T WE ALL BE ASKING OURSELVES WHO THE REAL MONSTERS ARE?
GENERAL—
SAVE IT, LUTHER. THESE ARE TERRORISTS, PURE AND SIMPLE.
THEY KNOW THEY DON'T HAVE THE NUMBERS OR THE TECH. NOT YET. SO THEY TRY TO HIDE BEHIND THE CONSTITUTION AND USE THE 2ND AMENDMENT AS A WEAPON. AL-QAEDA DID IT AND NOW THE BLOODS ARE DOING IT.
IT WAS BULLSHIT THEN AND IT'S BULLSHIT NOW.
I NEED YOU TO STAY FOCUSED. PUT A BAND-AID ON YOUR BLEEDING HEART AND GET BACK IN THE FUCKING GAME.

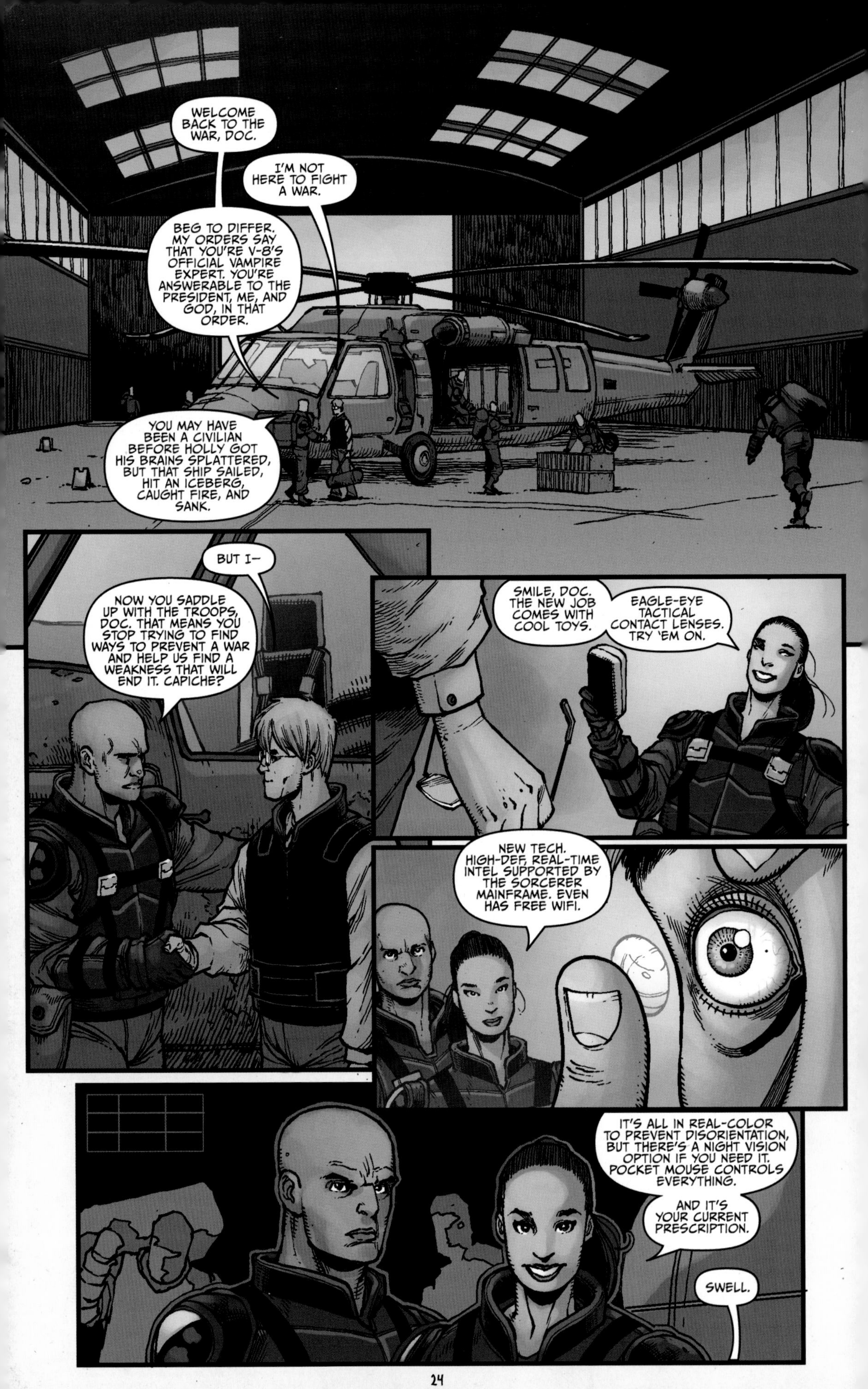
WELCOME BACK TO THE WAR, DOC.
I'M NOT HERE TO FIGHT A WAR.
BEG TO DIFFER. MY ORDERS SAY THAT YOU'RE V-8'S OFFICIAL VAMPIRE EXPERT. YOU'RE ANSWERABLE TO THE PRESIDENT, ME, AND GOD, IN THAT ORDER.
YOU MAY HAVE BEEN A CIVILIAN BEFORE HOLLY GOT HIS BRAINS SPLATTERED, BUT THAT SHIP SAILED, HIT AN ICEBERG, CAUGHT FIRE, AND SANK.
BUT I—
NOW YOU SADDLE UP WITH THE TROOPS, DOC. THAT MEANS YOU STOP TRYING TO FIND WAYS TO PREVENT A WAR AND HELP US FIND A WEAKNESS THAT WILL END IT. CAPICHE?
SMILE, DOC. THE NEW JOB COMES WITH COOL TOYS.
EAGLE-EYE TACTICAL CONTACT LENSES. TRY 'EM ON.
NEW TECH. HIGH-DEF, REAL-TIME INTEL SUPPORTED BY THE SORCERER MAINFRAME. EVEN HAS FREE WIFI.
IT'S ALL IN REAL-COLOR TO PREVENT DISORIENTATION, BUT THERE'S A NIGHT VISION OPTION IF YOU NEED IT. POCKET MOUSE CONTROLS EVERYTHING.
AND IT'S YOUR CURRENT PRESCRIPTION.
SWELL.

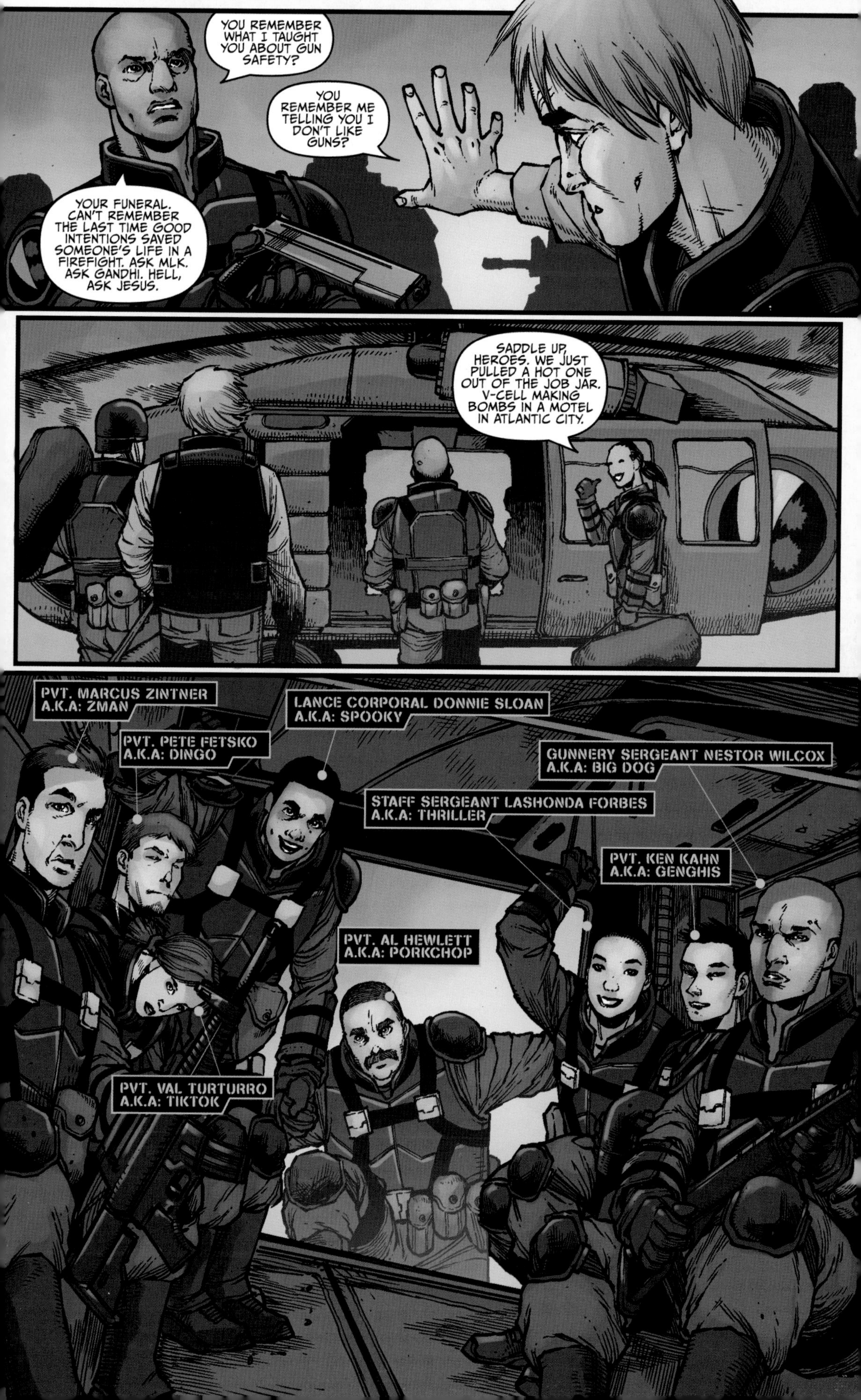
YOU REMEMBER WHAT I TAUGHT YOU ABOUT GUN SAFETY?
YOU REMEMBER ME TELLING YOU I DON'T LIKE GUNS?
YOUR FUNERAL. CAN'T REMEMBER THE LAST TIME GOOD INTENTIONS SAVED SOMEONE'S LIFE IN A FIREFIGHT. ASK MLK. ASK GANDHI. HELL, ASK JESUS.
SADDLE UP, HEROES. WE JUST PULLED A HOT ONE OUT OF THE JOB JAR. V-CELL MAKING BOMBS IN A MOTEL IN ATLANTIC CITY.
PVT. MARCUS ZINTNER A.K.A: ZMAN
PVT. PETE FETSKO A.K.A: DINGO
LANCE CORPORAL DONNIE SLOAN A.K.A: SPOOKY
GUNNERY SERGEANT NESTOR WILCOX A.K.A: BIG DOG
STAFF SERGEANT LASHONDA FORBES A.K.A: THRILLER
PVT. KEN KAHN A.K.A: GENGHIS
PVT. AL HEWLETT A.K.A: PORKCHOP
PVT. VAL TURTURRO A.K.A: TIKTOK

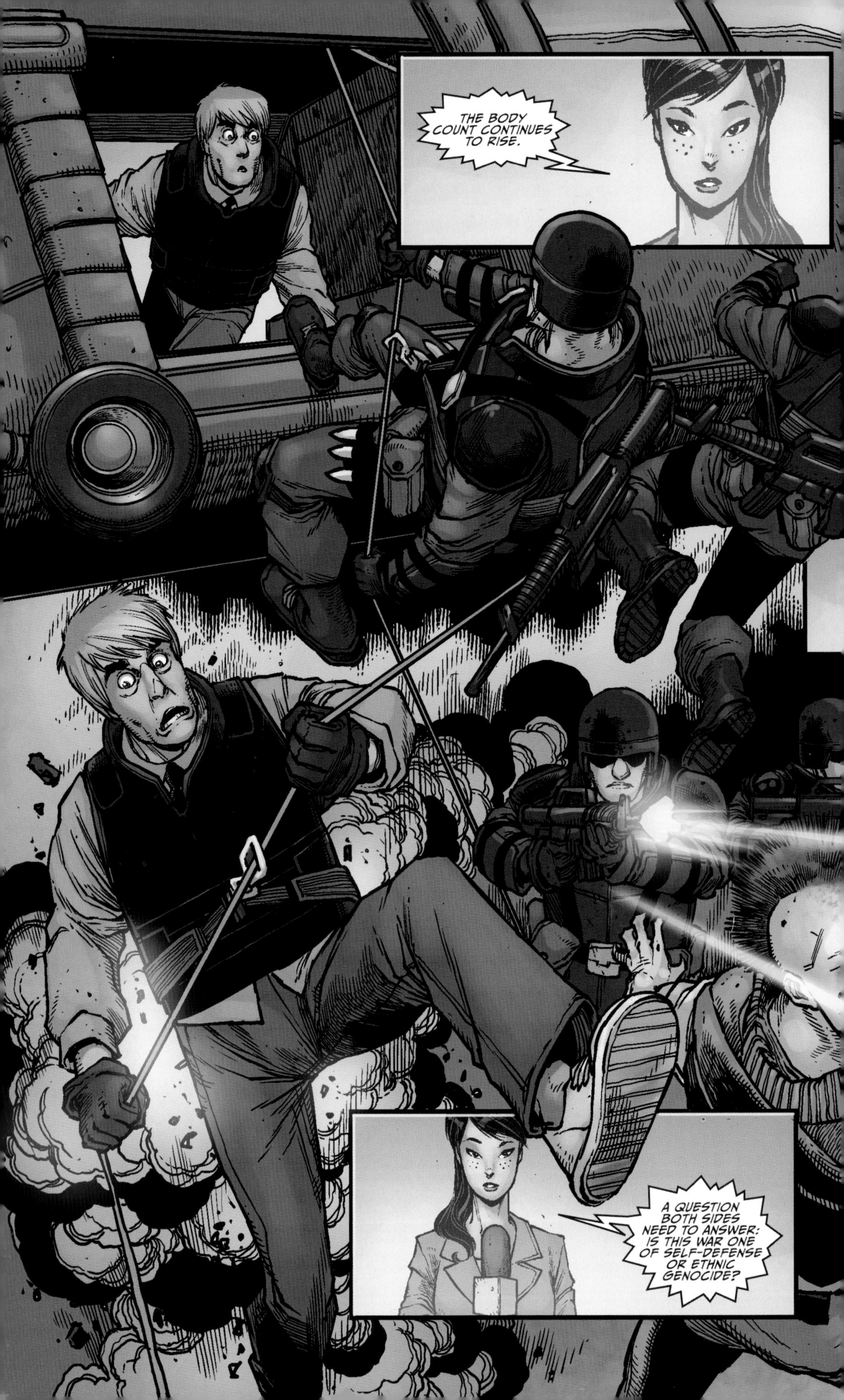
THE BODY COUNT CONTINUES TO RISE.
A QUESTION BOTH SIDES NEED TO ANSWER: IS THIS WAR ONE OF SELF-DEFENSE OR ETHNIC GENOCIDE?

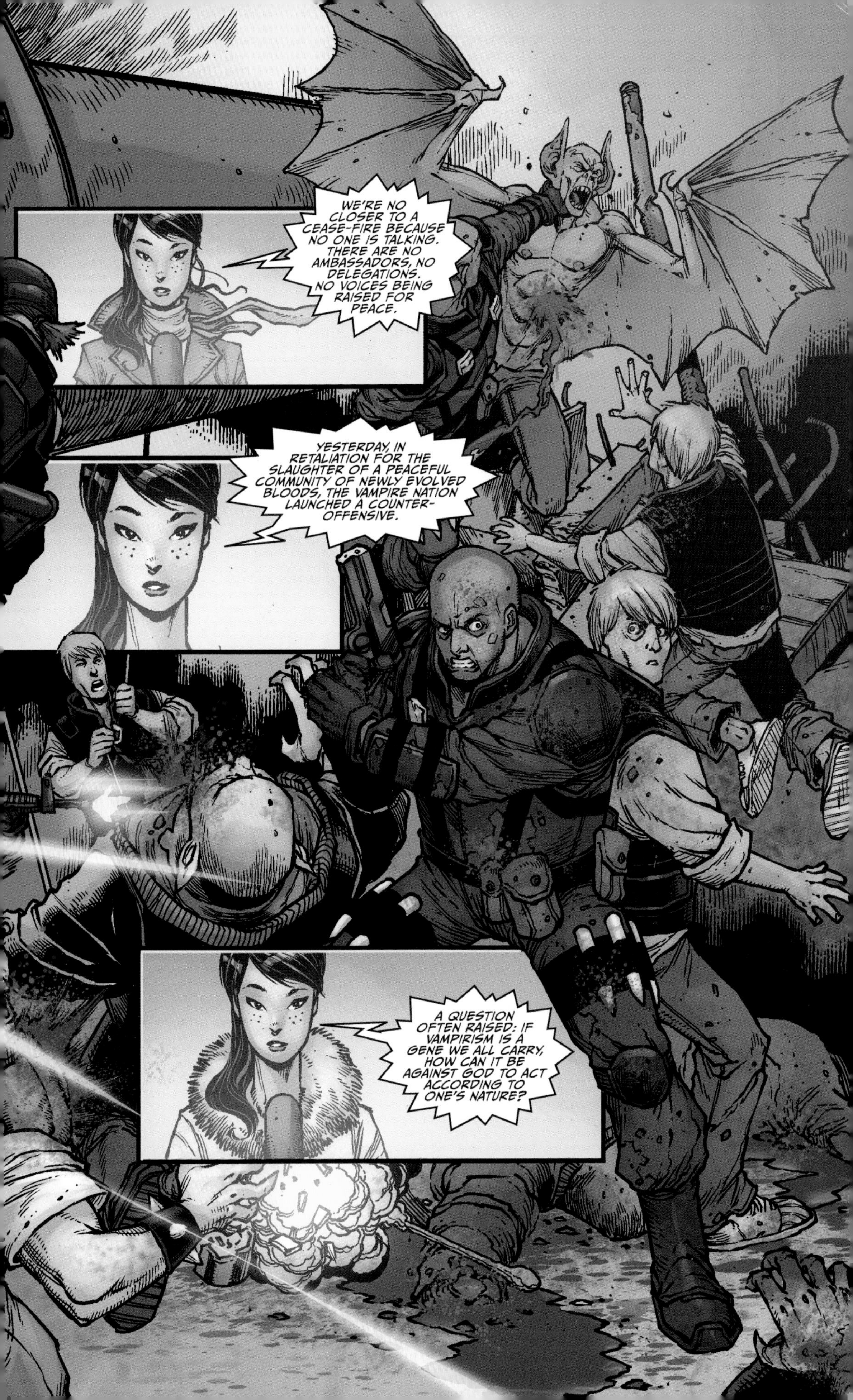
WE'RE NO CLOSER TO A CEASE-FIRE BECAUSE NO ONE IS TALKING. THERE ARE NO AMBASSADORS, NO DELEGATIONS. NO VOICES BEING RAISED FOR PEACE.
YESTERDAY, IN RETALIATION FOR THE SLAUGHTER OF A PEACEFUL COMMUNITY OF NEWLY EVOLVED BLOODS, THE VAMPIRE NATION LAUNCHED A COUNTER-OFFENSIVE.
A QUESTION OFTEN RAISED: IF VAMPIRISM IS A GENE WE ALL CARRY, HOW CAN IT BE AGAINST GOD TO ACT ACCORDING TO ONE'S NATURE?

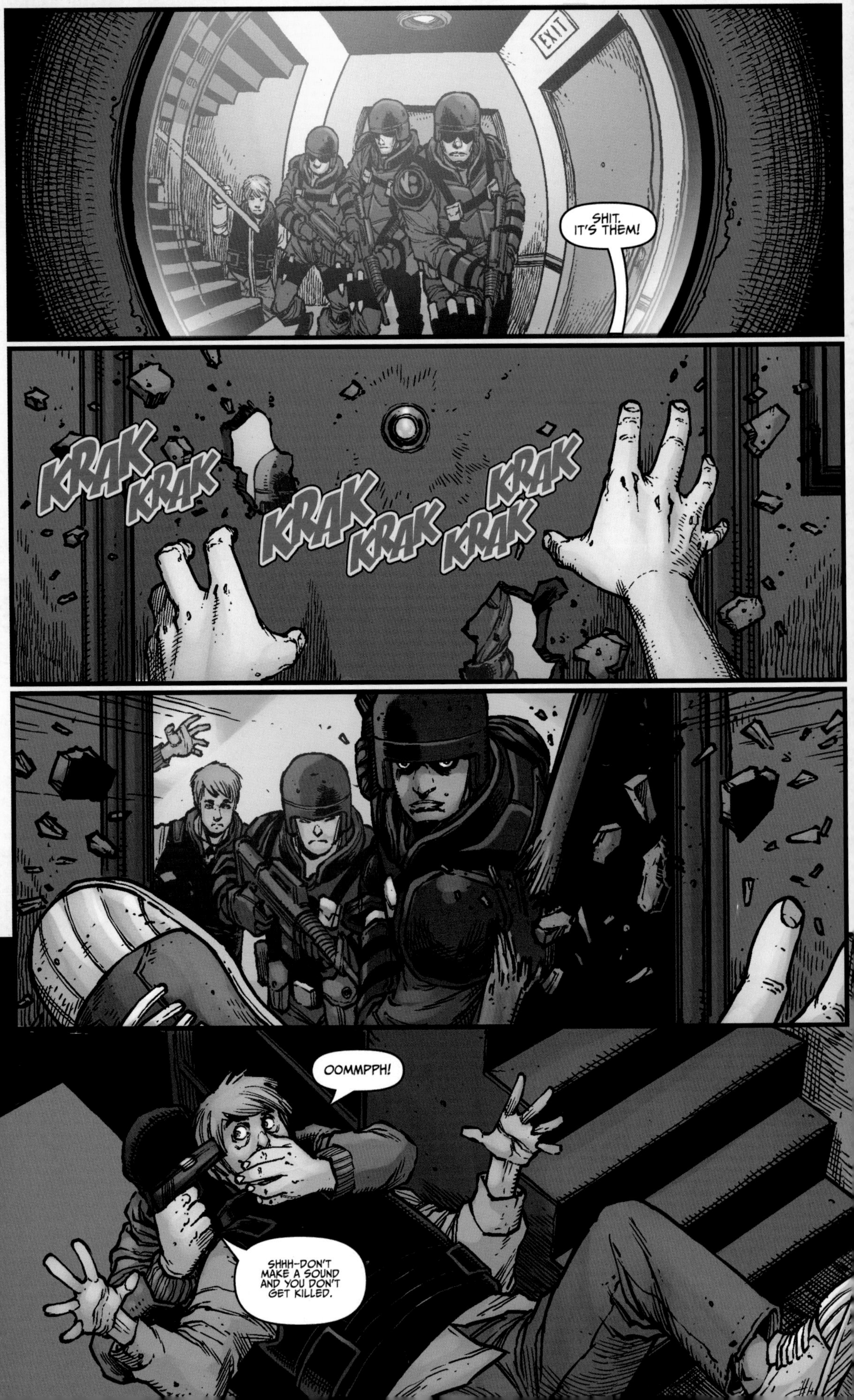
SHIT. IT'S THEM!
KRAK KRAK
KRAK KRAK KRAK KRAK
OOMMPPH!
SHHH–DON'T MAKE A SOUND AND YOU DON'T GET KILLED.

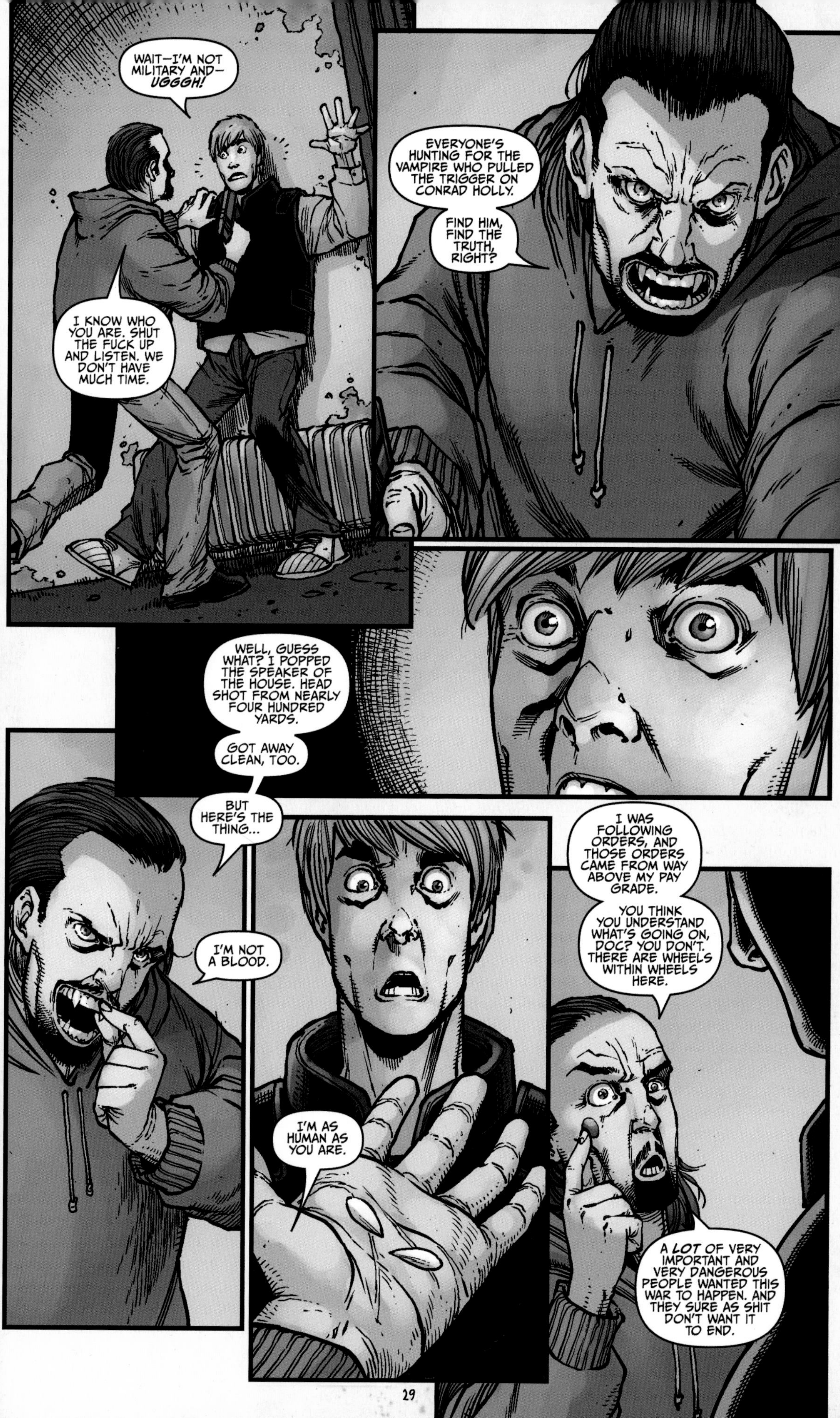

WAIT—I'M NOT MILITARY AND— *UGGGH!*
I KNOW WHO YOU ARE. SHUT THE FUCK UP AND LISTEN. WE DON'T HAVE MUCH TIME.
EVERYONE'S HUNTING FOR THE VAMPIRE WHO PULLED THE TRIGGER ON CONRAD HOLLY.
FIND HIM, FIND THE TRUTH, RIGHT?
WELL, GUESS WHAT? I POPPED THE SPEAKER OF THE HOUSE. HEAD SHOT FROM NEARLY FOUR HUNDRED YARDS.
GOT AWAY CLEAN, TOO.
BUT HERE'S THE THING...
I'M NOT A BLOOD.
I'M AS HUMAN AS YOU ARE.
I WAS FOLLOWING ORDERS, AND THOSE ORDERS CAME FROM WAY ABOVE MY PAY GRADE.
YOU THINK YOU UNDERSTAND WHAT'S GOING ON, DOC? YOU DON'T. THERE ARE WHEELS WITHIN WHEELS HERE.
A *LOT* OF VERY IMPORTANT AND VERY DANGEROUS PEOPLE WANTED THIS WAR TO HAPPEN. AND THEY SURE AS SHIT DON'T WANT IT TO END.

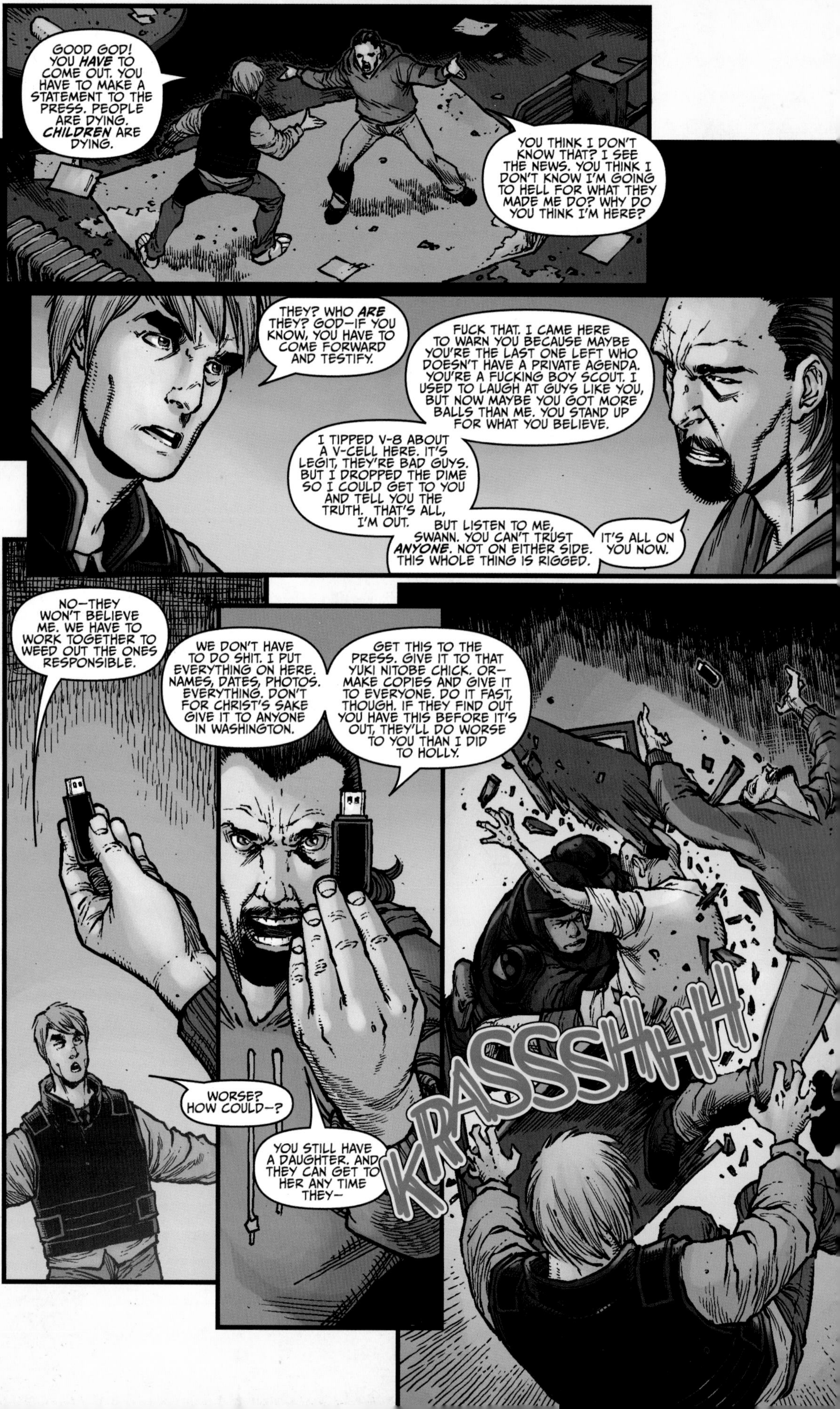
GOOD GOD! YOU HAVE TO COME OUT. YOU HAVE TO MAKE A STATEMENT TO THE PRESS. PEOPLE ARE DYING. CHILDREN ARE DYING.
YOU THINK I DON'T KNOW THAT? I SEE THE NEWS. YOU THINK I DON'T KNOW I'M GOING TO HELL FOR WHAT THEY MADE ME DO? WHY DO YOU THINK I'M HERE?
THEY? WHO ARE THEY? GOD—IF YOU KNOW, YOU HAVE TO COME FORWARD AND TESTIFY.
FUCK THAT. I CAME HERE TO WARN YOU BECAUSE MAYBE YOU'RE THE LAST ONE LEFT WHO DOESN'T HAVE A PRIVATE AGENDA. YOU'RE A FUCKING BOY SCOUT. I USED TO LAUGH AT GUYS LIKE YOU, BUT NOW MAYBE YOU GOT MORE BALLS THAN ME. YOU STAND UP FOR WHAT YOU BELIEVE.
I TIPPED V-8 ABOUT A V-CELL HERE. IT'S LEGIT, THEY'RE BAD GUYS. BUT I DROPPED THE DIME SO I COULD GET TO YOU AND TELL YOU THE TRUTH. THAT'S ALL, I'M OUT.
BUT LISTEN TO ME, SWANN. YOU CAN'T TRUST ANYONE. NOT ON EITHER SIDE. THIS WHOLE THING IS RIGGED.
IT'S ALL ON YOU NOW.
NO—THEY WON'T BELIEVE ME. WE HAVE TO WORK TOGETHER TO WEED OUT THE ONES RESPONSIBLE.
WE DON'T HAVE TO DO SHIT. I PUT EVERYTHING ON HERE. NAMES, DATES, PHOTOS. EVERYTHING. DON'T FOR CHRIST'S SAKE GIVE IT TO ANYONE IN WASHINGTON.
GET THIS TO THE PRESS. GIVE IT TO THAT YUKI NITOBE CHICK. OR—MAKE COPIES AND GIVE IT TO EVERYONE. DO IT FAST, THOUGH. IF THEY FIND OUT YOU HAVE THIS BEFORE IT'S OUT, THEY'LL DO WORSE TO YOU THAN I DID TO HOLLY.
WORSE? HOW COULD—?
YOU STILL HAVE A DAUGHTER. AND THEY CAN GET TO HER ANY TIME THEY—
KRASSSHHH

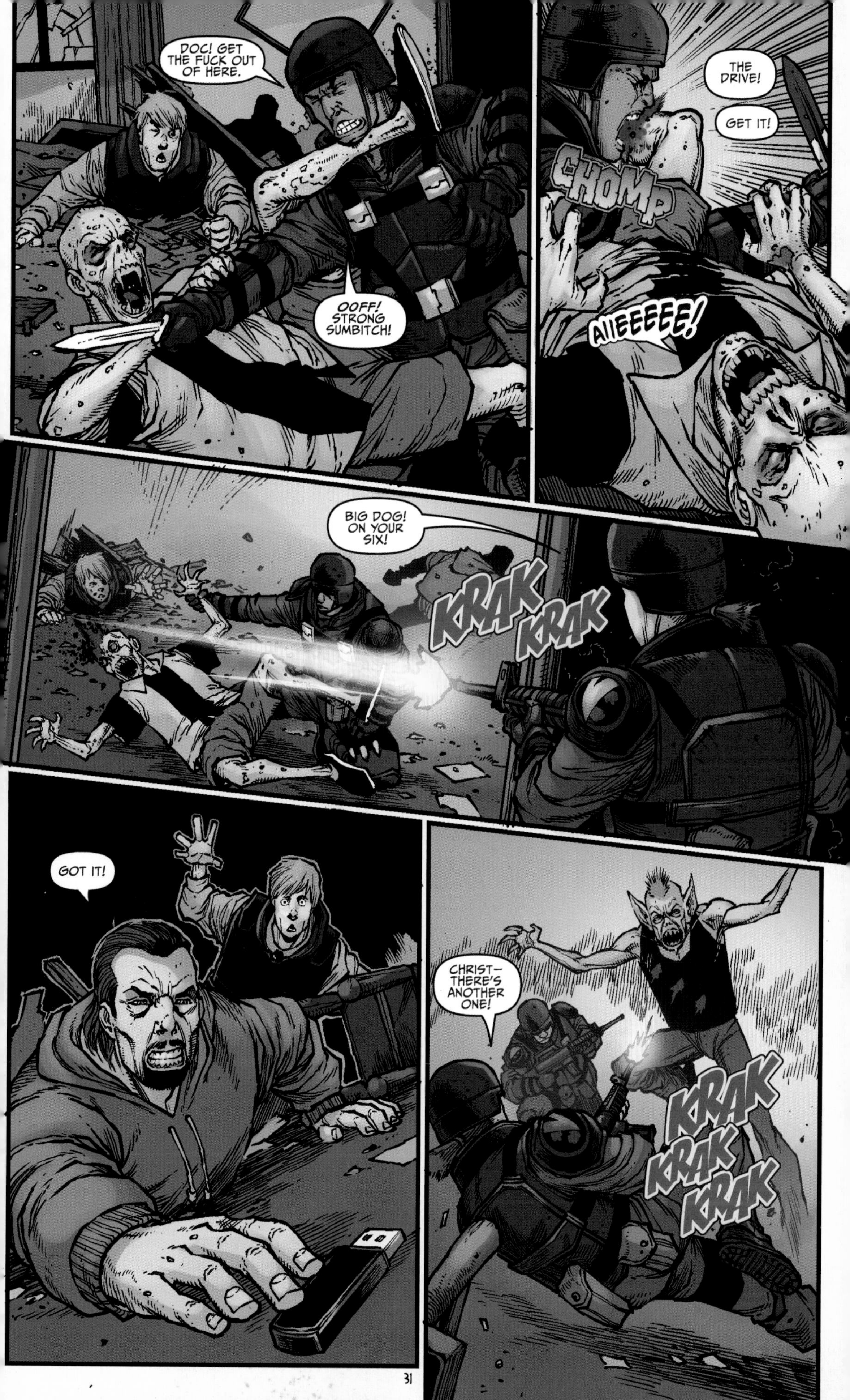
DOC! GET THE FUCK OUT OF HERE.
OOFF! STRONG SUMBITCH!
THE DRIVE!
GET IT!
CHOMP
AIIEEEEEE!
BIG DOG! ON YOUR SIX!
KRAK KRAK
GOT IT!
CHRIST— THERE'S ANOTHER ONE!
KRAK KRAK KRAK

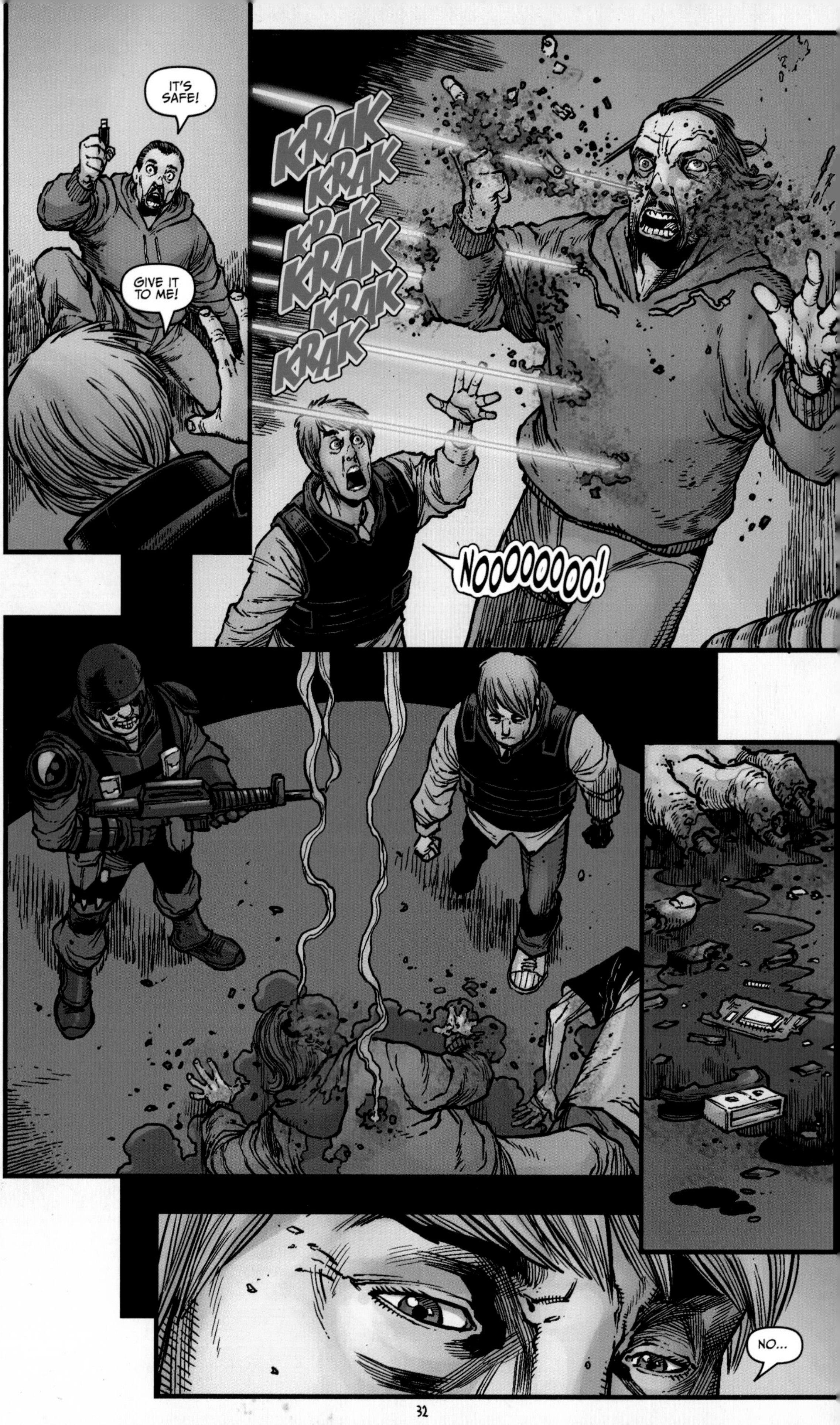
IT'S SAFE!
GIVE IT TO ME!
KRAK KRAK KRAK KRAK KRAK KRAK
NOOOOOOOO!
NO...

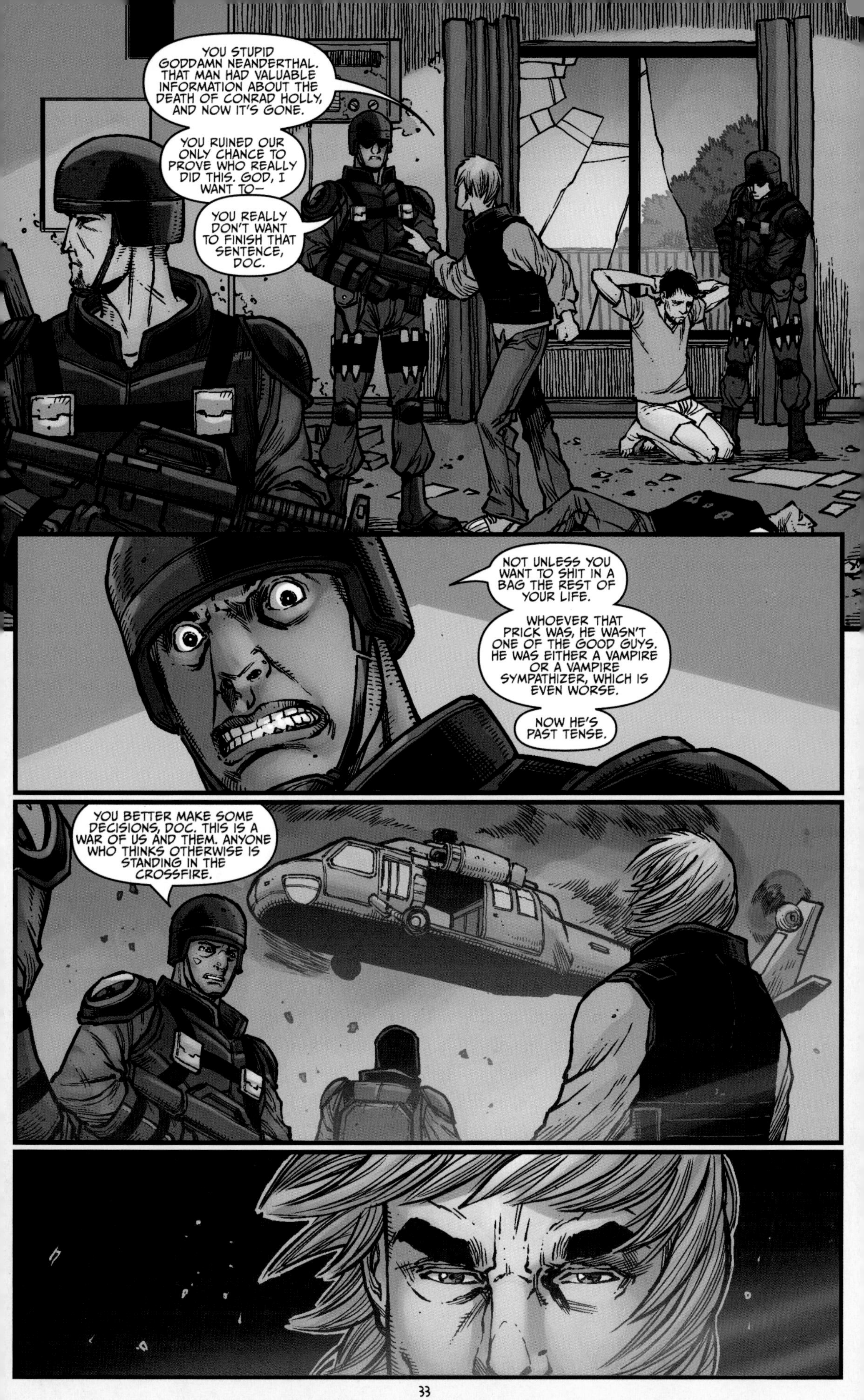
YOU STUPID GODDAMN NEANDERTHAL. THAT MAN HAD VALUABLE INFORMATION ABOUT THE DEATH OF CONRAD HOLLY, AND NOW IT'S GONE.
YOU RUINED OUR ONLY CHANCE TO PROVE WHO REALLY DID THIS. GOD, I WANT TO—
YOU REALLY DON'T WANT TO FINISH THAT SENTENCE, DOC.
NOT UNLESS YOU WANT TO SHIT IN A BAG THE REST OF YOUR LIFE.
WHOEVER THAT PRICK WAS, HE WASN'T ONE OF THE GOOD GUYS. HE WAS EITHER A VAMPIRE OR A VAMPIRE SYMPATHIZER, WHICH IS EVEN WORSE.
NOW HE'S PAST TENSE.
YOU BETTER MAKE SOME DECISIONS, DOC. THIS IS A WAR OF US AND THEM. ANYONE WHO THINKS OTHERWISE IS STANDING IN THE CROSSFIRE.

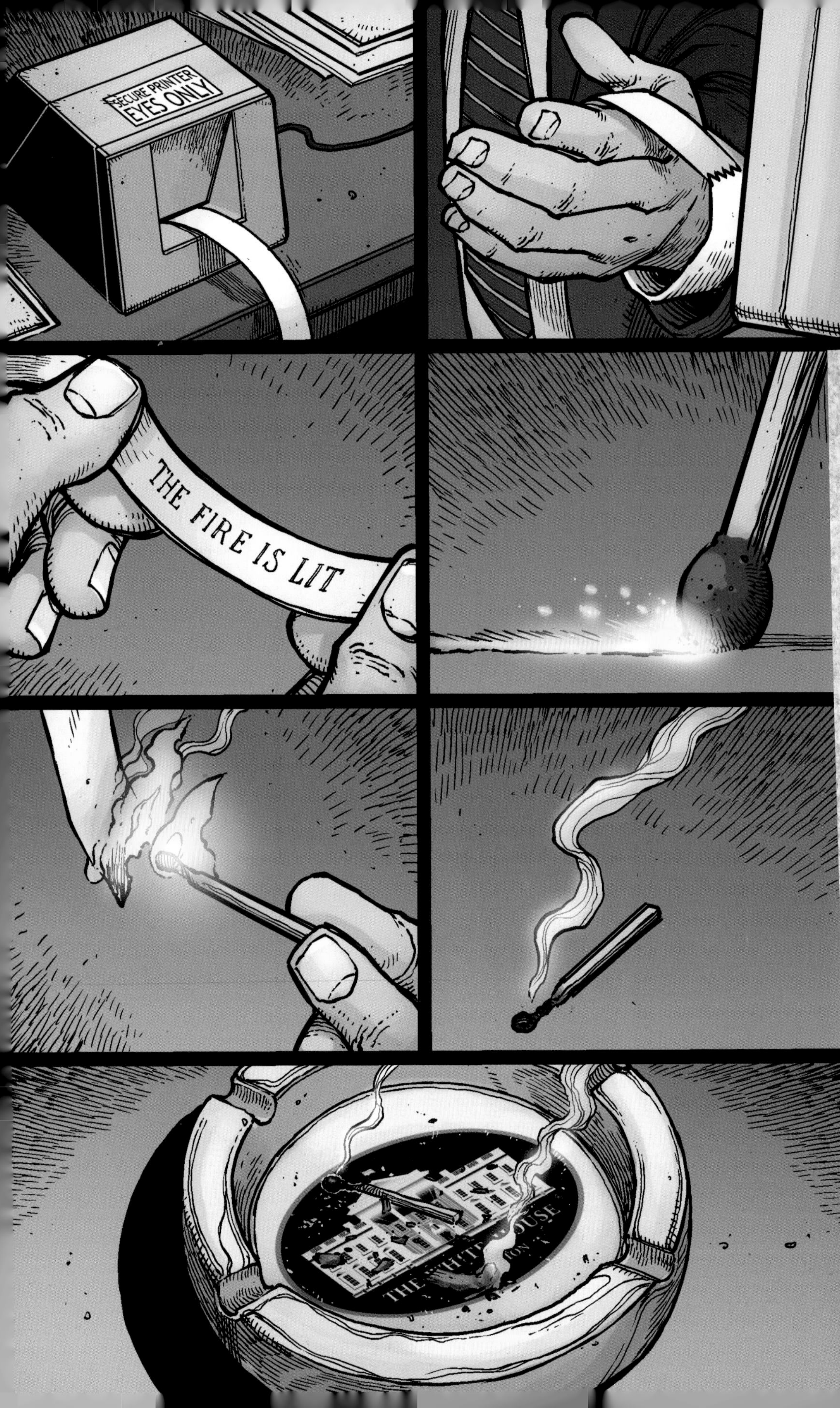
SECURE PRINTER
EYES ONLY
THE FIRE IS LIT

CHAPTER 2

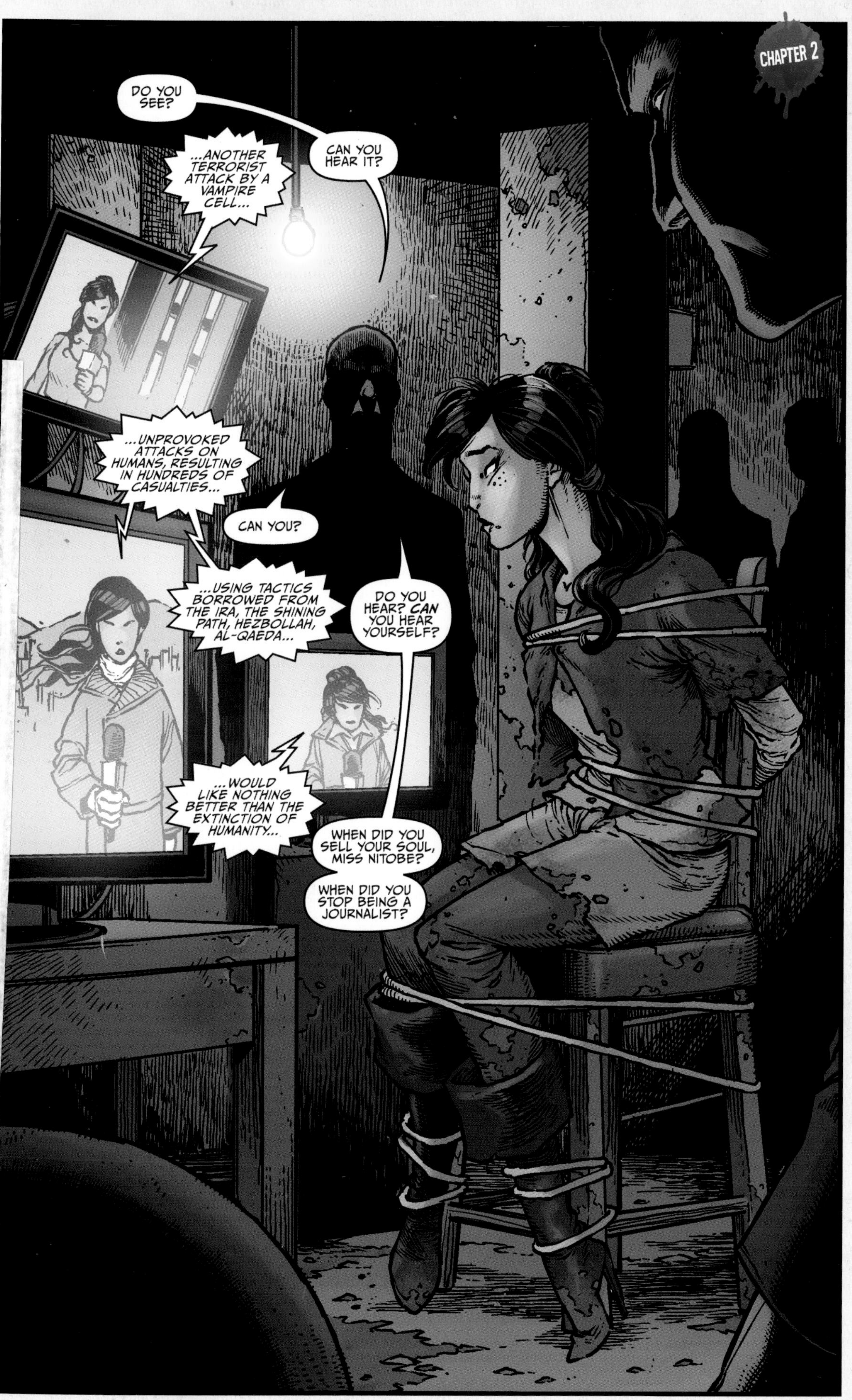
DO YOU SEE?
CAN YOU HEAR IT?
...ANOTHER TERRORIST ATTACK BY A VAMPIRE CELL...
...UNPROVOKED ATTACKS ON HUMANS, RESULTING IN HUNDREDS OF CASUALTIES...
CAN YOU?
...USING TACTICS BORROWED FROM THE IRA, THE SHINING PATH, HEZBOLLAH, AL-QAEDA...
DO YOU HEAR? CAN YOU HEAR YOURSELF?
...WOULD LIKE NOTHING BETTER THAN THE EXTINCTION OF HUMANITY...
WHEN DID YOU SELL YOUR SOUL, MISS NITOBE?
WHEN DID YOU STOP BEING A JOURNALIST?

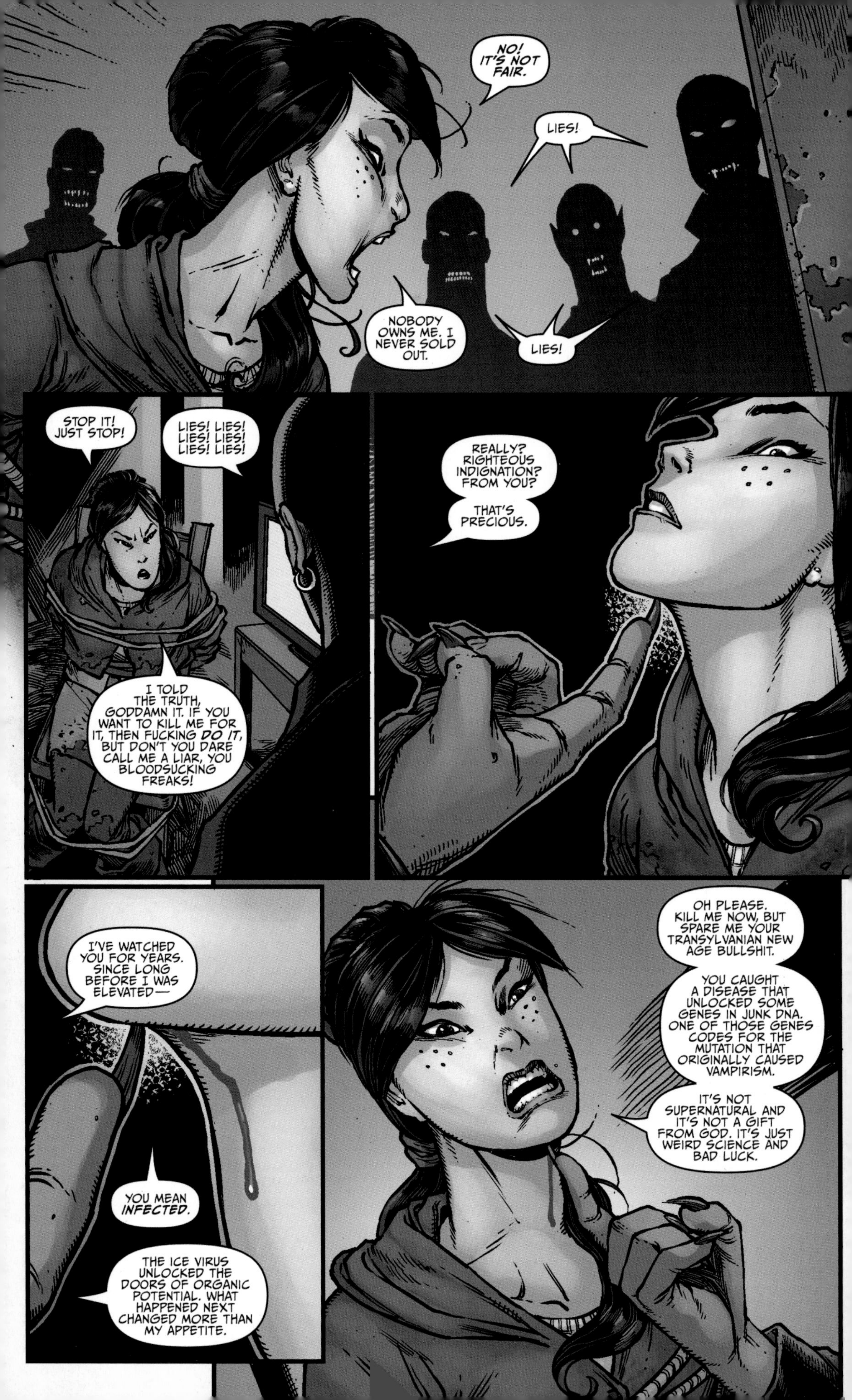
NO! IT'S NOT FAIR.
LIES!
NOBODY OWNS ME. I NEVER SOLD OUT.
LIES!
STOP IT! JUST STOP!
LIES! LIES! LIES! LIES! LIES! LIES!
I TOLD THE TRUTH, GODDAMN IT. IF YOU WANT TO KILL ME FOR IT, THEN FUCKING DO IT, BUT DON'T YOU DARE CALL ME A LIAR, YOU BLOODSUCKING FREAKS!
REALLY? RIGHTEOUS INDIGNATION? FROM YOU?
THAT'S PRECIOUS.
I'VE WATCHED YOU FOR YEARS. SINCE LONG BEFORE I WAS ELEVATED—
YOU MEAN INFECTED.
THE ICE VIRUS UNLOCKED THE DOORS OF ORGANIC POTENTIAL. WHAT HAPPENED NEXT CHANGED MORE THAN MY APPETITE.
OH PLEASE. KILL ME NOW, BUT SPARE ME YOUR TRANSYLVANIAN NEW AGE BULLSHIT.
YOU CAUGHT A DISEASE THAT UNLOCKED SOME GENES IN JUNK DNA. ONE OF THOSE GENES CODES FOR THE MUTATION THAT ORIGINALLY CAUSED VAMPIRISM.
IT'S NOT SUPERNATURAL AND IT'S NOT A GIFT FROM GOD. IT'S JUST WEIRD SCIENCE AND BAD LUCK.

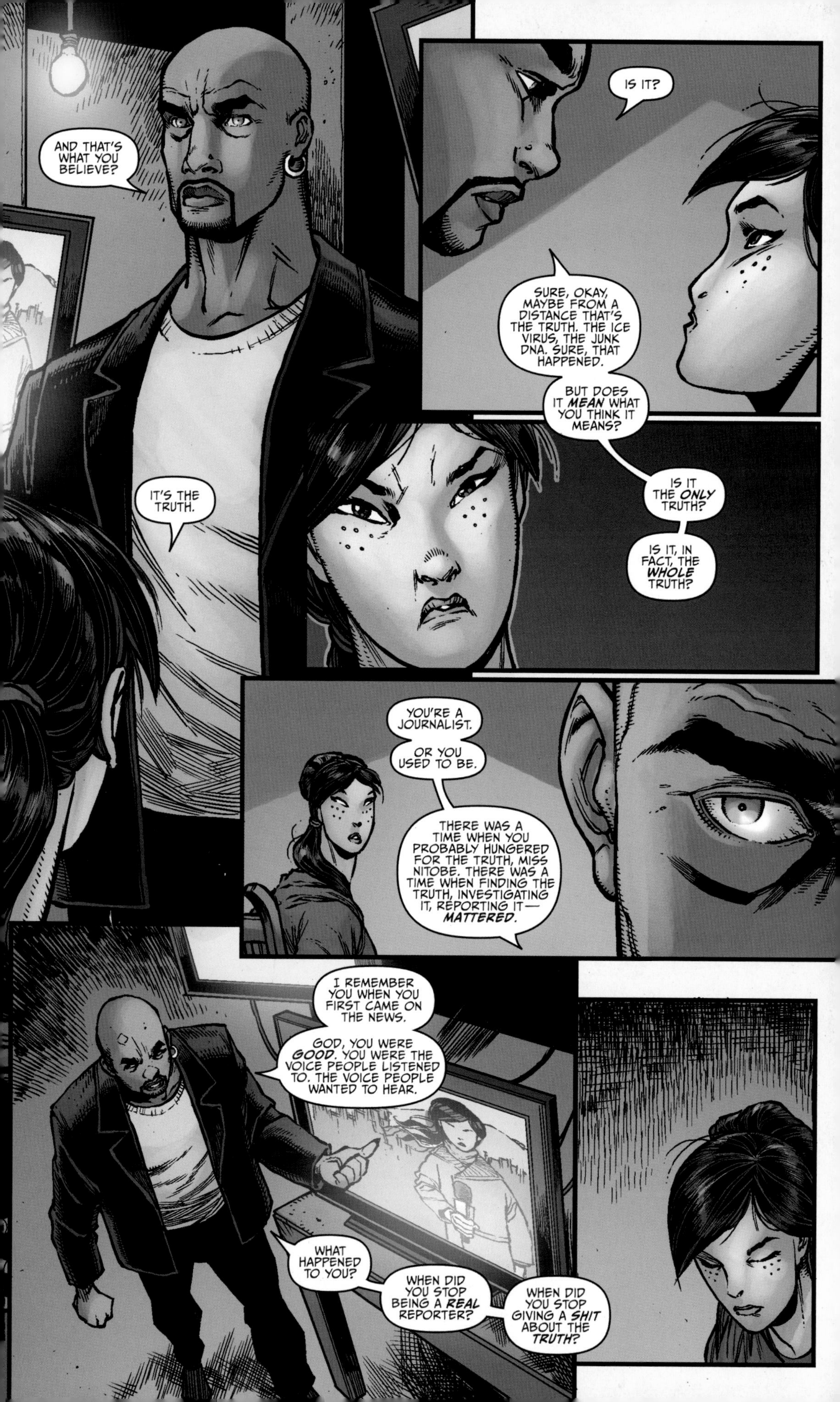
AND THAT'S WHAT YOU BELIEVE?
IS IT?
SURE, OKAY, MAYBE FROM A DISTANCE THAT'S THE TRUTH. THE ICE VIRUS, THE JUNK DNA. SURE, THAT HAPPENED.
BUT DOES IT *MEAN* WHAT YOU THINK IT MEANS?
IT'S THE TRUTH.
IS IT THE *ONLY* TRUTH?
IS IT, IN FACT, THE *WHOLE* TRUTH?
YOU'RE A JOURNALIST.
OR YOU USED TO BE.
THERE WAS A TIME WHEN YOU PROBABLY HUNGERED FOR THE TRUTH, MISS NITOBE. THERE WAS A TIME WHEN FINDING THE TRUTH, INVESTIGATING IT, REPORTING IT— *MATTERED.*
I REMEMBER YOU WHEN YOU FIRST CAME ON THE NEWS.
GOD, YOU WERE *GOOD*. YOU WERE THE VOICE PEOPLE LISTENED TO. THE VOICE PEOPLE WANTED TO HEAR.
WHAT HAPPENED TO YOU?
WHEN DID YOU STOP BEING A *REAL* REPORTER?
WHEN DID YOU STOP GIVING A *SHIT* ABOUT THE *TRUTH?*

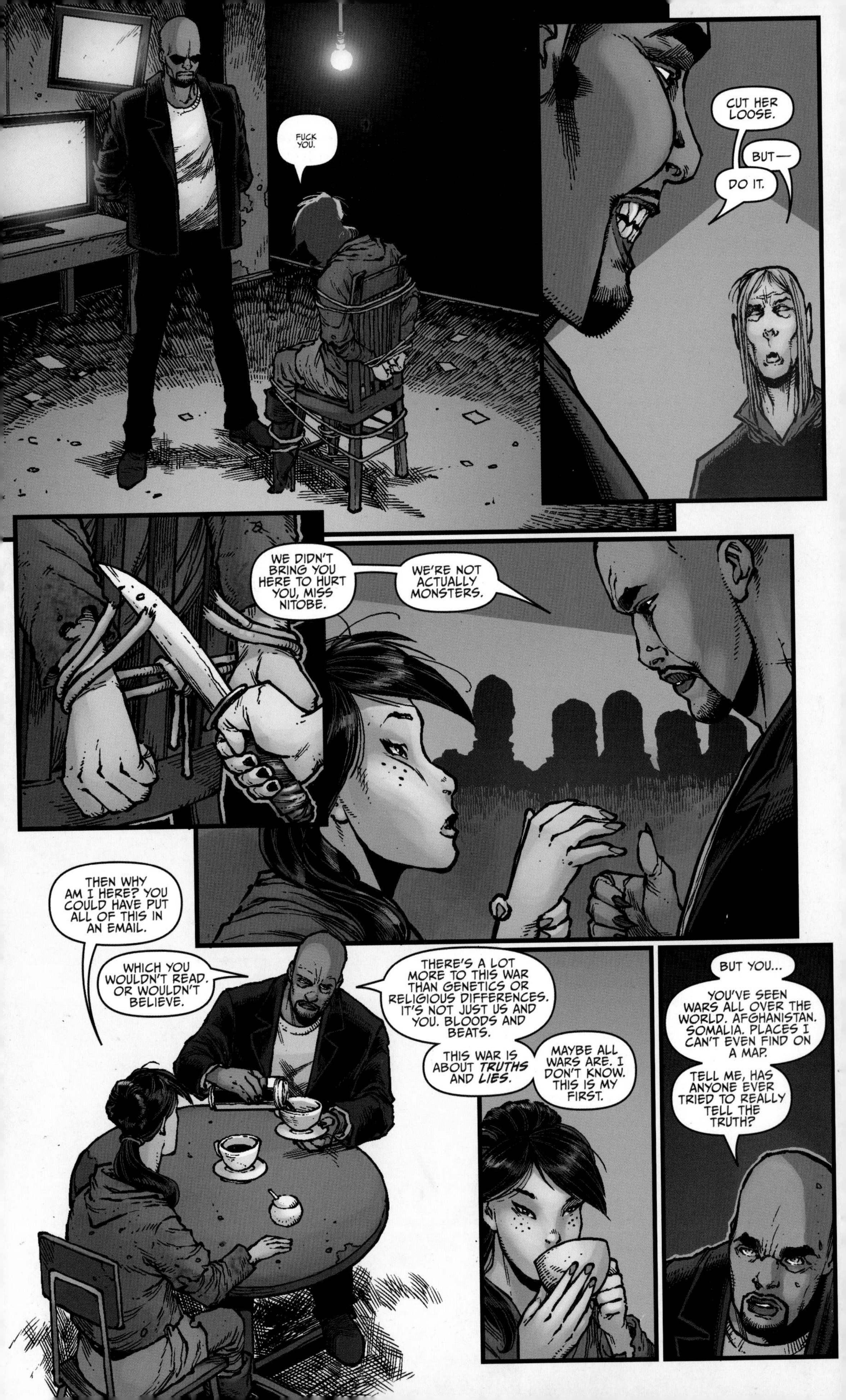
FUCK YOU.
CUT HER LOOSE.
BUT—
DO IT.
WE DIDN'T BRING YOU HERE TO HURT YOU, MISS NITOBE.
WE'RE NOT ACTUALLY MONSTERS.
THEN WHY AM I HERE? YOU COULD HAVE PUT ALL OF THIS IN AN EMAIL.
WHICH YOU WOULDN'T READ. OR WOULDN'T BELIEVE.
THERE'S A LOT MORE TO THIS WAR THAN GENETICS OR RELIGIOUS DIFFERENCES. IT'S NOT JUST US AND YOU. BLOODS AND BEATS.
THIS WAR IS ABOUT *TRUTHS* AND *LIES*.
MAYBE ALL WARS ARE. I DON'T KNOW. THIS IS MY FIRST.
BUT YOU...
YOU'VE SEEN WARS ALL OVER THE WORLD. AFGHANISTAN. SOMALIA. PLACES I CAN'T EVEN FIND ON A MAP.
TELL ME, HAS ANYONE EVER TRIED TO REALLY TELL THE TRUTH?

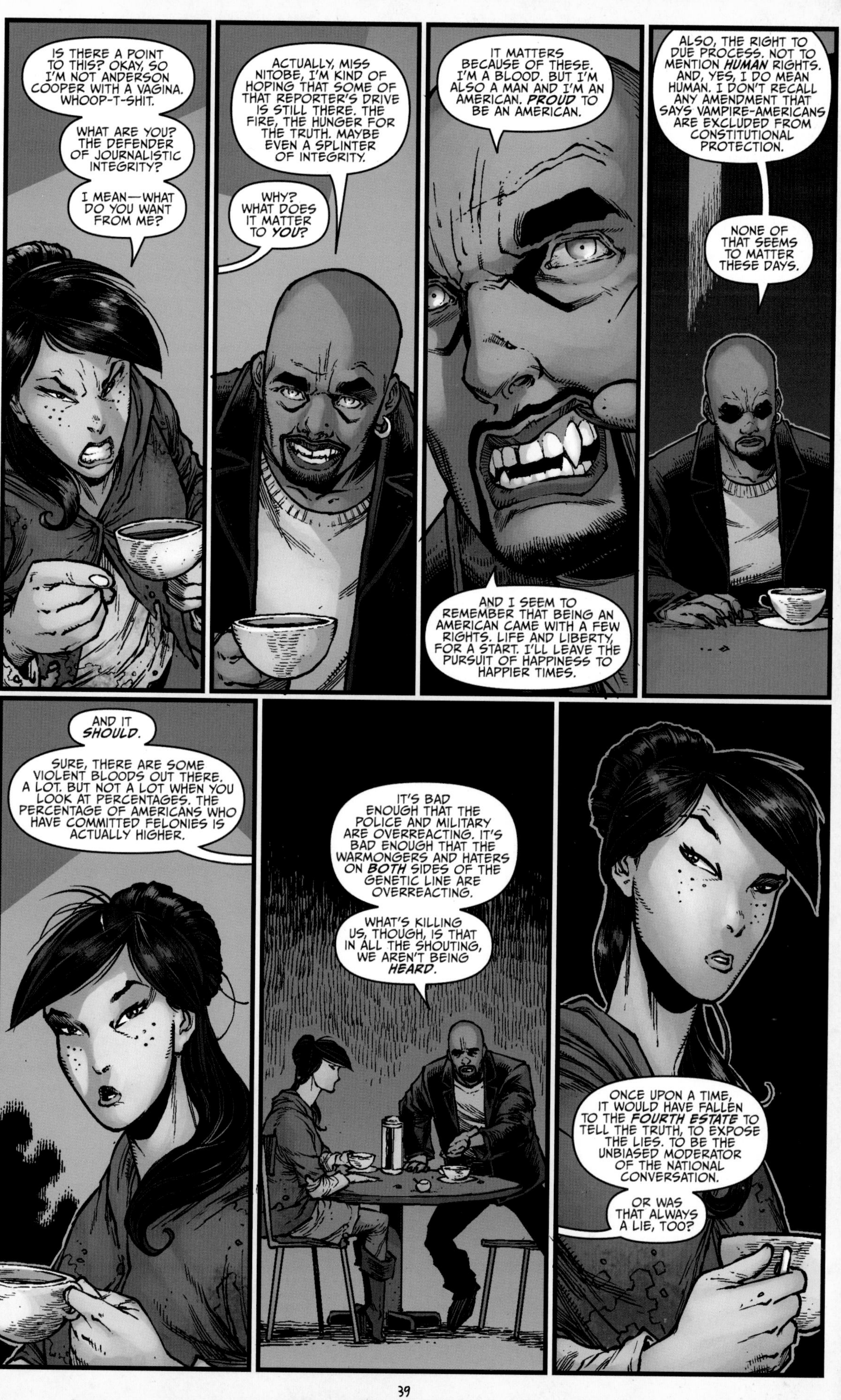
IS THERE A POINT TO THIS? OKAY, SO I'M NOT ANDERSON COOPER WITH A VAGINA. WHOOP-T-SHIT.
WHAT ARE YOU? THE DEFENDER OF JOURNALISTIC INTEGRITY?
I MEAN—WHAT DO YOU WANT FROM ME?
ACTUALLY, MISS NITOBE, I'M KIND OF HOPING THAT SOME OF THAT REPORTER'S DRIVE IS STILL THERE. THE FIRE, THE HUNGER FOR THE TRUTH. MAYBE EVEN A SPLINTER OF INTEGRITY.
WHY? WHAT DOES IT MATTER TO *YOU*?
IT MATTERS BECAUSE OF THESE. I'M A BLOOD. BUT I'M ALSO A MAN AND I'M AN AMERICAN. *PROUD* TO BE AN AMERICAN.
AND I SEEM TO REMEMBER THAT BEING AN AMERICAN CAME WITH A FEW RIGHTS. LIFE AND LIBERTY, FOR A START. I'LL LEAVE THE PURSUIT OF HAPPINESS TO HAPPIER TIMES.
ALSO, THE RIGHT TO DUE PROCESS. NOT TO MENTION *HUMAN* RIGHTS. AND, YES, I DO MEAN HUMAN. I DON'T RECALL ANY AMENDMENT THAT SAYS VAMPIRE-AMERICANS ARE EXCLUDED FROM CONSTITUTIONAL PROTECTION.
NONE OF THAT SEEMS TO MATTER THESE DAYS.
AND IT *SHOULD*.
SURE, THERE ARE SOME VIOLENT BLOODS OUT THERE. A LOT. BUT NOT A LOT WHEN YOU LOOK AT PERCENTAGES. THE PERCENTAGE OF AMERICANS WHO HAVE COMMITTED FELONIES IS ACTUALLY HIGHER.
IT'S BAD ENOUGH THAT THE POLICE AND MILITARY ARE OVERREACTING. IT'S BAD ENOUGH THAT THE WARMONGERS AND HATERS ON *BOTH* SIDES OF THE GENETIC LINE ARE OVERREACTING.
WHAT'S KILLING US, THOUGH, IS THAT IN ALL THE SHOUTING, WE AREN'T BEING *HEARD*.
ONCE UPON A TIME, IT WOULD HAVE FALLEN TO THE *FOURTH ESTATE* TO TELL THE TRUTH, TO EXPOSE THE LIES. TO BE THE UNBIASED MODERATOR OF THE NATIONAL CONVERSATION.
OR WAS THAT ALWAYS A LIE, TOO?

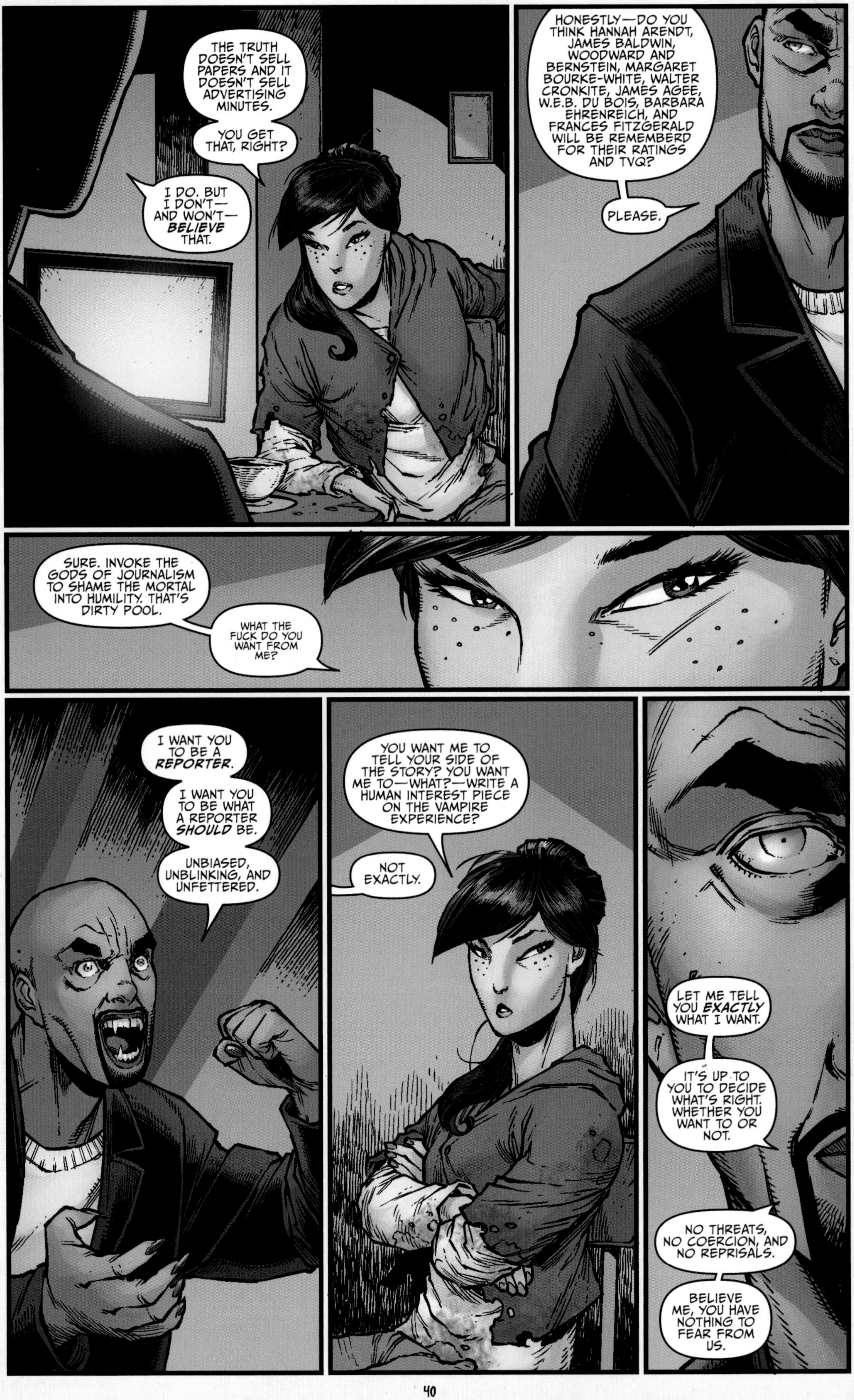
THE TRUTH DOESN'T SELL PAPERS AND IT DOESN'T SELL ADVERTISING MINUTES.
YOU GET THAT, RIGHT?
I DO. BUT I DON'T— AND WON'T— BELIEVE THAT.
HONESTLY—DO YOU THINK HANNAH ARENDT, JAMES BALDWIN, WOODWARD AND BERNSTEIN, MARGARET BOURKE-WHITE, WALTER CRONKITE, JAMES AGEE, W.E.B. DU BOIS, BARBARA EHRENREICH, AND FRANCES FITZGERALD WILL BE REMEMBERD FOR THEIR RATINGS AND TVQ?
PLEASE.
SURE. INVOKE THE GODS OF JOURNALISM TO SHAME THE MORTAL INTO HUMILITY. THAT'S DIRTY POOL.
WHAT THE FUCK DO YOU WANT FROM ME?
I WANT YOU TO BE A REPORTER.
I WANT YOU TO BE WHAT A REPORTER SHOULD BE.
UNBIASED, UNBLINKING, AND UNFETTERED.
YOU WANT ME TO TELL YOUR SIDE OF THE STORY? YOU WANT ME TO—WHAT?—WRITE A HUMAN INTEREST PIECE ON THE VAMPIRE EXPERIENCE?
NOT EXACTLY.
LET ME TELL YOU EXACTLY WHAT I WANT.
IT'S UP TO YOU TO DECIDE WHAT'S RIGHT. WHETHER YOU WANT TO OR NOT.
NO THREATS, NO COERCION, AND NO REPRISALS.
BELIEVE ME, YOU HAVE NOTHING TO FEAR FROM US.

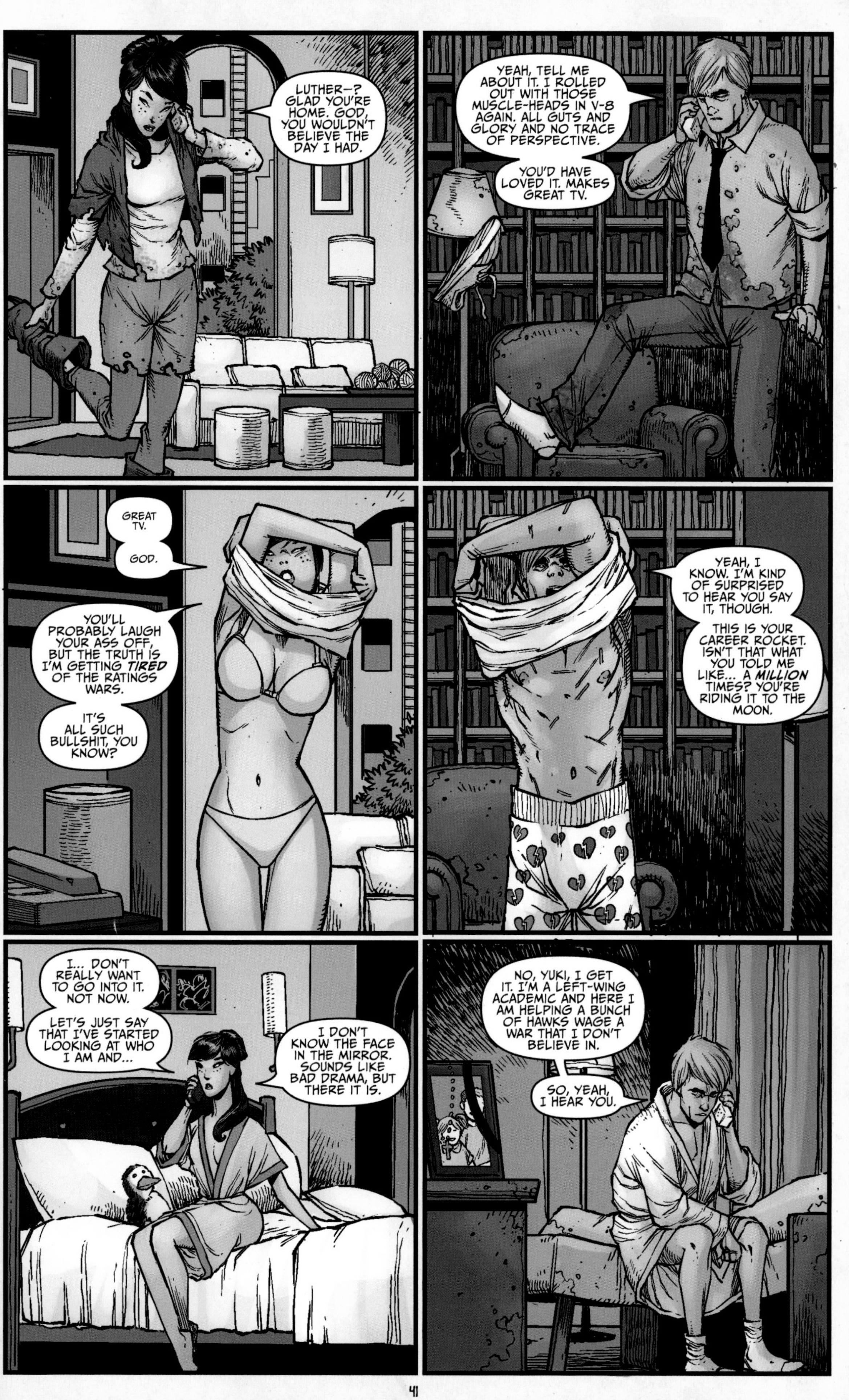
LUTHER–? GLAD YOU'RE HOME. GOD, YOU WOULDN'T BELIEVE THE DAY I HAD.
YEAH, TELL ME ABOUT IT. I ROLLED OUT WITH THOSE MUSCLE-HEADS IN V-8 AGAIN. ALL GUTS AND GLORY AND NO TRACE OF PERSPECTIVE.
YOU'D HAVE LOVED IT. MAKES GREAT TV.
GREAT TV.
GOD.
YOU'LL PROBABLY LAUGH YOUR ASS OFF, BUT THE TRUTH IS I'M GETTING TIRED OF THE RATINGS WARS.
IT'S ALL SUCH BULLSHIT, YOU KNOW?
YEAH, I KNOW. I'M KIND OF SURPRISED TO HEAR YOU SAY IT, THOUGH.
THIS IS YOUR CAREER ROCKET. ISN'T THAT WHAT YOU TOLD ME LIKE... A MILLION TIMES? YOU'RE RIDING IT TO THE MOON.
I... DON'T REALLY WANT TO GO INTO IT. NOT NOW.
LET'S JUST SAY THAT I'VE STARTED LOOKING AT WHO I AM AND...
I DON'T KNOW THE FACE IN THE MIRROR. SOUNDS LIKE BAD DRAMA, BUT THERE IT IS.
NO, YUKI, I GET IT. I'M A LEFT-WING ACADEMIC AND HERE I AM HELPING A BUNCH OF HAWKS WAGE A WAR THAT I DON'T BELIEVE IN.
SO, YEAH, I HEAR YOU.

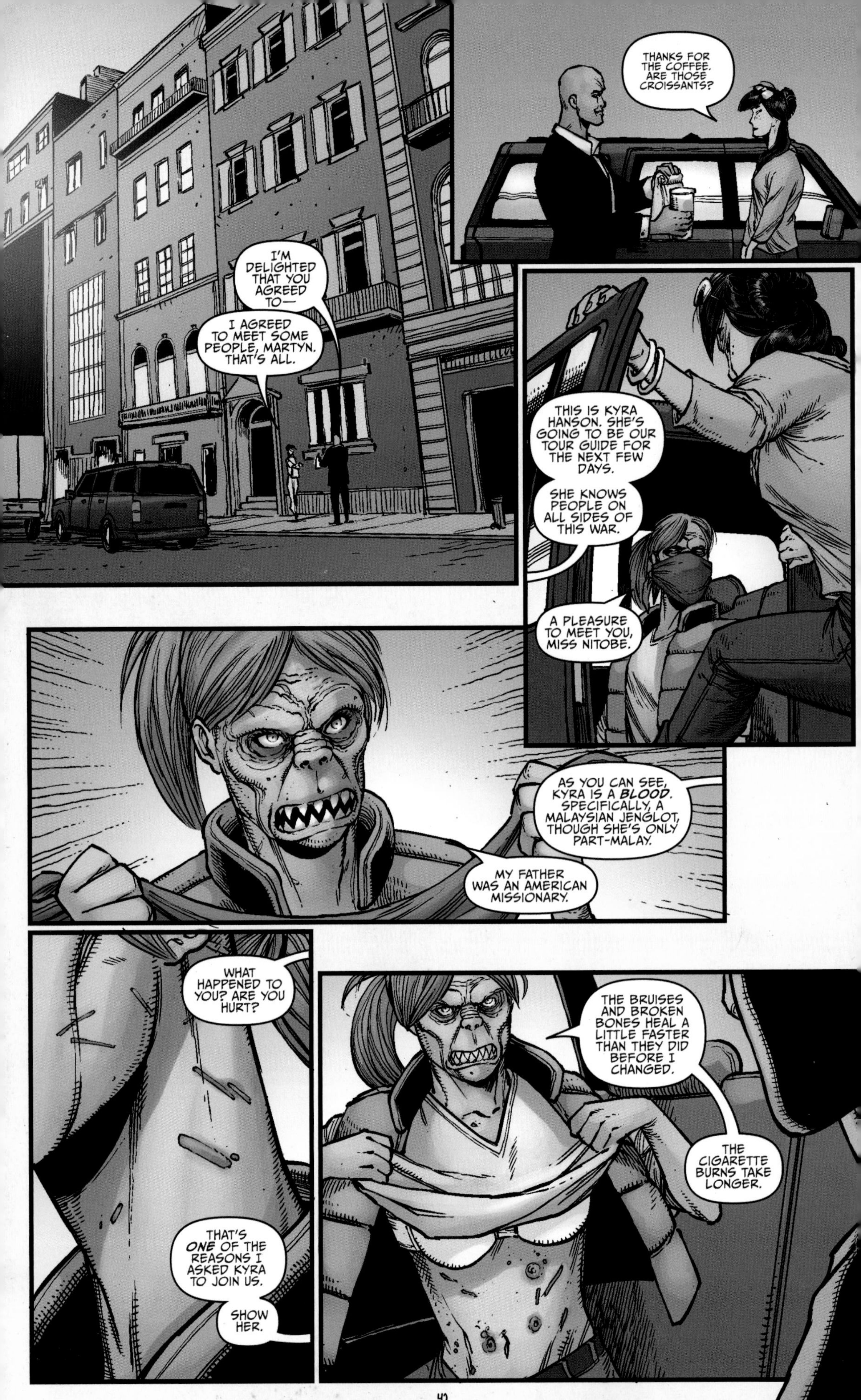
THANKS FOR THE COFFEE. ARE THOSE CROISSANTS?
I'M DELIGHTED THAT YOU AGREED TO—
I AGREED TO MEET SOME PEOPLE, MARTYN. THAT'S ALL.
THIS IS KYRA HANSON. SHE'S GOING TO BE OUR TOUR GUIDE FOR THE NEXT FEW DAYS.
SHE KNOWS PEOPLE ON ALL SIDES OF THIS WAR.
A PLEASURE TO MEET YOU, MISS NITOBE.
AS YOU CAN SEE, KYRA IS A *BLOOD*. SPECIFICALLY, A MALAYSIAN JENGLOT, THOUGH SHE'S ONLY PART-MALAY.
MY FATHER WAS AN AMERICAN MISSIONARY.
WHAT HAPPENED TO YOU? ARE YOU HURT?
THAT'S *ONE* OF THE REASONS I ASKED KYRA TO JOIN US.
SHOW HER.
THE BRUISES AND BROKEN BONES HEAL A LITTLE FASTER THAN THEY DID BEFORE I CHANGED.
THE CIGARETTE BURNS TAKE LONGER.

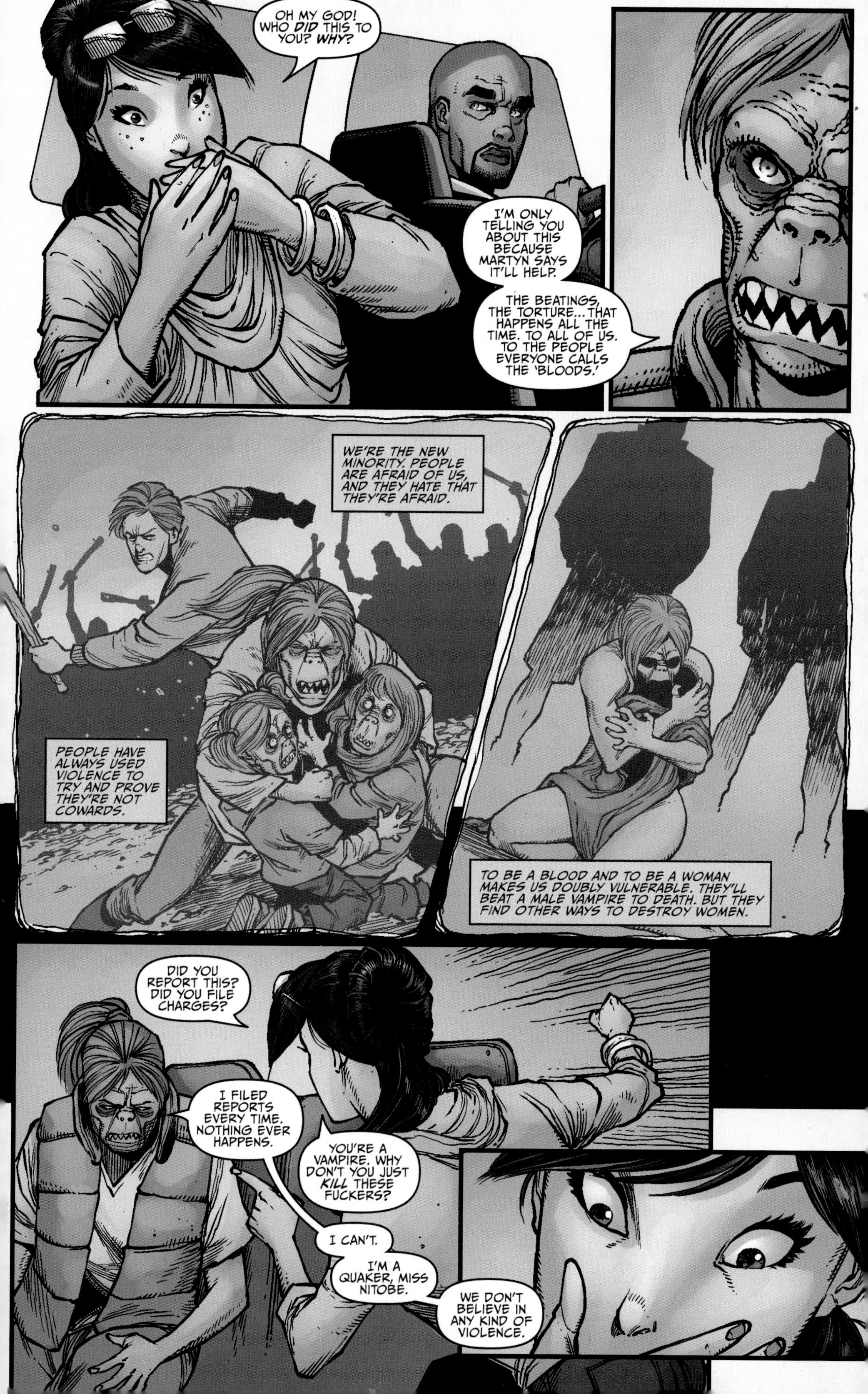

OH MY GOD! WHO DID THIS TO YOU? WHY?
I'M ONLY TELLING YOU ABOUT THIS BECAUSE MARTYN SAYS IT'LL HELP.
THE BEATINGS, THE TORTURE... THAT HAPPENS ALL THE TIME. TO ALL OF US. TO THE PEOPLE EVERYONE CALLS THE 'BLOODS.'
WE'RE THE NEW MINORITY. PEOPLE ARE AFRAID OF US, AND THEY HATE THAT THEY'RE AFRAID.
PEOPLE HAVE ALWAYS USED VIOLENCE TO TRY AND PROVE THEY'RE NOT COWARDS.
TO BE A BLOOD AND TO BE A WOMAN MAKES US DOUBLY VULNERABLE. THEY'LL BEAT A MALE VAMPIRE TO DEATH. BUT THEY FIND OTHER WAYS TO DESTROY WOMEN.
DID YOU REPORT THIS? DID YOU FILE CHARGES?
I FILED REPORTS EVERY TIME. NOTHING EVER HAPPENS.
YOU'RE A VAMPIRE. WHY DON'T YOU JUST KILL THESE FUCKERS?
I CAN'T.
I'M A QUAKER, MISS NITOBE.
WE DON'T BELIEVE IN ANY KIND OF VIOLENCE.

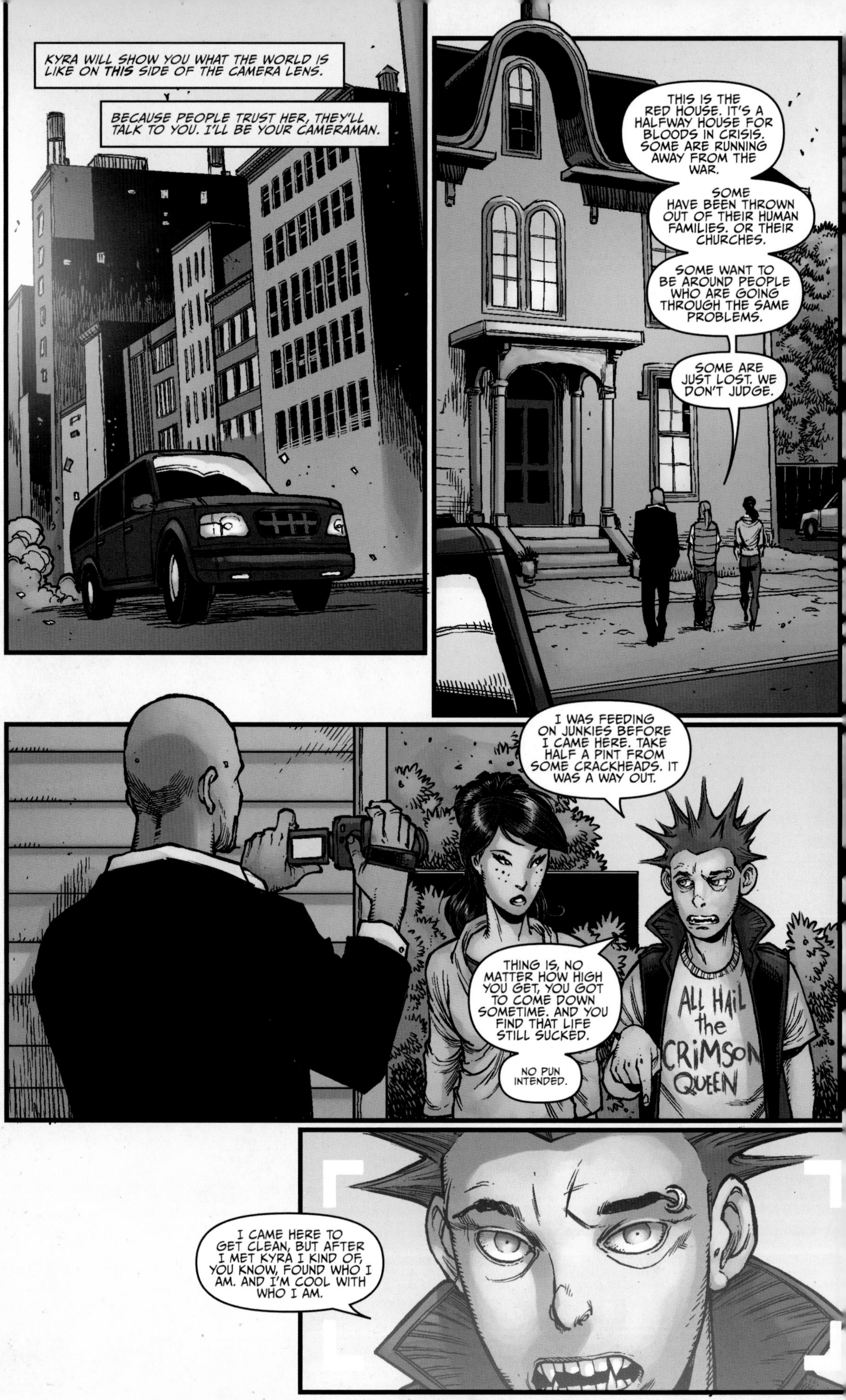
KYRA WILL SHOW YOU WHAT THE WORLD IS LIKE ON THIS SIDE OF THE CAMERA LENS.
BECAUSE PEOPLE TRUST HER, THEY'LL TALK TO YOU. I'LL BE YOUR CAMERAMAN.
THIS IS THE RED HOUSE. IT'S A HALFWAY HOUSE FOR BLOODS IN CRISIS. SOME ARE RUNNING AWAY FROM THE WAR.
SOME HAVE BEEN THROWN OUT OF THEIR HUMAN FAMILIES. OR THEIR CHURCHES.
SOME WANT TO BE AROUND PEOPLE WHO ARE GOING THROUGH THE SAME PROBLEMS.
SOME ARE JUST LOST. WE DON'T JUDGE.
I WAS FEEDING ON JUNKIES BEFORE I CAME HERE. TAKE HALF A PINT FROM SOME CRACKHEADS. IT WAS A WAY OUT.
THING IS, NO MATTER HOW HIGH YOU GET, YOU GOT TO COME DOWN SOMETIME. AND YOU FIND THAT LIFE STILL SUCKED.
NO PUN INTENDED.
ALL HAIL the CRIMSON QUEEN
I CAME HERE TO GET CLEAN, BUT AFTER I MET KYRA I KIND OF, YOU KNOW, FOUND WHO I AM. AND I'M COOL WITH WHO I AM.

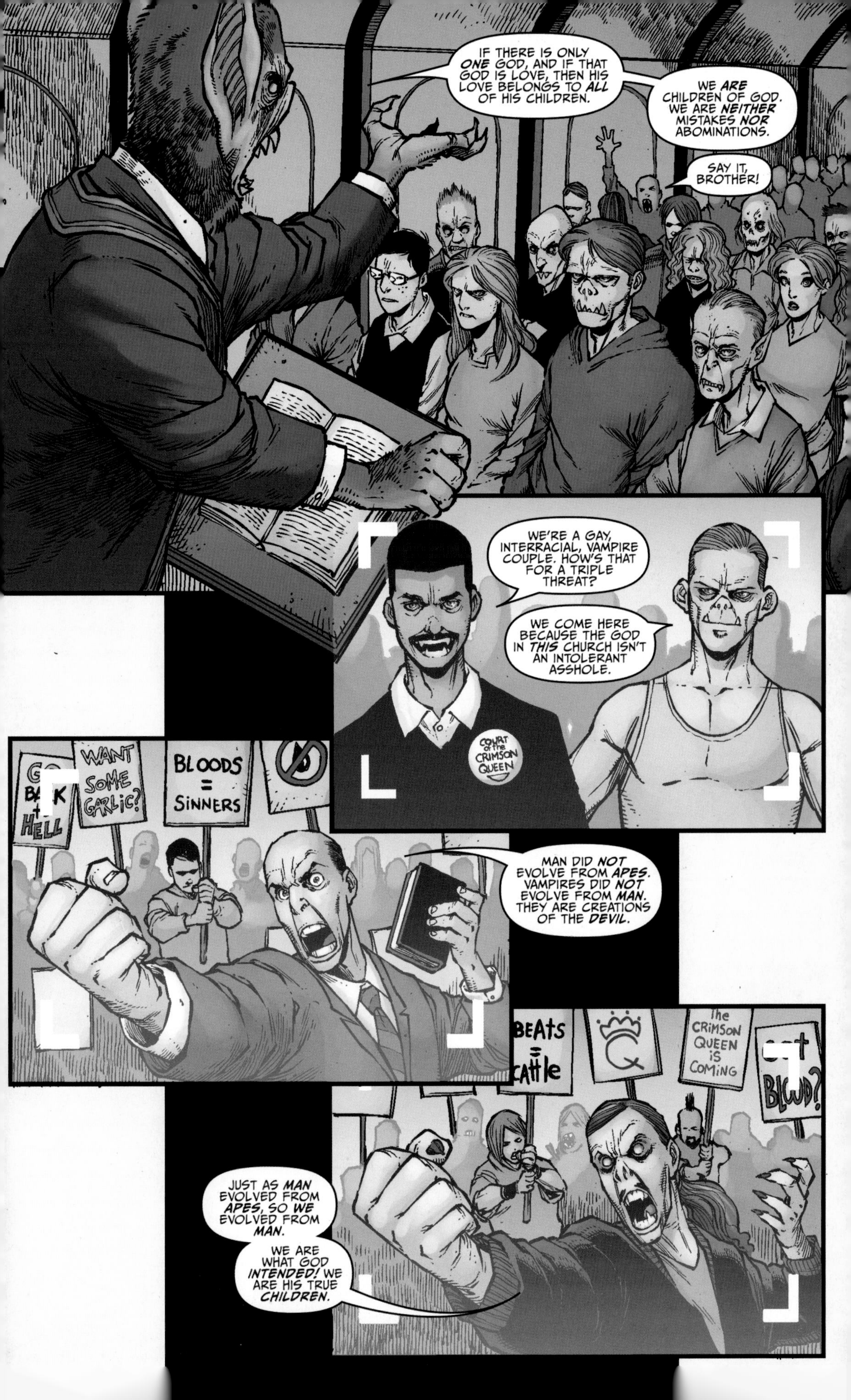
IF THERE IS ONLY *ONE* GOD, AND IF THAT GOD IS LOVE, THEN HIS LOVE BELONGS TO *ALL* OF HIS CHILDREN.
WE *ARE* CHILDREN OF GOD. WE ARE *NEITHER* MISTAKES *NOR* ABOMINATIONS.
SAY IT, BROTHER!
WE'RE A GAY, INTERRACIAL, VAMPIRE COUPLE. HOW'S THAT FOR A TRIPLE THREAT?
WE COME HERE BECAUSE THE GOD IN *THIS* CHURCH ISN'T AN INTOLERANT ASSHOLE.
COURT of the CRIMSON QUEEN
WANT SOME GARLIC?
BLOODS = SINNERS
MAN DID *NOT* EVOLVE FROM *APES*. VAMPIRES DID *NOT* EVOLVE FROM *MAN*. THEY ARE CREATIONS OF THE *DEVIL*.
BEATS = cattle
The CRIMSON QUEEN IS COMING
JUST AS *MAN* EVOLVED FROM *APES*, SO *WE* EVOLVED FROM *MAN*.
WE ARE WHAT GOD *INTENDED!* WE ARE HIS TRUE *CHILDREN*.

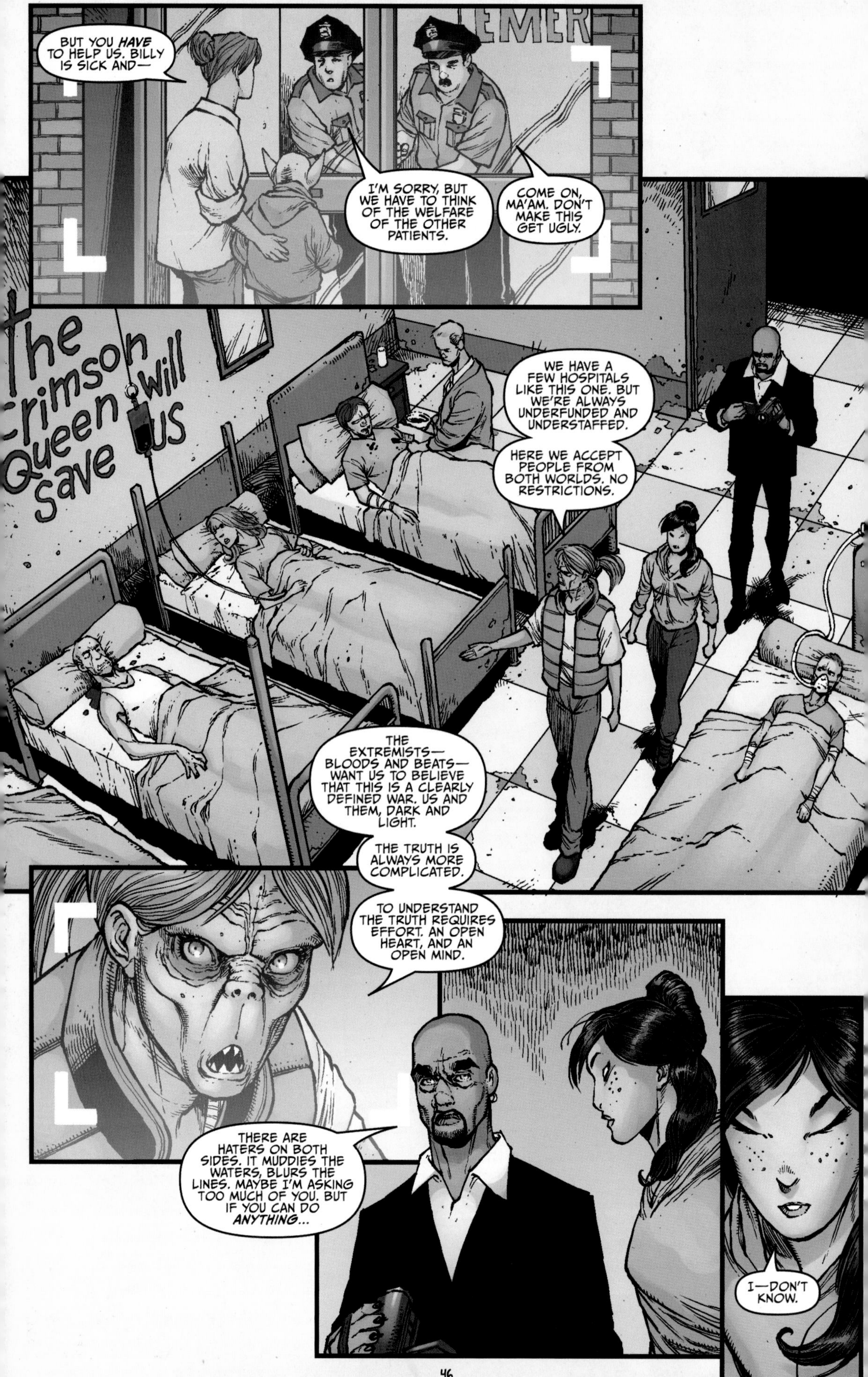
EMER
BUT YOU *HAVE* TO HELP US. BILLY IS SICK AND—
I'M SORRY, BUT WE HAVE TO THINK OF THE WELFARE OF THE OTHER PATIENTS.
COME ON, MA'AM. DON'T MAKE THIS GET UGLY.
The Crimson Queen will save us
WE HAVE A FEW HOSPITALS LIKE THIS ONE. BUT WE'RE ALWAYS UNDERFUNDED AND UNDERSTAFFED.
HERE WE ACCEPT PEOPLE FROM BOTH WORLDS. NO RESTRICTIONS.
THE EXTREMISTS—BLOODS AND BEATS—WANT US TO BELIEVE THAT THIS IS A CLEARLY DEFINED WAR. US AND THEM, DARK AND LIGHT.
THE TRUTH IS ALWAYS MORE COMPLICATED.
TO UNDERSTAND THE TRUTH REQUIRES EFFORT. AN OPEN HEART, AND AN OPEN MIND.
THERE ARE HATERS ON BOTH SIDES. IT MUDDIES THE WATERS, BLURS THE LINES. MAYBE I'M ASKING TOO MUCH OF YOU. BUT IF YOU CAN DO *ANYTHING*...
I—DON'T KNOW.

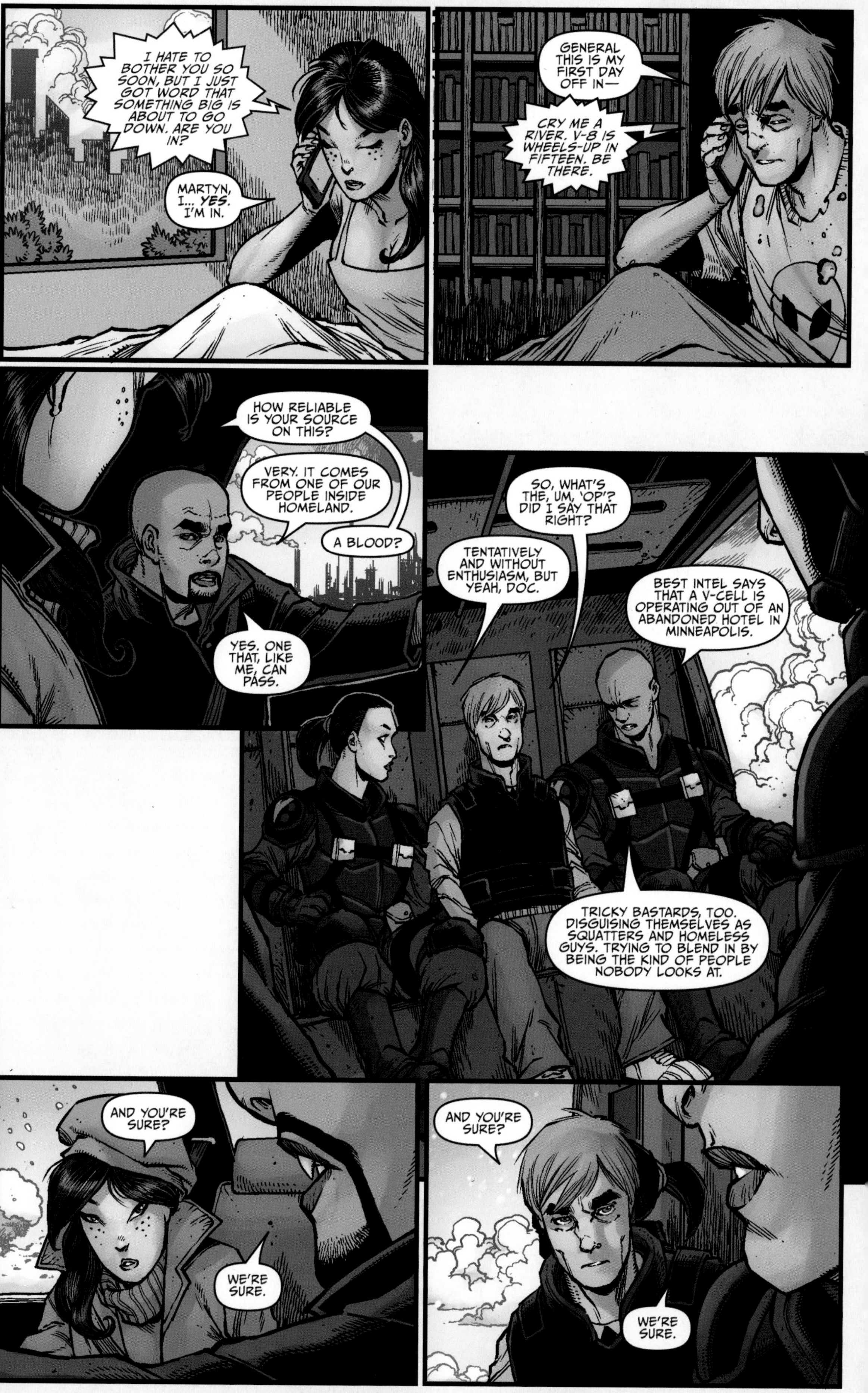
I HATE TO BOTHER YOU SO SOON, BUT I JUST GOT WORD THAT SOMETHING BIG IS ABOUT TO GO DOWN. ARE YOU IN?
MARTYN, I... YES. I'M IN.
GENERAL THIS IS MY FIRST DAY OFF IN—
CRY ME A RIVER. V-8 IS WHEELS-UP IN FIFTEEN. BE THERE.
HOW RELIABLE IS YOUR SOURCE ON THIS?
VERY. IT COMES FROM ONE OF OUR PEOPLE INSIDE HOMELAND.
A BLOOD?
YES. ONE THAT, LIKE ME, CAN PASS.
SO, WHAT'S THE, UM, 'OP'? DID I SAY THAT RIGHT?
TENTATIVELY AND WITHOUT ENTHUSIASM, BUT YEAH, DOC.
BEST INTEL SAYS THAT A V-CELL IS OPERATING OUT OF AN ABANDONED HOTEL IN MINNEAPOLIS.
TRICKY BASTARDS, TOO. DISGUISING THEMSELVES AS SQUATTERS AND HOMELESS GUYS. TRYING TO BLEND IN BY BEING THE KIND OF PEOPLE NOBODY LOOKS AT.
AND YOU'RE SURE?
WE'RE SURE.
AND YOU'RE SURE?
WE'RE SURE.

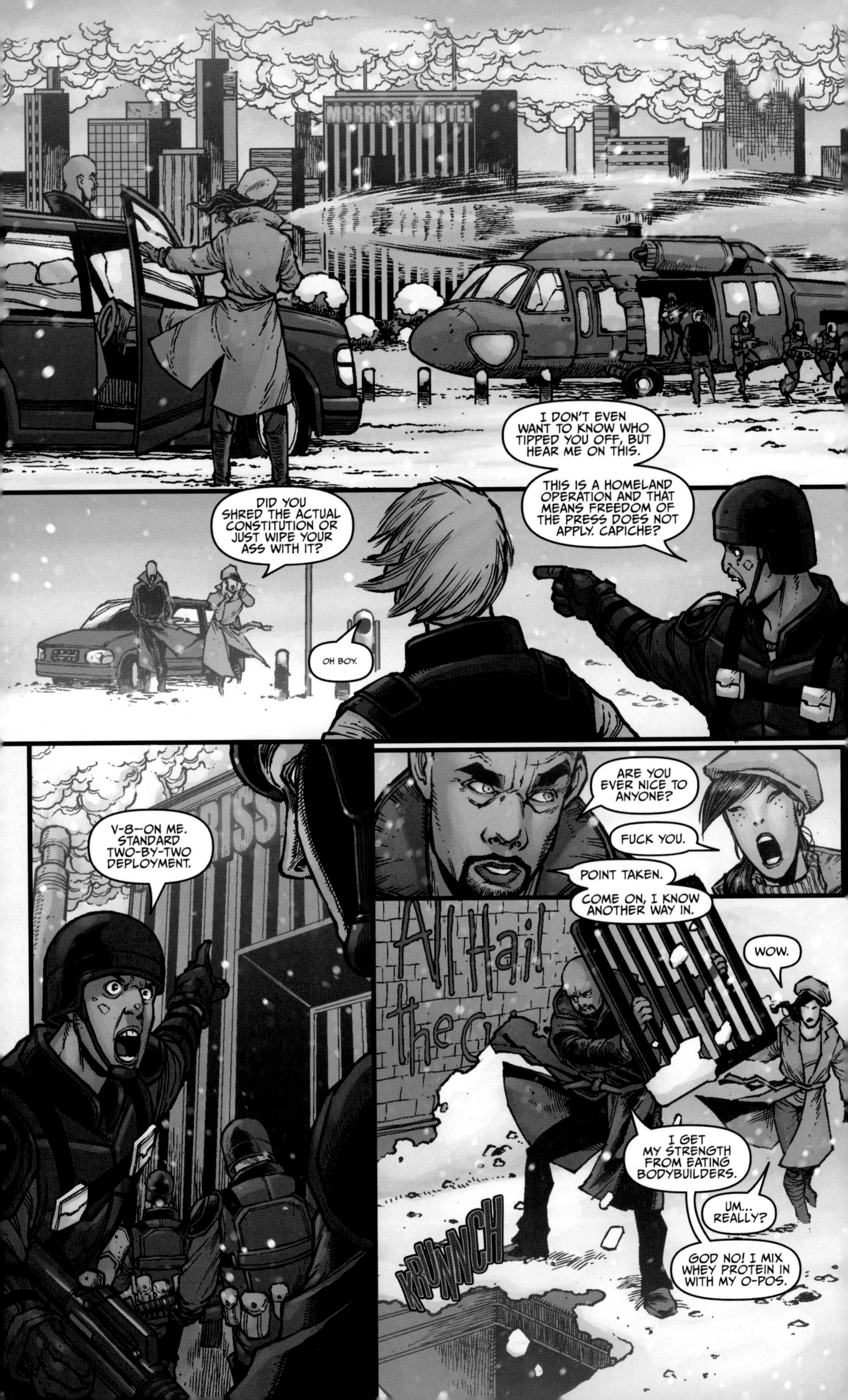
MORRISSEY HOTEL
I DON'T EVEN WANT TO KNOW WHO TIPPED YOU OFF, BUT HEAR ME ON THIS.
THIS IS A HOMELAND OPERATION AND THAT MEANS FREEDOM OF THE PRESS DOES NOT APPLY. CAPICHE?
DID YOU SHRED THE ACTUAL CONSTITUTION OR JUST WIPE YOUR ASS WITH IT?
OH BOY.
V-8—ON ME. STANDARD TWO-BY-TWO DEPLOYMENT.
ARE YOU EVER NICE TO ANYONE?
FUCK YOU.
POINT TAKEN.
COME ON, I KNOW ANOTHER WAY IN.
All Hail the G
WOW.
I GET MY STRENGTH FROM EATING BODYBUILDERS.
UM... REALLY?
GOD NO! I MIX WHEY PROTEIN IN WITH MY O-POS.
KRUNNCH

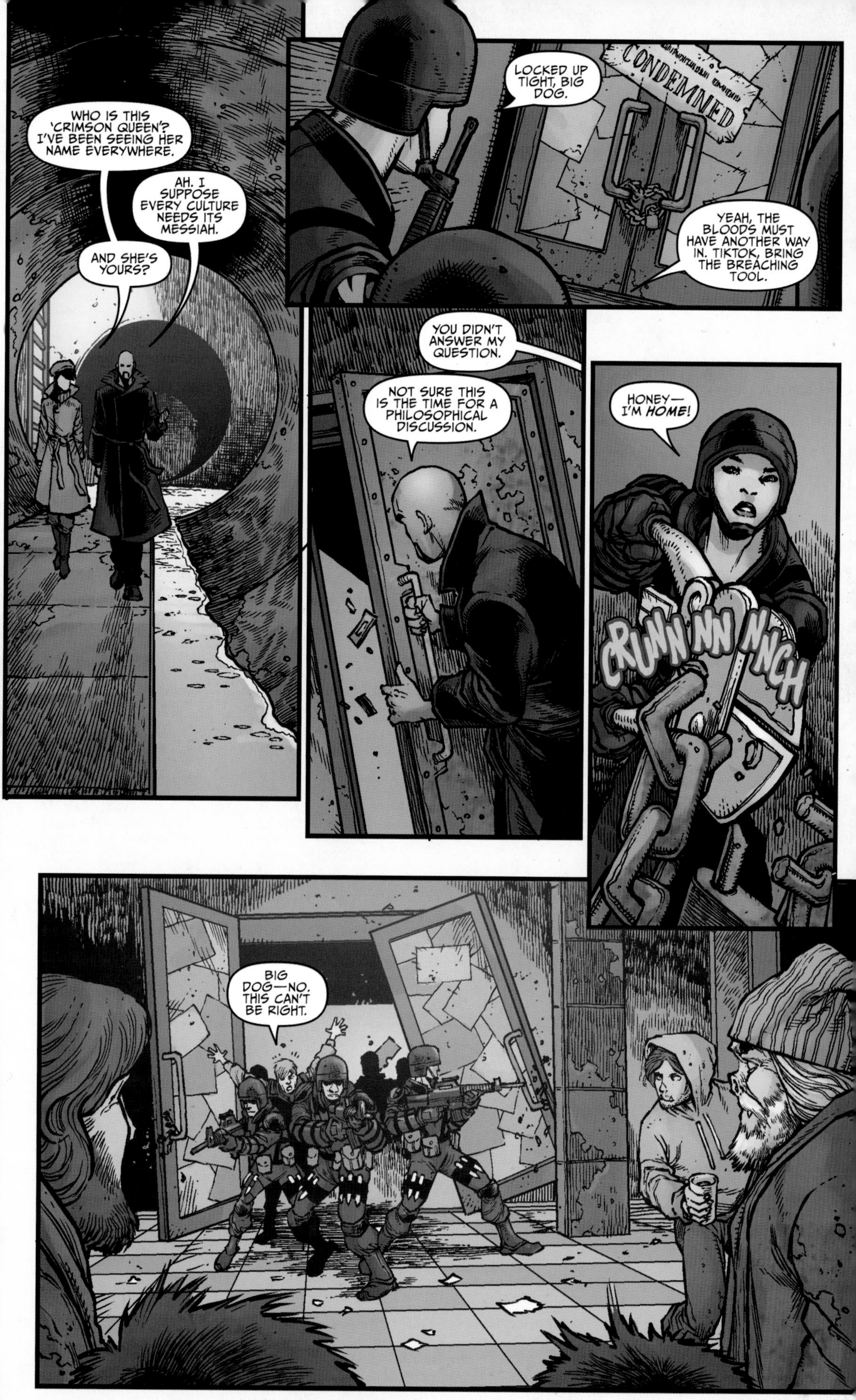
WHO IS THIS 'CRIMSON QUEEN'? I'VE BEEN SEEING HER NAME EVERYWHERE.
AH. I SUPPOSE EVERY CULTURE NEEDS ITS MESSIAH.
AND SHE'S YOURS?
CONDEMNED
LOCKED UP TIGHT, BIG DOG.
YEAH, THE BLOODS MUST HAVE ANOTHER WAY IN. TIKTOK, BRING THE BREACHING TOOL.
YOU DIDN'T ANSWER MY QUESTION.
NOT SURE THIS IS THE TIME FOR A PHILOSOPHICAL DISCUSSION.
HONEY— I'M *HOME*!
CRUNNNNNNCH
BIG DOG—NO. THIS CAN'T BE RIGHT.

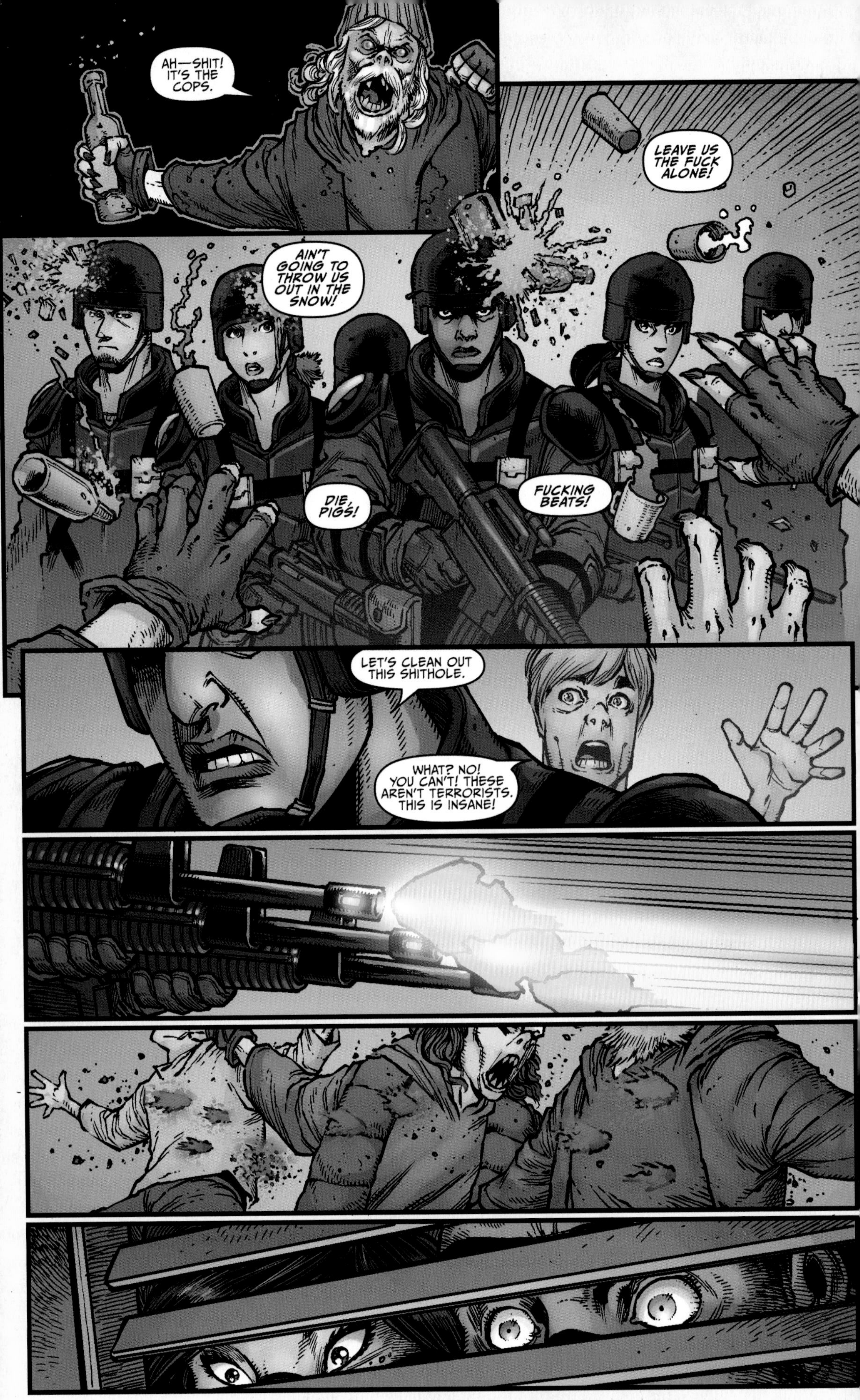

AH—SHIT! IT'S THE COPS.
LEAVE US THE FUCK ALONE!
AIN'T GOING TO THROW US OUT IN THE SNOW!
DIE, PIGS!
FUCKING BEATS!
LET'S CLEAN OUT THIS SHITHOLE.
WHAT? NO! YOU CAN'T! THESE AREN'T TERRORISTS. THIS IS INSANE!

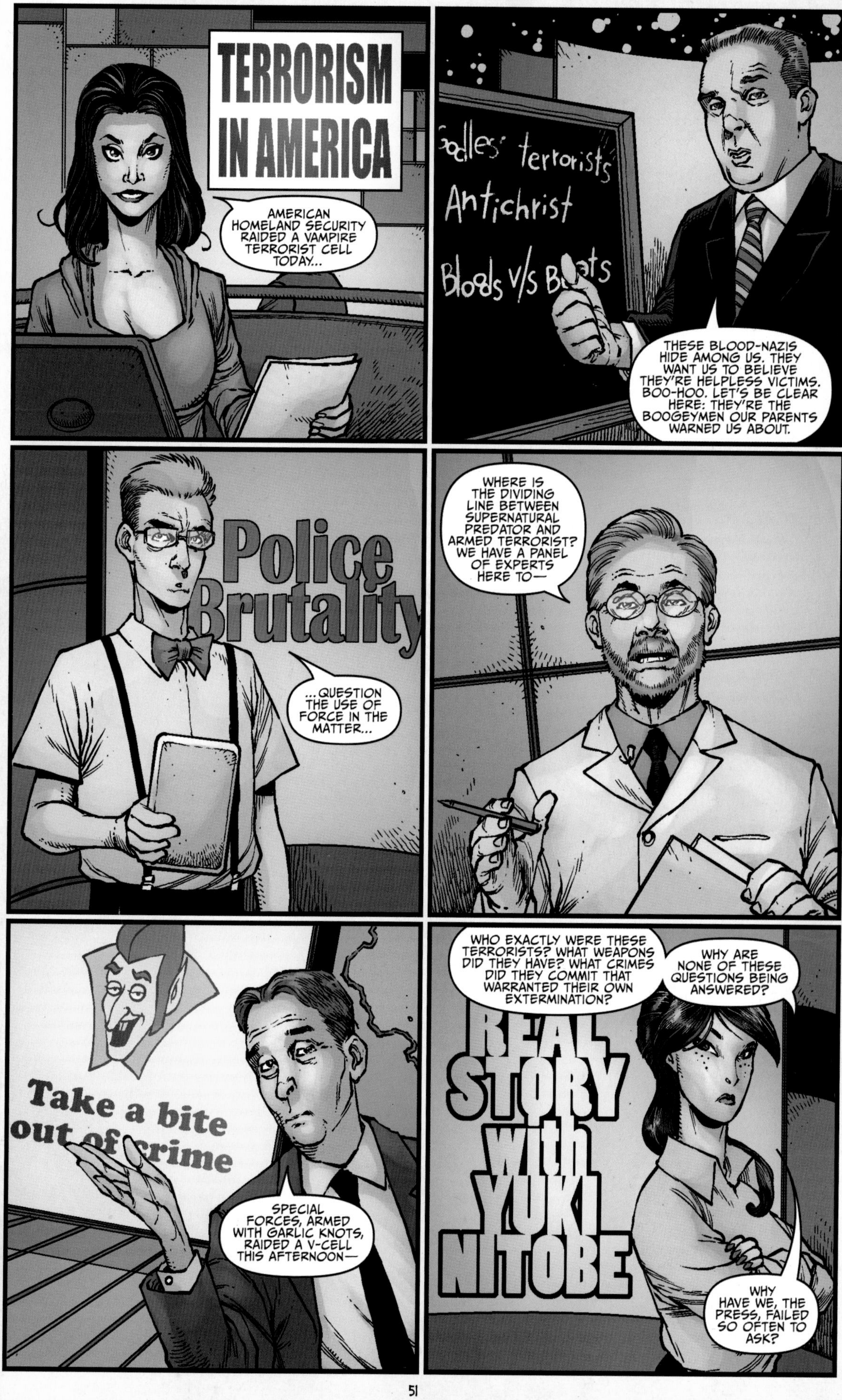
TERRORISM IN AMERICA
AMERICAN HOMELAND SECURITY RAIDED A VAMPIRE TERRORIST CELL TODAY...
Godless terrorists
Antichrist
THESE BLOOD-NAZIS HIDE AMONG US. THEY WANT US TO BELIEVE THEY'RE HELPLESS VICTIMS. BOO-HOO. LET'S BE CLEAR HERE: THEY'RE THE BOOGEYMEN OUR PARENTS WARNED US ABOUT.
Police Brutality
...QUESTION THE USE OF FORCE IN THE MATTER...
WHERE IS THE DIVIDING LINE BETWEEN SUPERNATURAL PREDATOR AND ARMED TERRORIST? WE HAVE A PANEL OF EXPERTS HERE TO—
Take a bite out of crime
SPECIAL FORCES, ARMED WITH GARLIC KNOTS, RAIDED A V-CELL THIS AFTERNOON—
WHO EXACTLY WERE THESE TERRORISTS? WHAT WEAPONS DID THEY HAVE? WHAT CRIMES DID THEY COMMIT THAT WARRANTED THEIR OWN EXTERMINATION?
WHY ARE NONE OF THESE QUESTIONS BEING ANSWERED?
STORY with YUKI NITOBE
WHY HAVE WE, THE PRESS, FAILED SO OFTEN TO ASK?

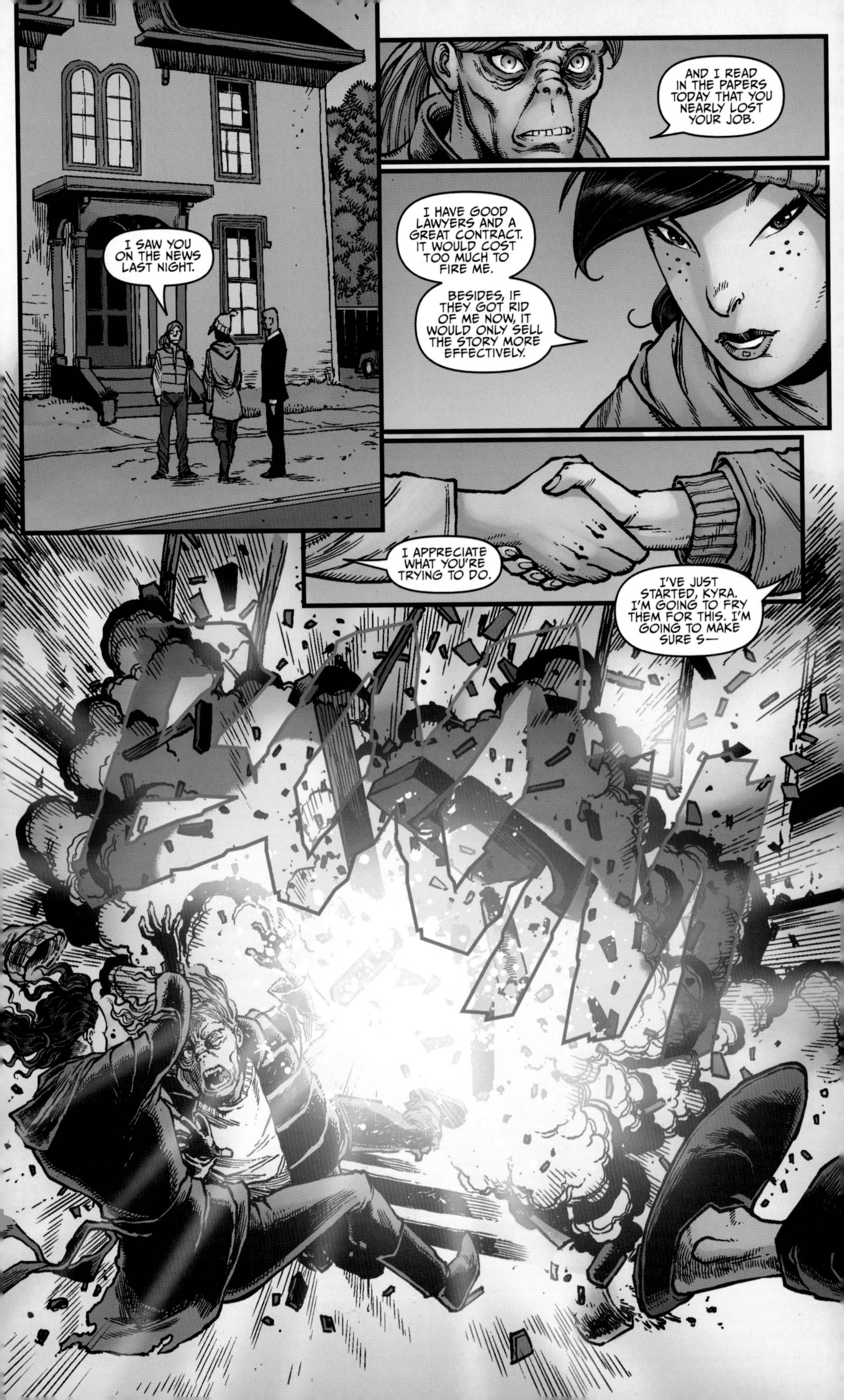
I SAW YOU ON THE NEWS LAST NIGHT.
AND I READ IN THE PAPERS TODAY THAT YOU NEARLY LOST YOUR JOB.
I HAVE GOOD LAWYERS AND A GREAT CONTRACT. IT WOULD COST TOO MUCH TO FIRE ME.
BESIDES, IF THEY GOT RID OF ME NOW, IT WOULD ONLY SELL THE STORY MORE EFFECTIVELY.
I APPRECIATE WHAT YOU'RE TRYING TO DO.
I'VE JUST STARTED, KYRA. I'M GOING TO FRY THEM FOR THIS. I'M GOING TO MAKE SURE S—

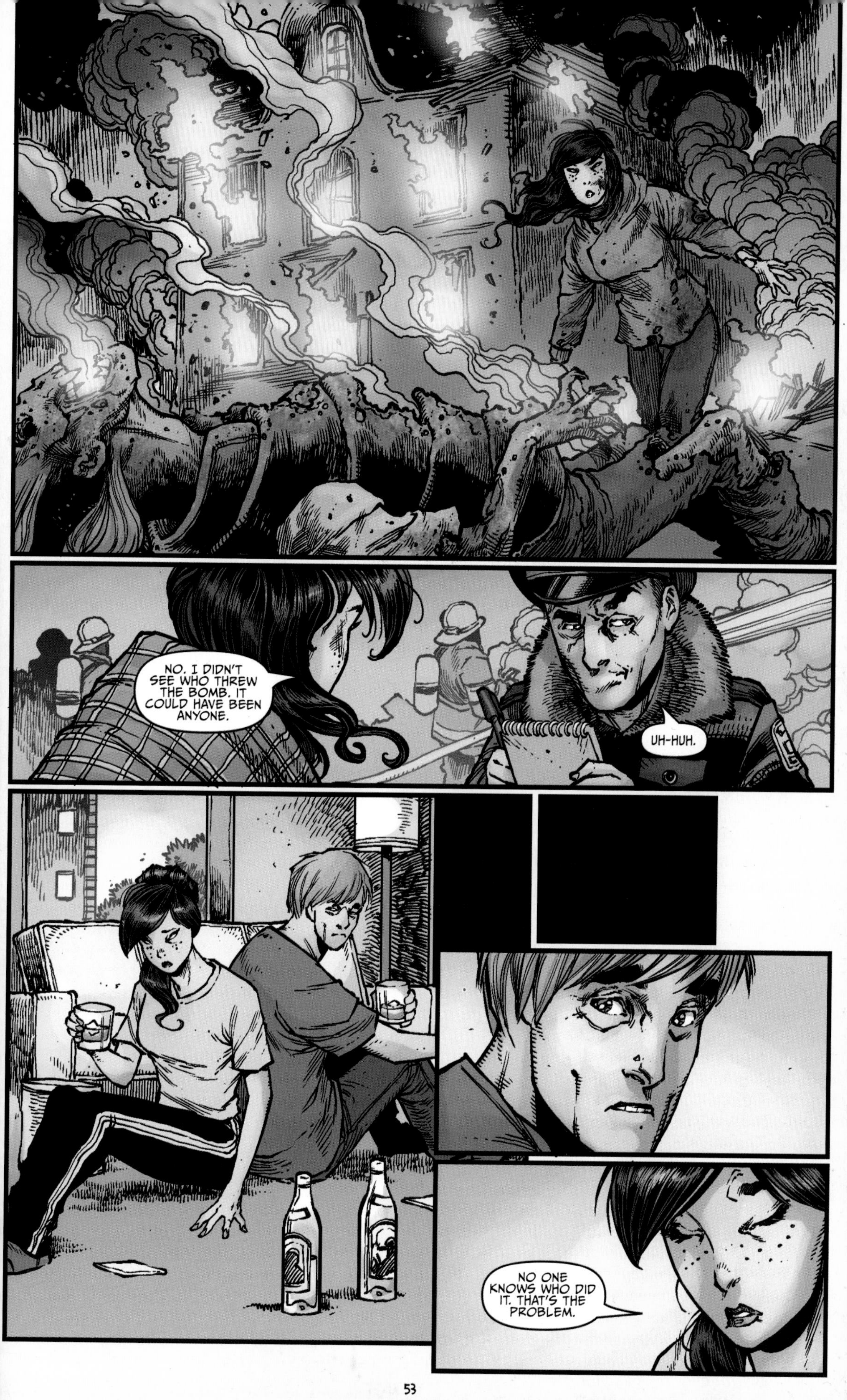
NO. I DIDN'T SEE WHO THREW THE BOMB. IT COULD HAVE BEEN ANYONE.
UH-HUH.
NO ONE KNOWS WHO DID IT. THAT'S THE PROBLEM.

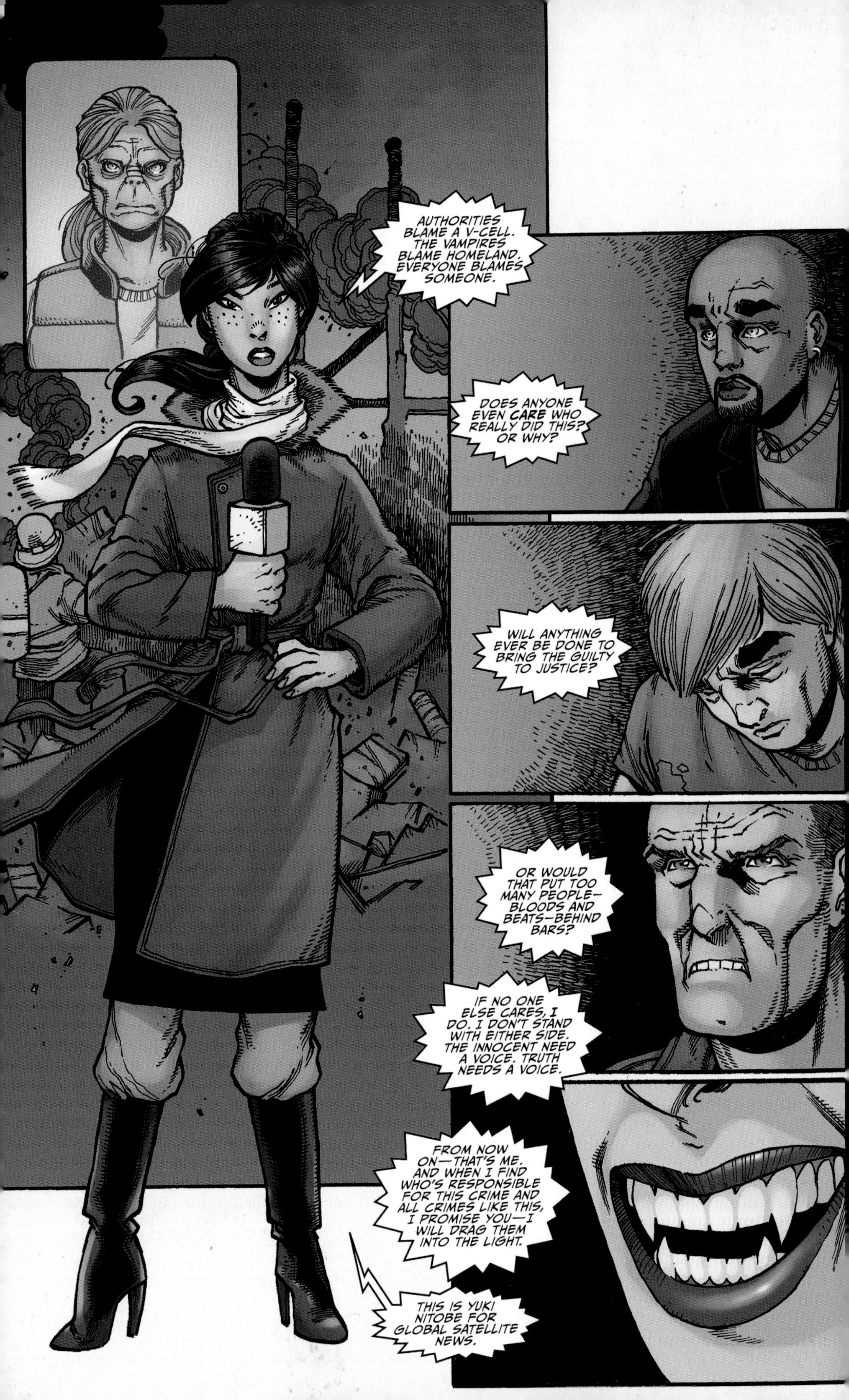
AUTHORITIES BLAME A V-CELL. THE VAMPIRES BLAME HOMELAND. EVERYONE BLAMES SOMEONE.
DOES ANYONE EVEN CARE WHO REALLY DID THIS? OR WHY?
WILL ANYTHING EVER BE DONE TO BRING THE GUILTY TO JUSTICE?
OR WOULD THAT PUT TOO MANY PEOPLE—BLOODS AND BEATS—BEHIND BARS?
IF NO ONE ELSE CARES, I DO. I DON'T STAND WITH EITHER SIDE. THE INNOCENT NEED A VOICE. TRUTH NEEDS A VOICE.
FROM NOW ON—THAT'S ME. AND WHEN I FIND WHO'S RESPONSIBLE FOR THIS CRIME AND ALL CRIMES LIKE THIS, I PROMISE YOU—I WILL DRAG THEM INTO THE LIGHT.
THIS IS YUKI NITOBE FOR GLOBAL SATELLITE NEWS.

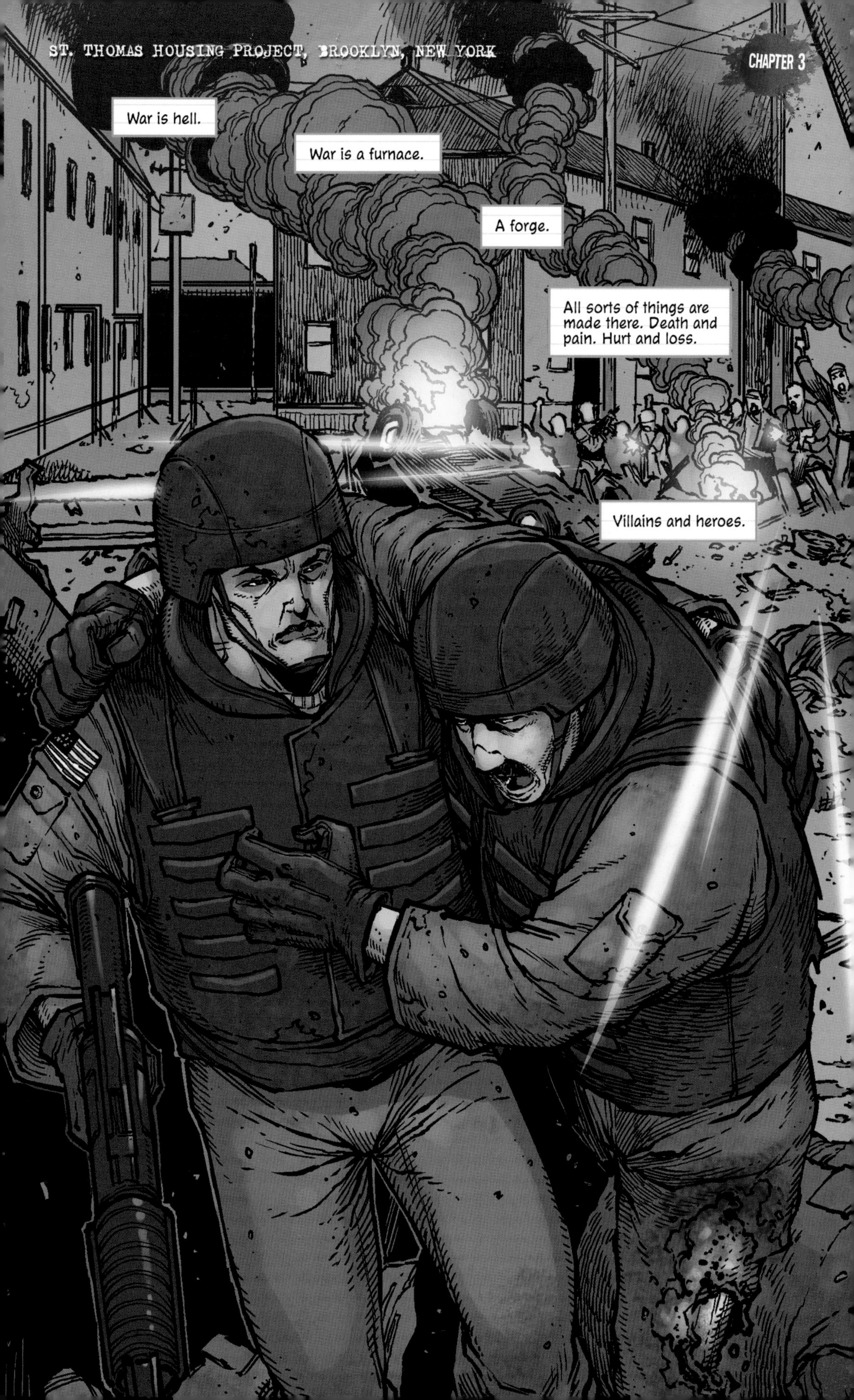
ST. THOMAS HOUSING PROJECT, BROOKLYN, NEW YORK
CHAPTER 3
War is hell.
War is a furnace.
A forge.
All sorts of things are made there. Death and pain. Hurt and loss.
Villains and heroes.

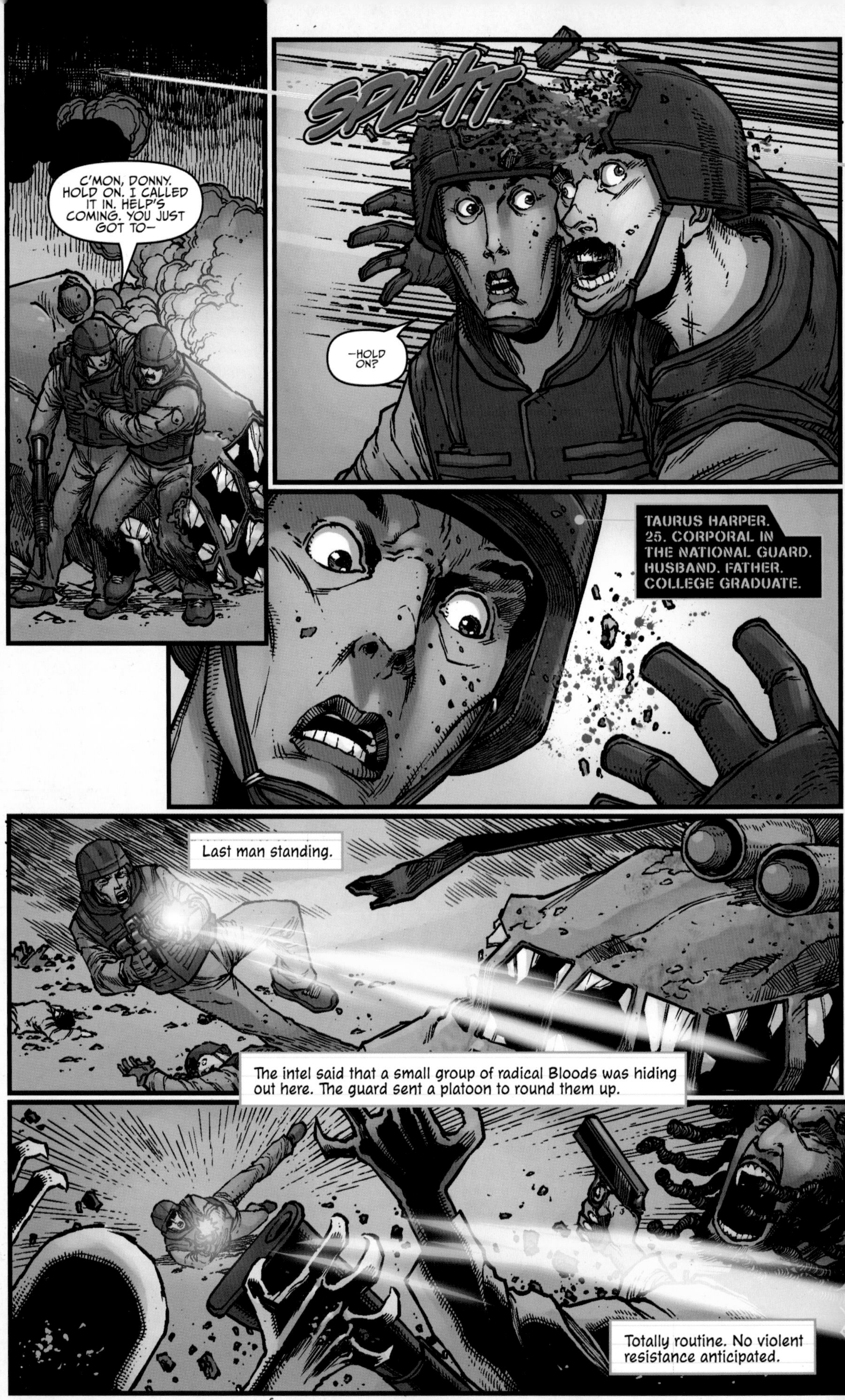
C'MON, DONNY. HOLD ON. I CALLED IT IN. HELP'S COMING. YOU JUST GOT TO—
SPLUTT
—HOLD ON?
TAURUS HARPER. 25. CORPORAL IN THE NATIONAL GUARD. HUSBAND. FATHER. COLLEGE GRADUATE.
Last man standing.
The intel said that a small group of radical Bloods was hiding out here. The guard sent a platoon to round them up.
Totally routine. No violent resistance anticipated.

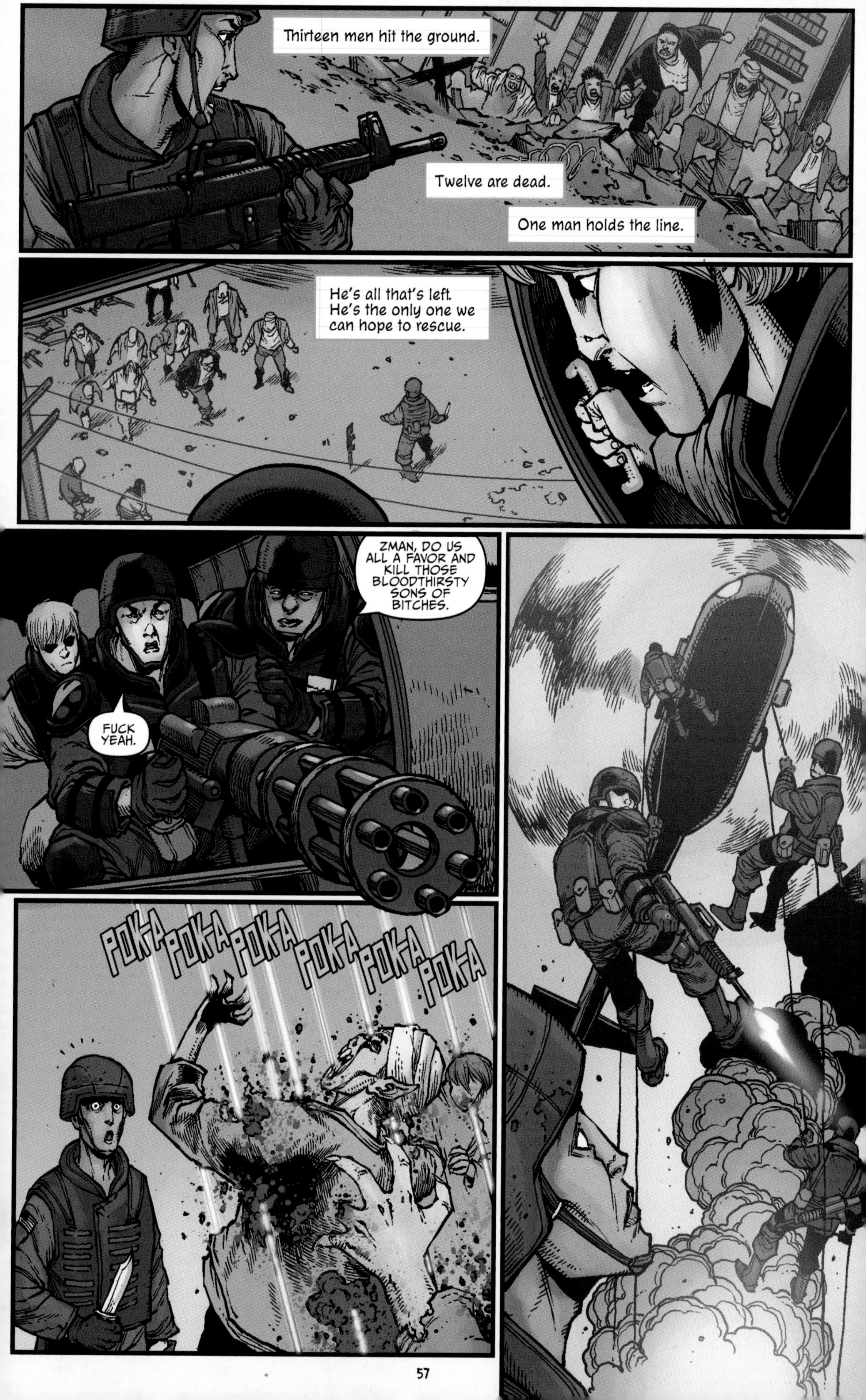
Thirteen men hit the ground.
Twelve are dead.
One man holds the line.
He's all that's left. He's the only one we can hope to rescue.
ZMAN, DO US ALL A FAVOR AND KILL THOSE BLOODTHIRSTY SONS OF BITCHES.
FUCK YEAH.
POKA POKA POKA POKA POKA POKA

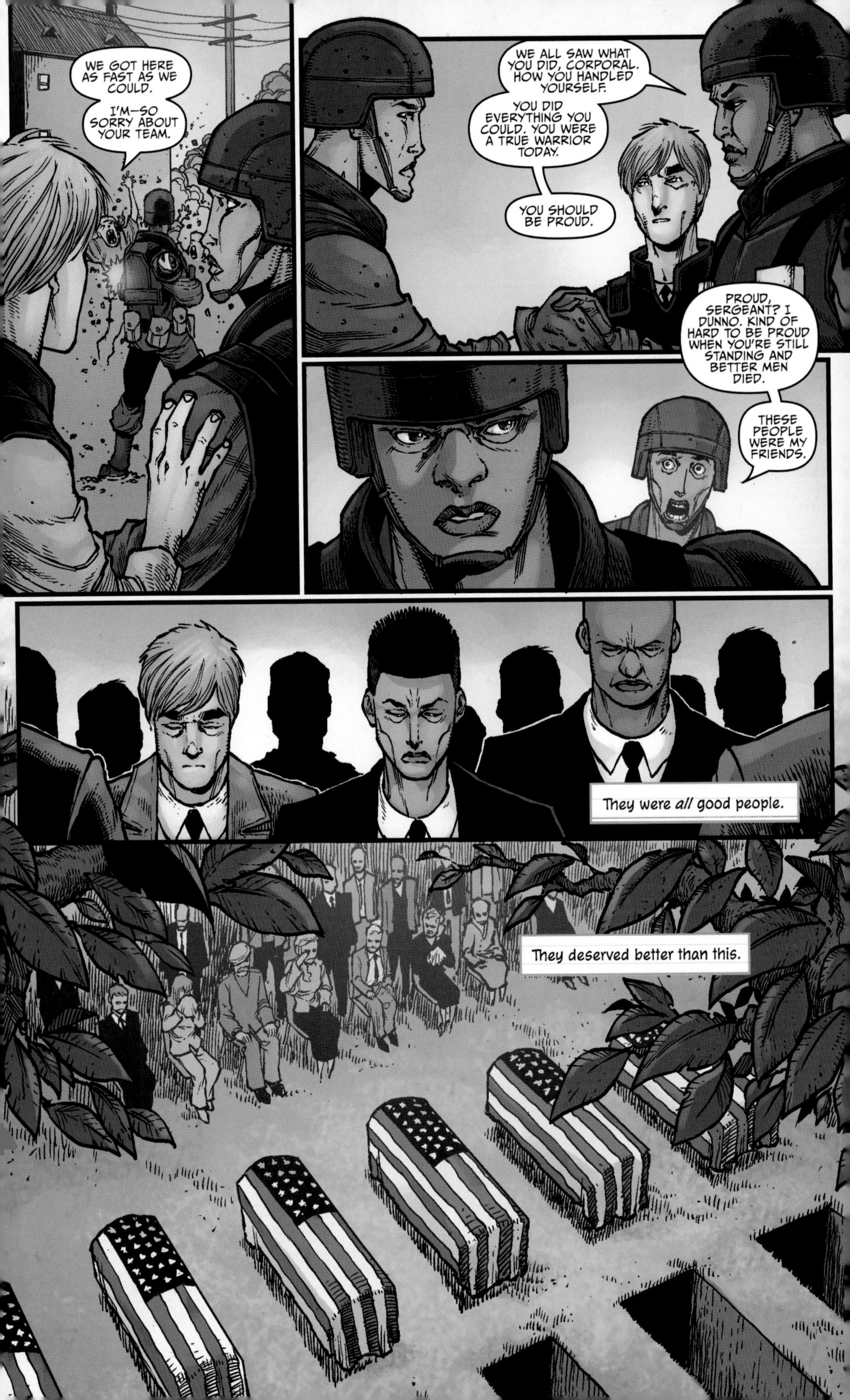
WE GOT HERE AS FAST AS WE COULD.
I'M—SO SORRY ABOUT YOUR TEAM.
WE ALL SAW WHAT YOU DID, CORPORAL. HOW YOU HANDLED YOURSELF.
YOU DID EVERYTHING YOU COULD. YOU WERE A TRUE WARRIOR TODAY.
YOU SHOULD BE PROUD.
PROUD, SERGEANT? I DUNNO. KIND OF HARD TO BE PROUD WHEN YOU'RE STILL STANDING AND BETTER MEN DIED.
THESE PEOPLE WERE MY FRIENDS.
They were *all* good people.
They deserved better than this.

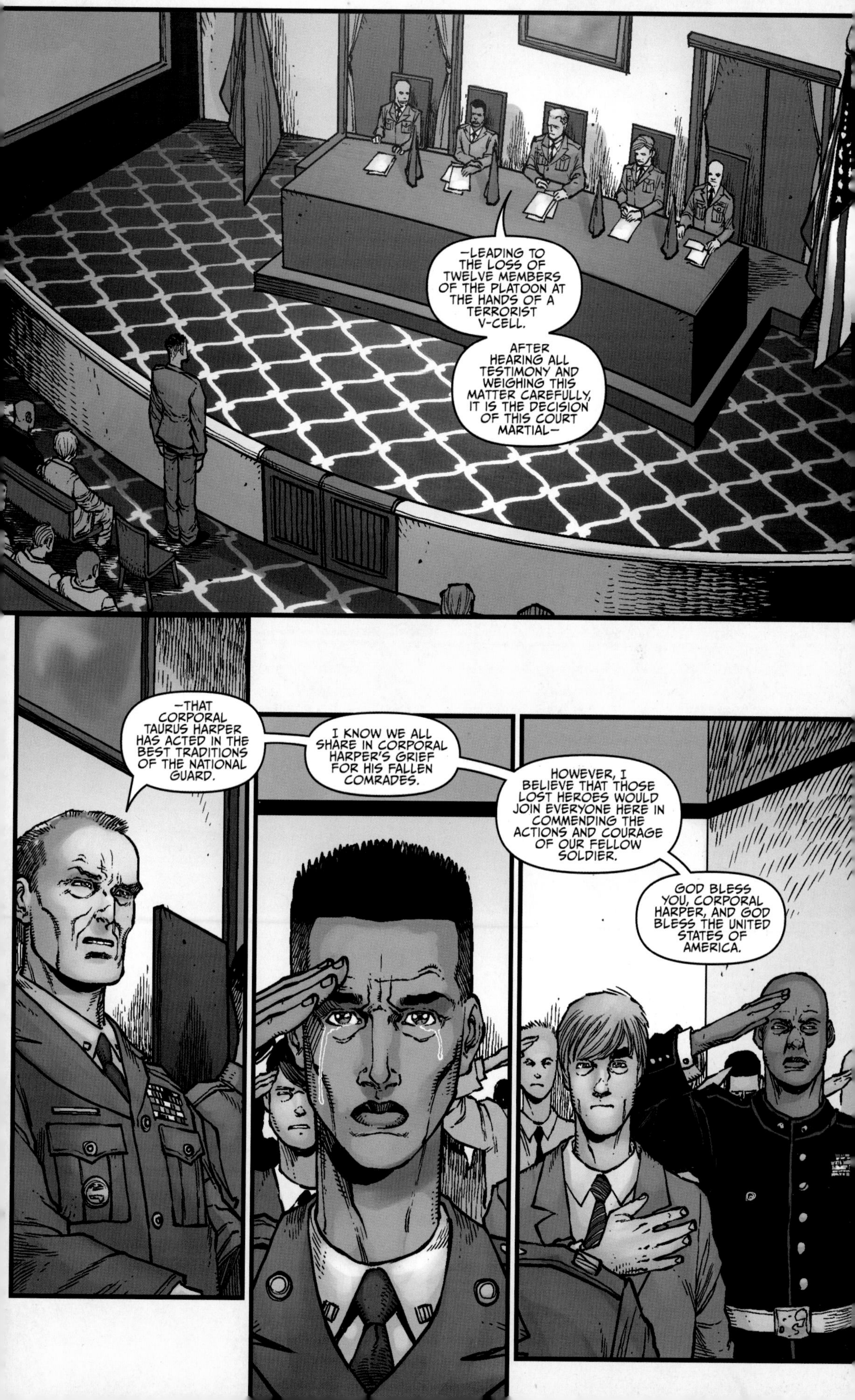

—LEADING TO THE LOSS OF TWELVE MEMBERS OF THE PLATOON AT THE HANDS OF A TERRORIST V-CELL.
AFTER HEARING ALL TESTIMONY AND WEIGHING THIS MATTER CAREFULLY, IT IS THE DECISION OF THIS COURT MARTIAL—
—THAT CORPORAL TAURUS HARPER HAS ACTED IN THE BEST TRADITIONS OF THE NATIONAL GUARD.
I KNOW WE ALL SHARE IN CORPORAL HARPER'S GRIEF FOR HIS FALLEN COMRADES.
HOWEVER, I BELIEVE THAT THOSE LOST HEROES WOULD JOIN EVERYONE HERE IN COMMENDING THE ACTIONS AND COURAGE OF OUR FELLOW SOLDIER.
GOD BLESS YOU, CORPORAL HARPER, AND GOD BLESS THE UNITED STATES OF AMERICA.

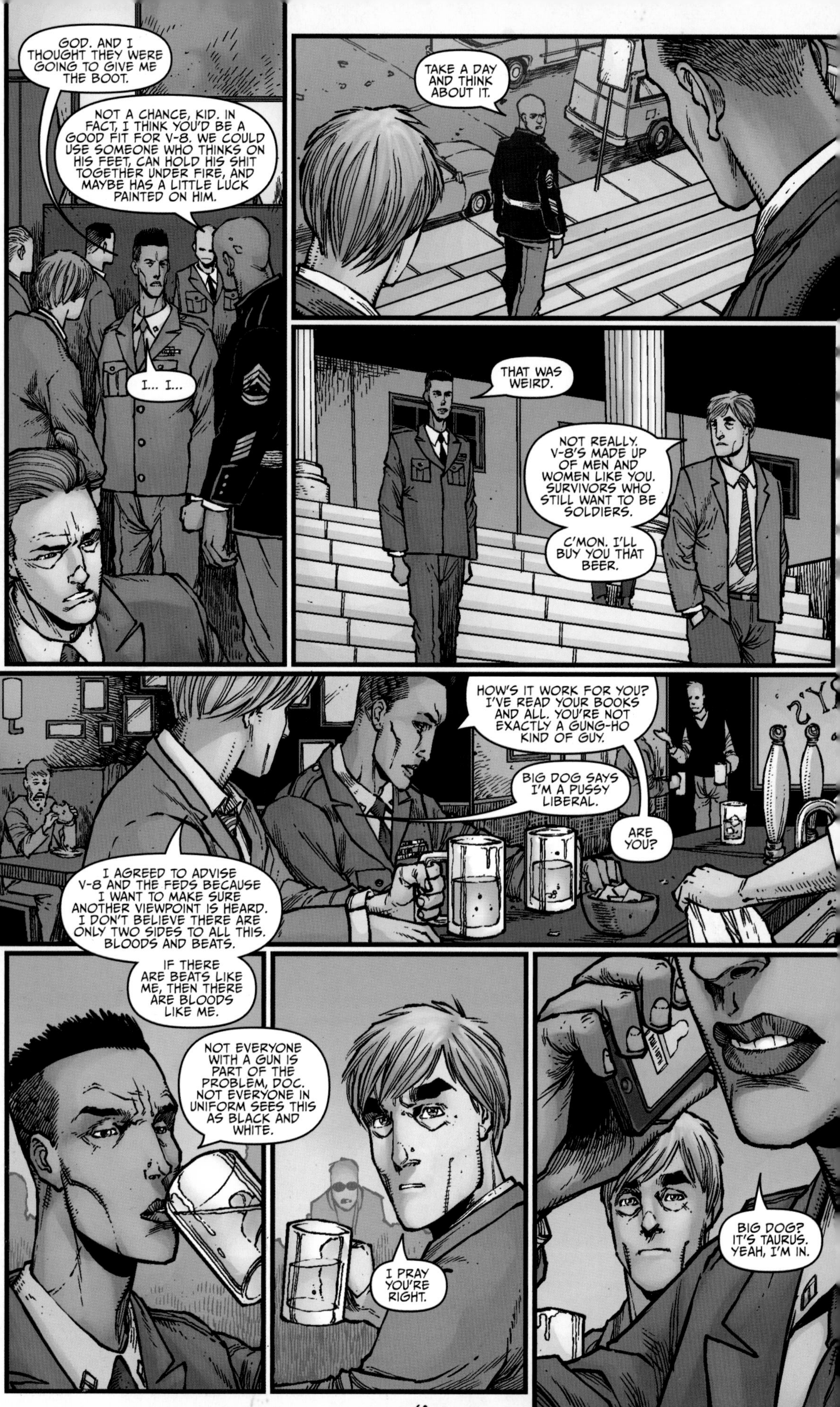
GOD. AND I THOUGHT THEY WERE GOING TO GIVE ME THE BOOT.
NOT A CHANCE, KID. IN FACT, I THINK YOU'D BE A GOOD FIT FOR V-8. WE COULD USE SOMEONE WHO THINKS ON HIS FEET, CAN HOLD HIS SHIT TOGETHER UNDER FIRE, AND MAYBE HAS A LITTLE LUCK PAINTED ON HIM.
I... I...
TAKE A DAY AND THINK ABOUT IT.
THAT WAS WEIRD.
NOT REALLY. V-8'S MADE UP OF MEN AND WOMEN LIKE YOU. SURVIVORS WHO STILL WANT TO BE SOLDIERS.
C'MON. I'LL BUY YOU THAT BEER.
HOW'S IT WORK FOR YOU? I'VE READ YOUR BOOKS AND ALL. YOU'RE NOT EXACTLY A GUNG-HO KIND OF GUY.
BIG DOG SAYS I'M A PUSSY LIBERAL.
ARE YOU?
I AGREED TO ADVISE V-8 AND THE FEDS BECAUSE I WANT TO MAKE SURE ANOTHER VIEWPOINT IS HEARD. I DON'T BELIEVE THERE ARE ONLY TWO SIDES TO ALL THIS. BLOODS AND BEATS.
IF THERE ARE BEATS LIKE ME, THEN THERE ARE BLOODS LIKE ME.
NOT EVERYONE WITH A GUN IS PART OF THE PROBLEM, DOC. NOT EVERYONE IN UNIFORM SEES THIS AS BLACK AND WHITE.
I PRAY YOU'RE RIGHT.
BIG DOG? IT'S TAURUS. YEAH, I'M IN.

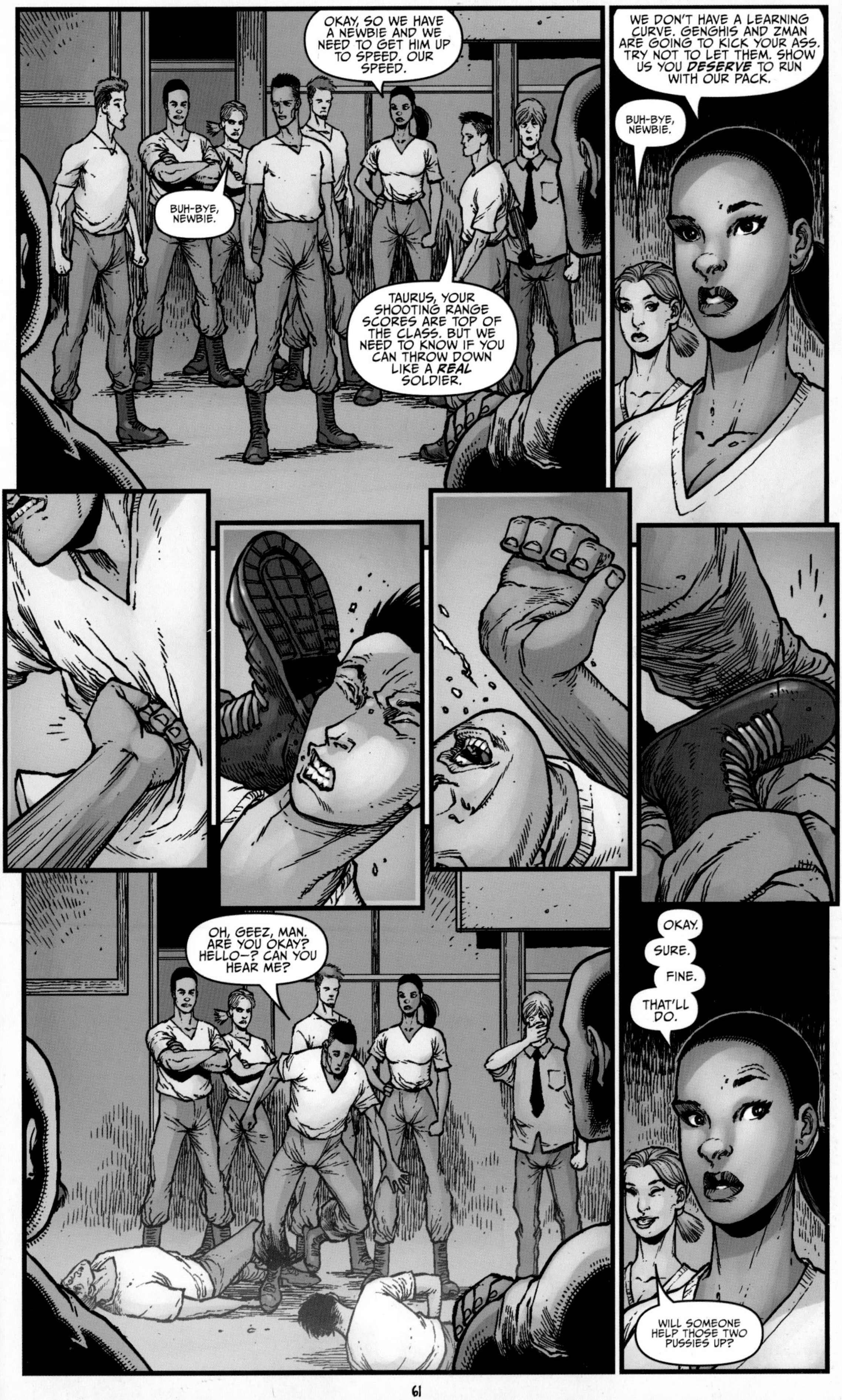
OKAY, SO WE HAVE A NEWBIE AND WE NEED TO GET HIM UP TO SPEED. OUR SPEED.
BUH-BYE, NEWBIE.
TAURUS, YOUR SHOOTING RANGE SCORES ARE TOP OF THE CLASS. BUT WE NEED TO KNOW IF YOU CAN THROW DOWN LIKE A REAL SOLDIER.
WE DON'T HAVE A LEARNING CURVE. GENGHIS AND ZMAN ARE GOING TO KICK YOUR ASS. TRY NOT TO LET THEM. SHOW US YOU DESERVE TO RUN WITH OUR PACK.
BUH-BYE, NEWBIE.
OH, GEEZ, MAN. ARE YOU OKAY? HELLO--? CAN YOU HEAR ME?
OKAY.
SURE.
FINE.
THAT'LL DO.
WILL SOMEONE HELP THOSE TWO PUSSIES UP?

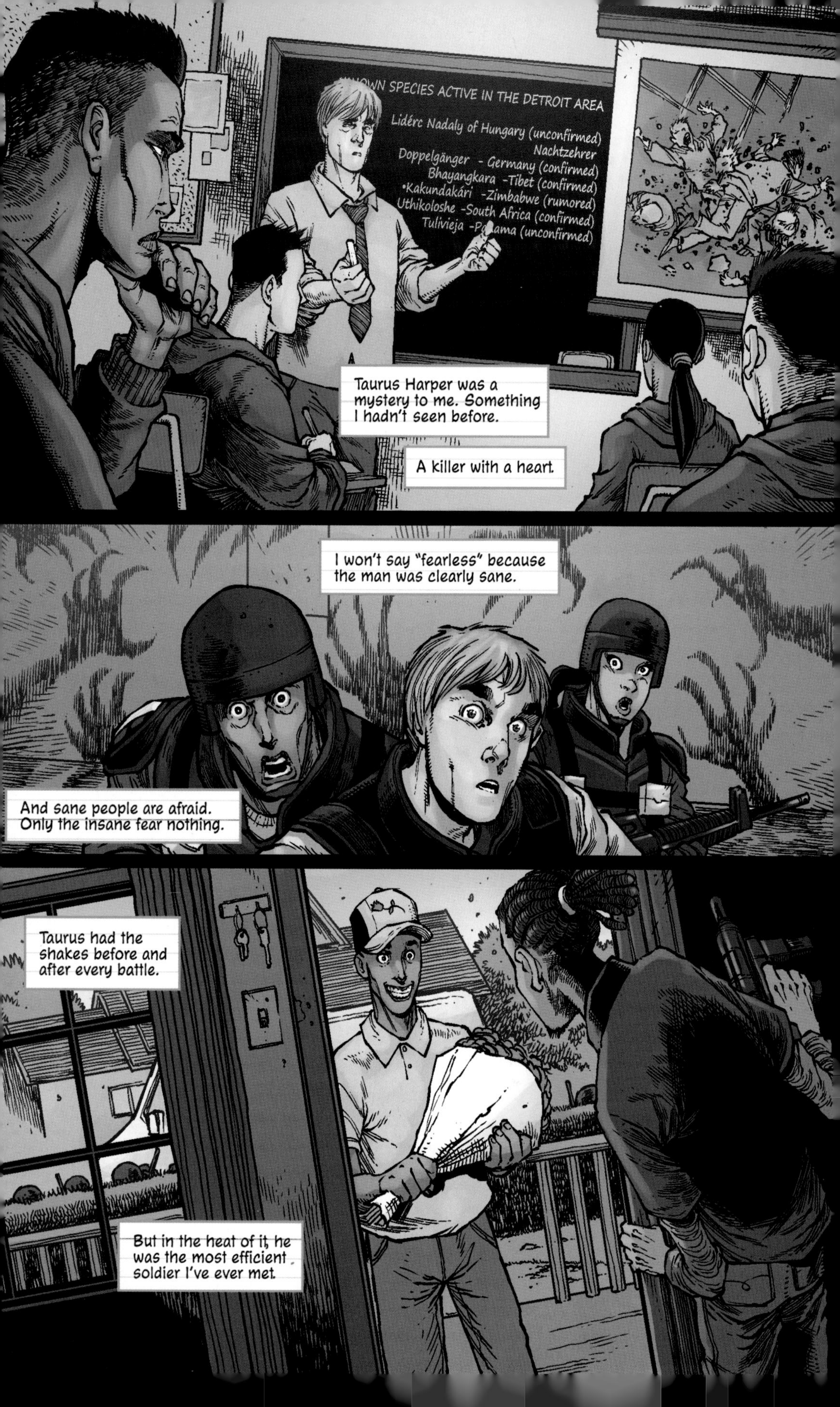

OWN SPECIES ACTIVE IN THE DETROIT AREA
Lidérc Nadaly of Hungary (unconfirmed)
Nachtzehrer
Doppelgänger - Germany (confirmed)
Bhayangkara -Tibet (confirmed)
•Kakundakári -Zimbabwe (rumored)
Uthikoloshe -South Africa (confirmed)
Tulívieja -Panama (unconfirmed)
Taurus Harper was a mystery to me. Something I hadn't seen before.
A killer with a heart.
I won't say "fearless" because the man was clearly sane.
And sane people are afraid. Only the insane fear nothing.
Taurus had the shakes before and after every battle.
But in the heat of it, he was the most efficient soldier I've ever met.

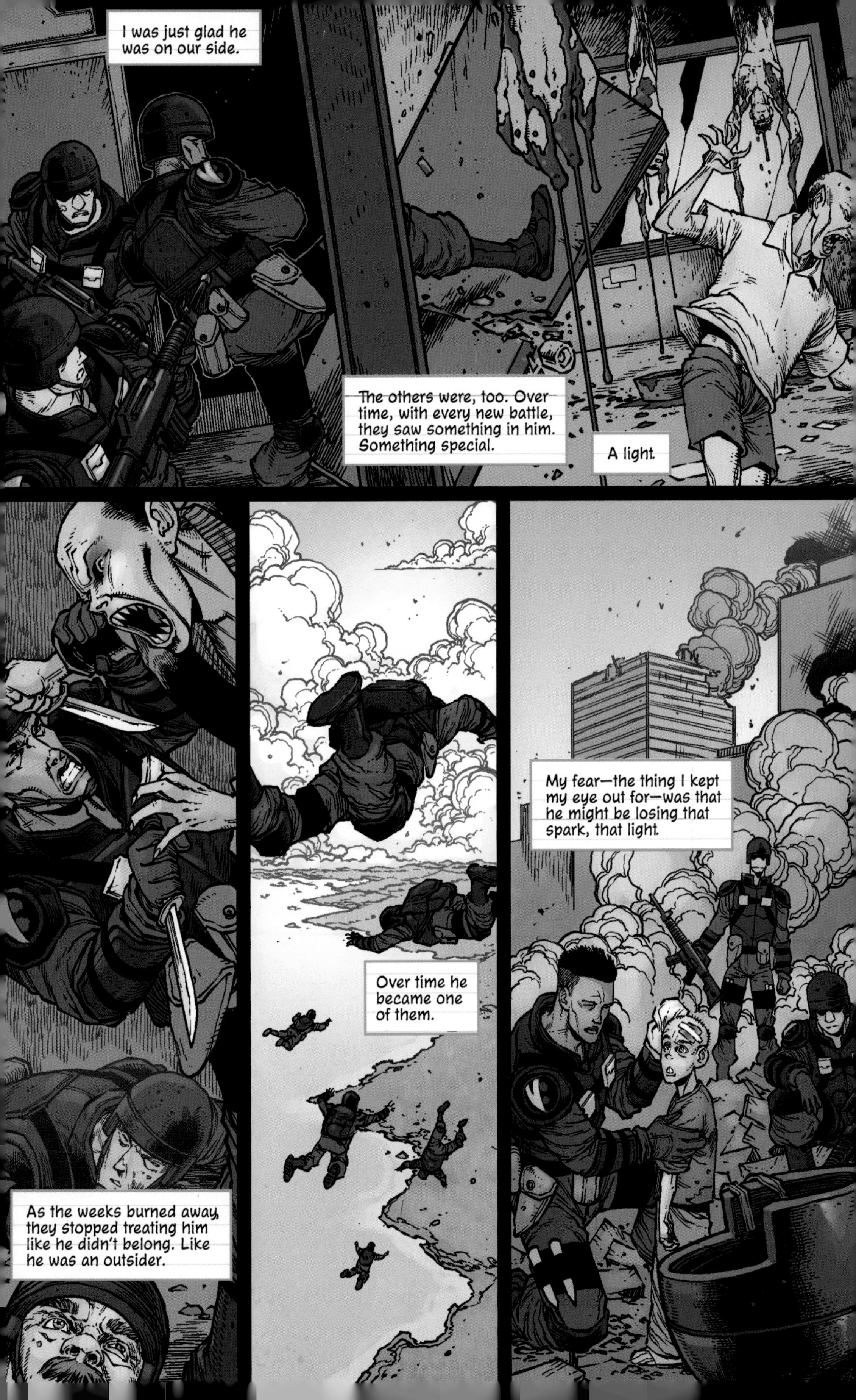
I was just glad he was on our side.
The others were, too. Over time, with every new battle, they saw something in him. Something special.
A light.
As the weeks burned away, they stopped treating him like he didn't belong. Like he was an outsider.
Over time he became one of them.
My fear—the thing I kept my eye out for—was that he might be losing that spark, that light.

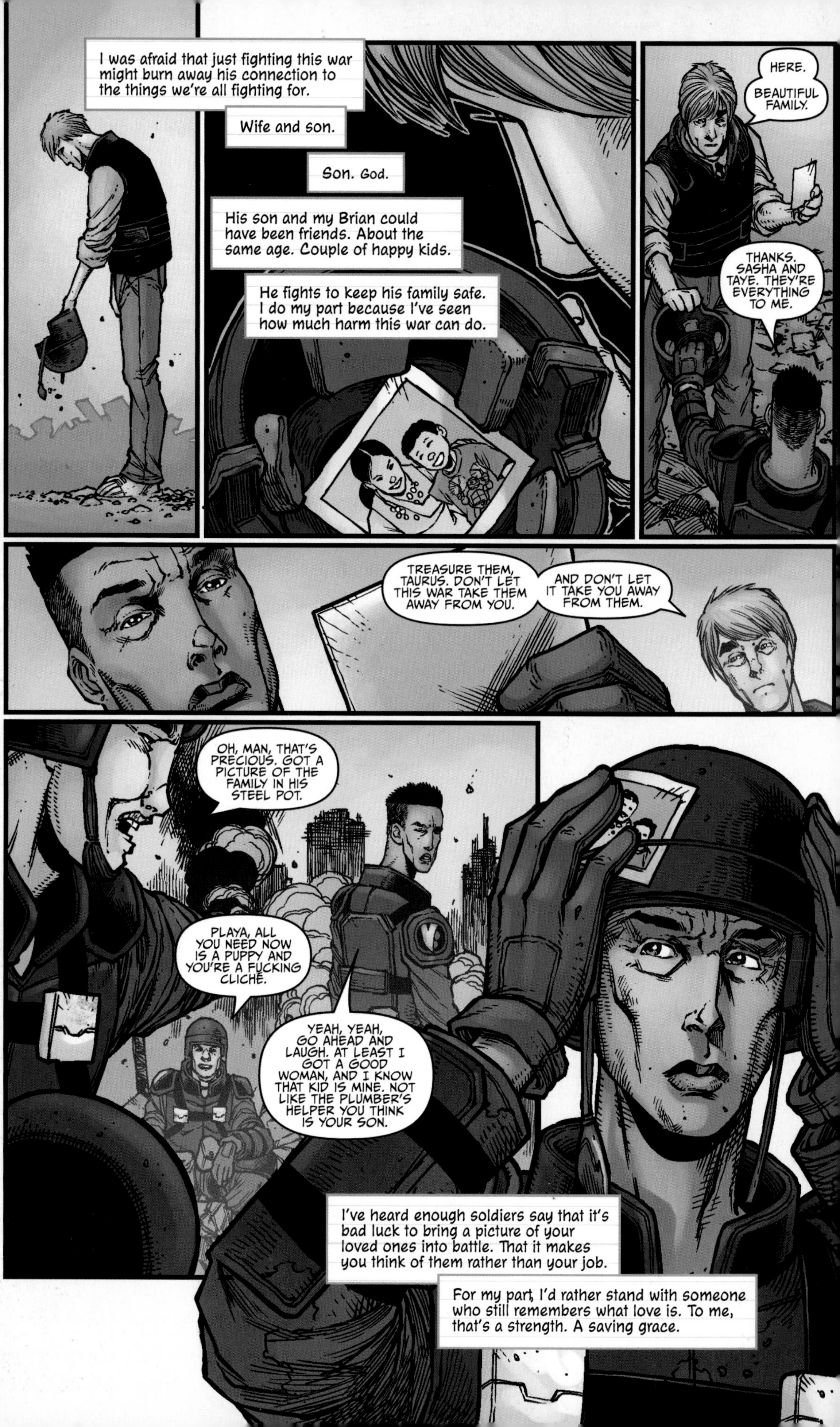
I was afraid that just fighting this war might burn away his connection to the things we're all fighting for.
Wife and son.
Son. God.
His son and my Brian could have been friends. About the same age. Couple of happy kids.
He fights to keep his family safe. I do my part because I've seen how much harm this war can do.
HERE.
BEAUTIFUL FAMILY.
THANKS. SASHA AND TAYE. THEY'RE EVERYTHING TO ME.
TREASURE THEM, TAURUS. DON'T LET THIS WAR TAKE THEM AWAY FROM YOU.
AND DON'T LET IT TAKE YOU AWAY FROM THEM.
OH, MAN, THAT'S PRECIOUS. GOT A PICTURE OF THE FAMILY IN HIS STEEL POT.
PLAYA, ALL YOU NEED NOW IS A PUPPY AND YOU'RE A FUCKING CLICHÉ.
YEAH, YEAH, GO AHEAD AND LAUGH. AT LEAST I GOT A GOOD WOMAN, AND I KNOW THAT KID IS MINE. NOT LIKE THE PLUMBER'S HELPER YOU THINK IS YOUR SON.
I've heard enough soldiers say that it's bad luck to bring a picture of your loved ones into battle. That it makes you think of them rather than your job.
For my part, I'd rather stand with someone who still remembers what love is. To me, that's a strength. A saving grace.

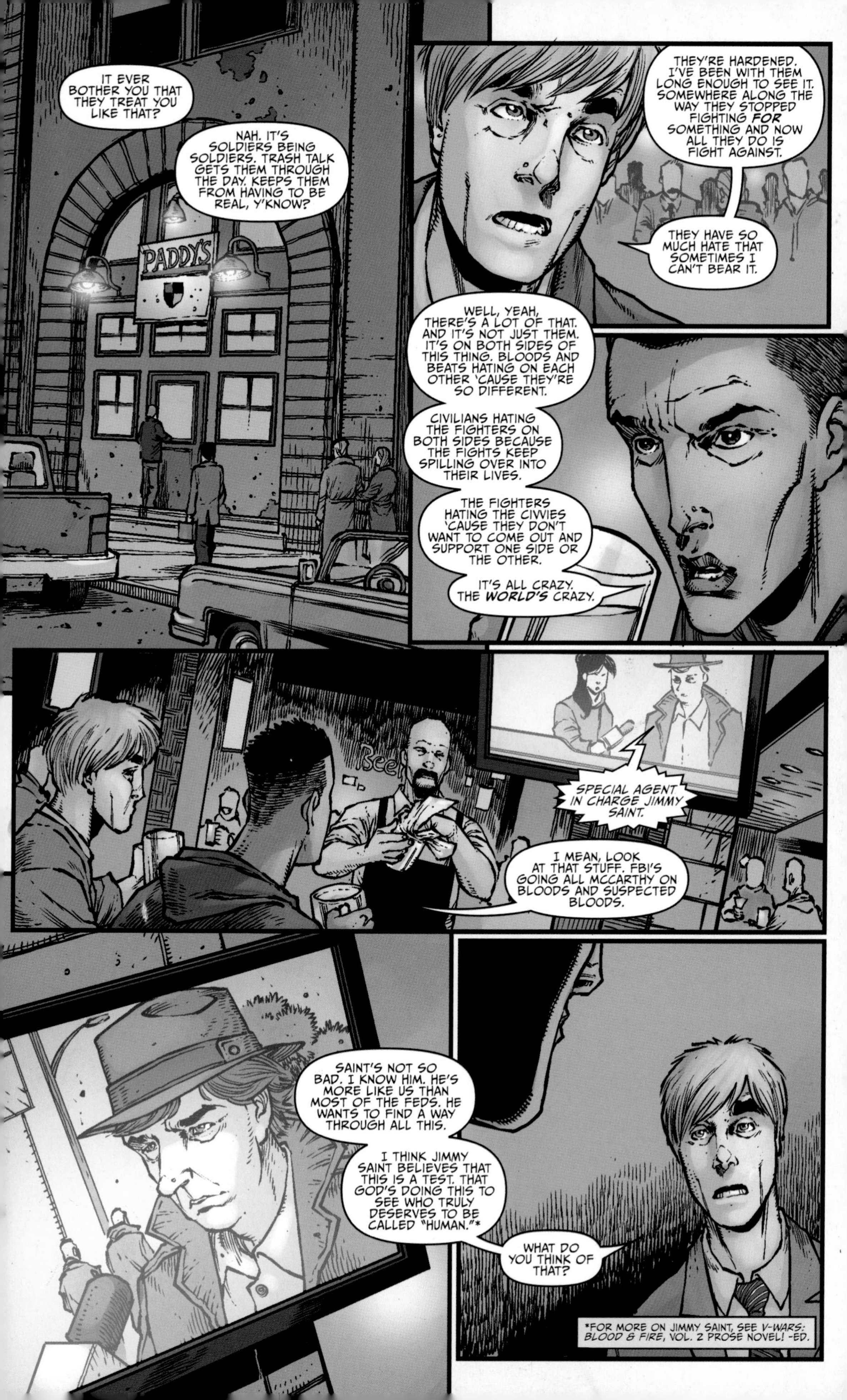
IT EVER BOTHER YOU THAT THEY TREAT YOU LIKE THAT?
NAH. IT'S SOLDIERS BEING SOLDIERS. TRASH TALK GETS THEM THROUGH THE DAY. KEEPS THEM FROM HAVING TO BE REAL, Y'KNOW?
PADDY'S
THEY'RE HARDENED. I'VE BEEN WITH THEM LONG ENOUGH TO SEE IT. SOMEWHERE ALONG THE WAY THEY STOPPED FIGHTING *FOR* SOMETHING AND NOW ALL THEY DO IS FIGHT AGAINST.
THEY HAVE SO MUCH HATE THAT SOMETIMES I CAN'T BEAR IT.
WELL, YEAH, THERE'S A LOT OF THAT. AND IT'S NOT JUST THEM. IT'S ON BOTH SIDES OF THIS THING. BLOODS AND BEATS HATING ON EACH OTHER 'CAUSE THEY'RE SO DIFFERENT.
CIVILIANS HATING THE FIGHTERS ON BOTH SIDES BECAUSE THE FIGHTS KEEP SPILLING OVER INTO THEIR LIVES.
THE FIGHTERS HATING THE CIVVIES 'CAUSE THEY DON'T WANT TO COME OUT AND SUPPORT ONE SIDE OR THE OTHER.
IT'S ALL CRAZY. THE ***WORLD'S*** CRAZY.
Beer
SPECIAL AGENT IN CHARGE JIMMY SAINT.
I MEAN, LOOK AT THAT STUFF. FBI'S GOING ALL MCCARTHY ON BLOODS AND SUSPECTED BLOODS.
SAINT'S NOT SO BAD. I KNOW HIM. HE'S MORE LIKE US THAN MOST OF THE FEDS. HE WANTS TO FIND A WAY THROUGH ALL THIS.
I THINK JIMMY SAINT BELIEVES THAT THIS IS A TEST. THAT GOD'S DOING THIS TO SEE WHO TRULY DESERVES TO BE CALLED "HUMAN."*
WHAT DO YOU THINK OF THAT?
*FOR MORE ON JIMMY SAINT, SEE *V-WARS: BLOOD & FIRE*, VOL. 2 PROSE NOVEL! -ED.

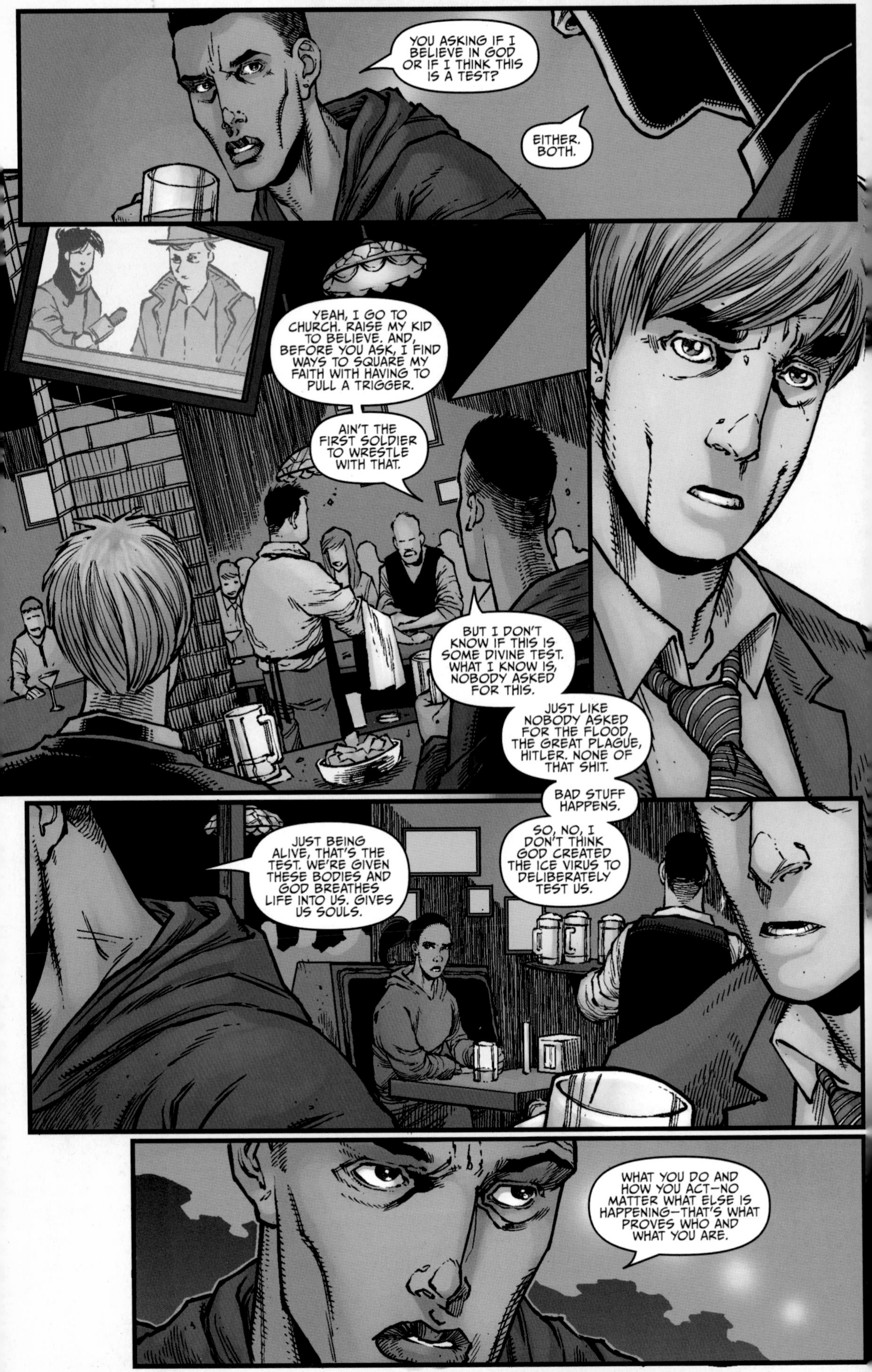
YOU ASKING IF I BELIEVE IN GOD OR IF I THINK THIS IS A TEST?
EITHER. BOTH.
YEAH, I GO TO CHURCH. RAISE MY KID TO BELIEVE. AND, BEFORE YOU ASK, I FIND WAYS TO SQUARE MY FAITH WITH HAVING TO PULL A TRIGGER.
AIN'T THE FIRST SOLDIER TO WRESTLE WITH THAT.
BUT I DON'T KNOW IF THIS IS SOME DIVINE TEST. WHAT I KNOW IS, NOBODY ASKED FOR THIS.
JUST LIKE NOBODY ASKED FOR THE FLOOD, THE GREAT PLAGUE, HITLER. NONE OF THAT SHIT.
BAD STUFF HAPPENS.
SO, NO, I DON'T THINK GOD CREATED THE ICE VIRUS TO DELIBERATELY TEST US.
JUST BEING ALIVE, THAT'S THE TEST. WE'RE GIVEN THESE BODIES AND GOD BREATHES LIFE INTO US. GIVES US SOULS.
WHAT YOU DO AND HOW YOU ACT—NO MATTER WHAT ELSE IS HAPPENING—THAT'S WHAT PROVES WHO AND WHAT YOU ARE.

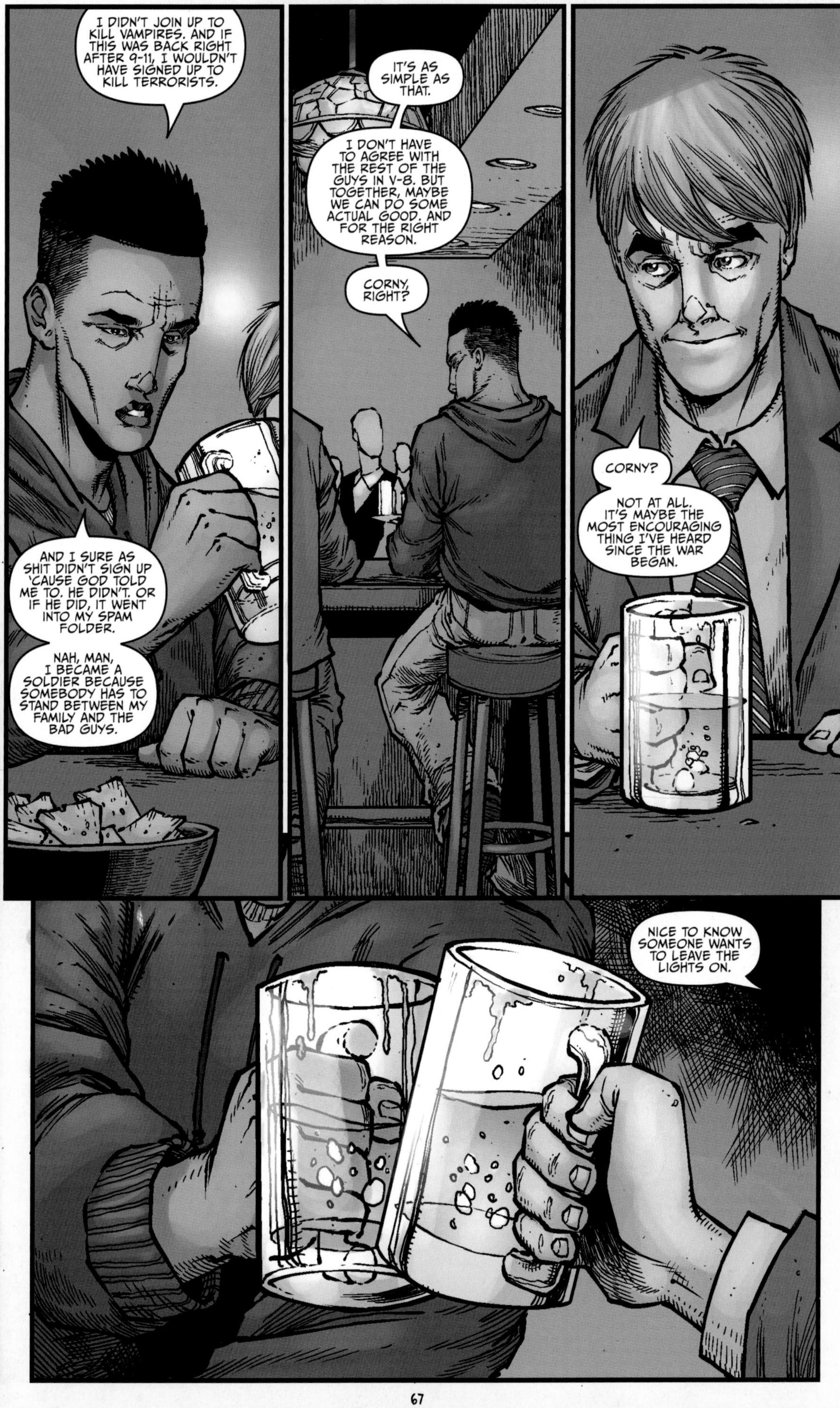

I DIDN'T JOIN UP TO KILL VAMPIRES. AND IF THIS WAS BACK RIGHT AFTER 9-11, I WOULDN'T HAVE SIGNED UP TO KILL TERRORISTS.
AND I SURE AS SHIT DIDN'T SIGN UP 'CAUSE GOD TOLD ME TO. HE DIDN'T. OR IF HE DID, IT WENT INTO MY SPAM FOLDER.
NAH, MAN, I BECAME A SOLDIER BECAUSE SOMEBODY HAS TO STAND BETWEEN MY FAMILY AND THE BAD GUYS.
IT'S AS SIMPLE AS THAT.
I DON'T HAVE TO AGREE WITH THE REST OF THE GUYS IN V-8. BUT TOGETHER, MAYBE WE CAN DO SOME ACTUAL GOOD. AND FOR THE RIGHT REASON.
CORNY, RIGHT?
CORNY?
NOT AT ALL. IT'S MAYBE THE MOST ENCOURAGING THING I'VE HEARD SINCE THE WAR BEGAN.
NICE TO KNOW SOMEONE WANTS TO LEAVE THE LIGHTS ON.

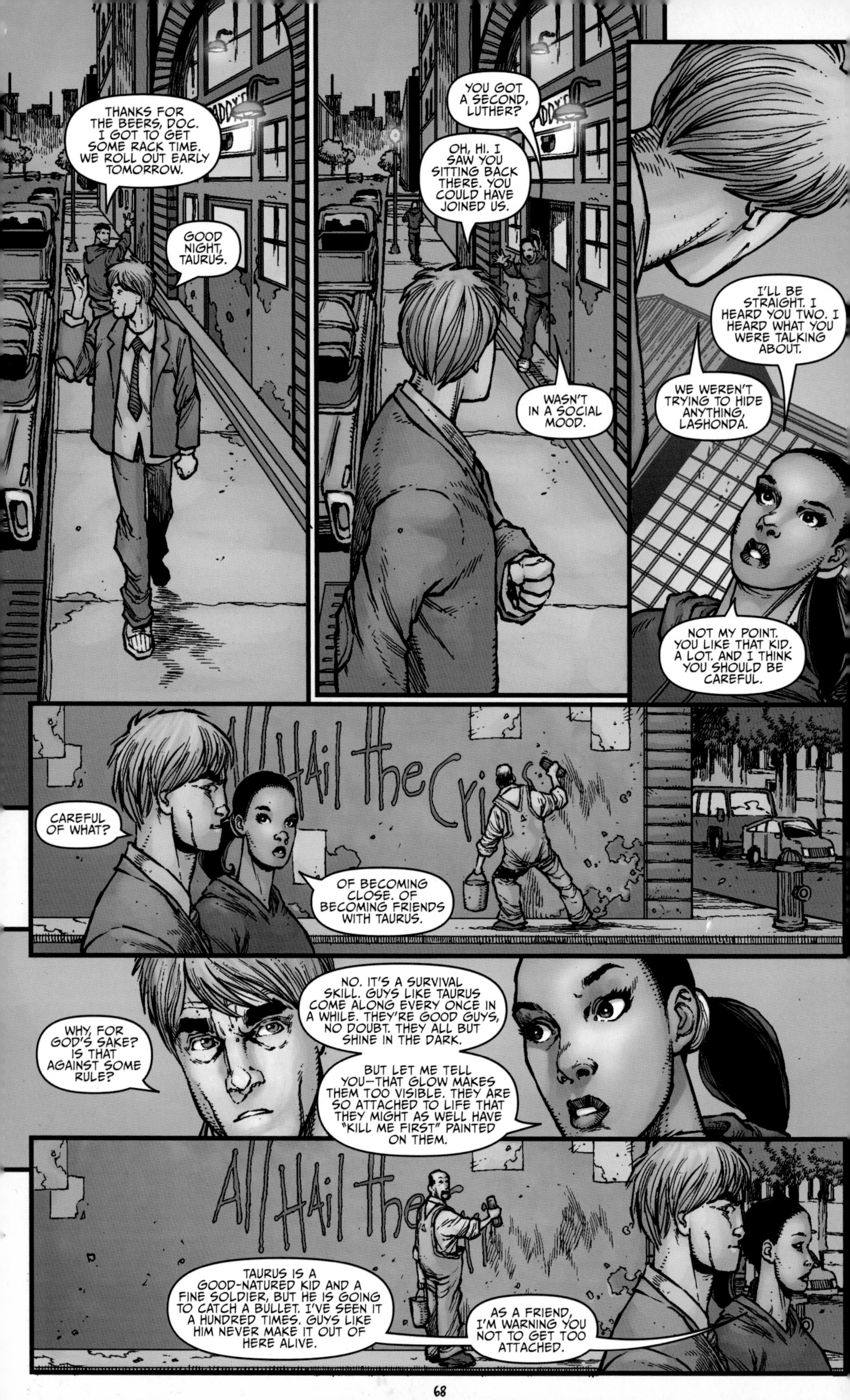

THANKS FOR THE BEERS, DOC. I GOT TO GET SOME RACK TIME. WE ROLL OUT EARLY TOMORROW.
GOOD NIGHT, TAURUS.
YOU GOT A SECOND, LUTHER?
OH, HI. I SAW YOU SITTING BACK THERE. YOU COULD HAVE JOINED US.
WASN'T IN A SOCIAL MOOD.
I'LL BE STRAIGHT. I HEARD YOU TWO. I HEARD WHAT YOU WERE TALKING ABOUT.
WE WEREN'T TRYING TO HIDE ANYTHING, LASHONDA.
NOT MY POINT. YOU LIKE THAT KID. A LOT. AND I THINK YOU SHOULD BE CAREFUL.
All Hail the Cris
CAREFUL OF WHAT?
OF BECOMING CLOSE. OF BECOMING FRIENDS WITH TAURUS.
WHY, FOR GOD'S SAKE? IS THAT AGAINST SOME RULE?
NO. IT'S A SURVIVAL SKILL. GUYS LIKE TAURUS COME ALONG EVERY ONCE IN A WHILE. THEY'RE GOOD GUYS, NO DOUBT. THEY ALL BUT SHINE IN THE DARK.
BUT LET ME TELL YOU—THAT GLOW MAKES THEM TOO VISIBLE. THEY ARE SO ATTACHED TO LIFE THAT THEY MIGHT AS WELL HAVE "KILL ME FIRST" PAINTED ON THEM.
All Hail the
TAURUS IS A GOOD-NATURED KID AND A FINE SOLDIER, BUT HE IS GOING TO CATCH A BULLET. I'VE SEEN IT A HUNDRED TIMES. GUYS LIKE HIM NEVER MAKE IT OUT OF HERE ALIVE.
AS A FRIEND, I'M WARNING YOU NOT TO GET TOO ATTACHED.

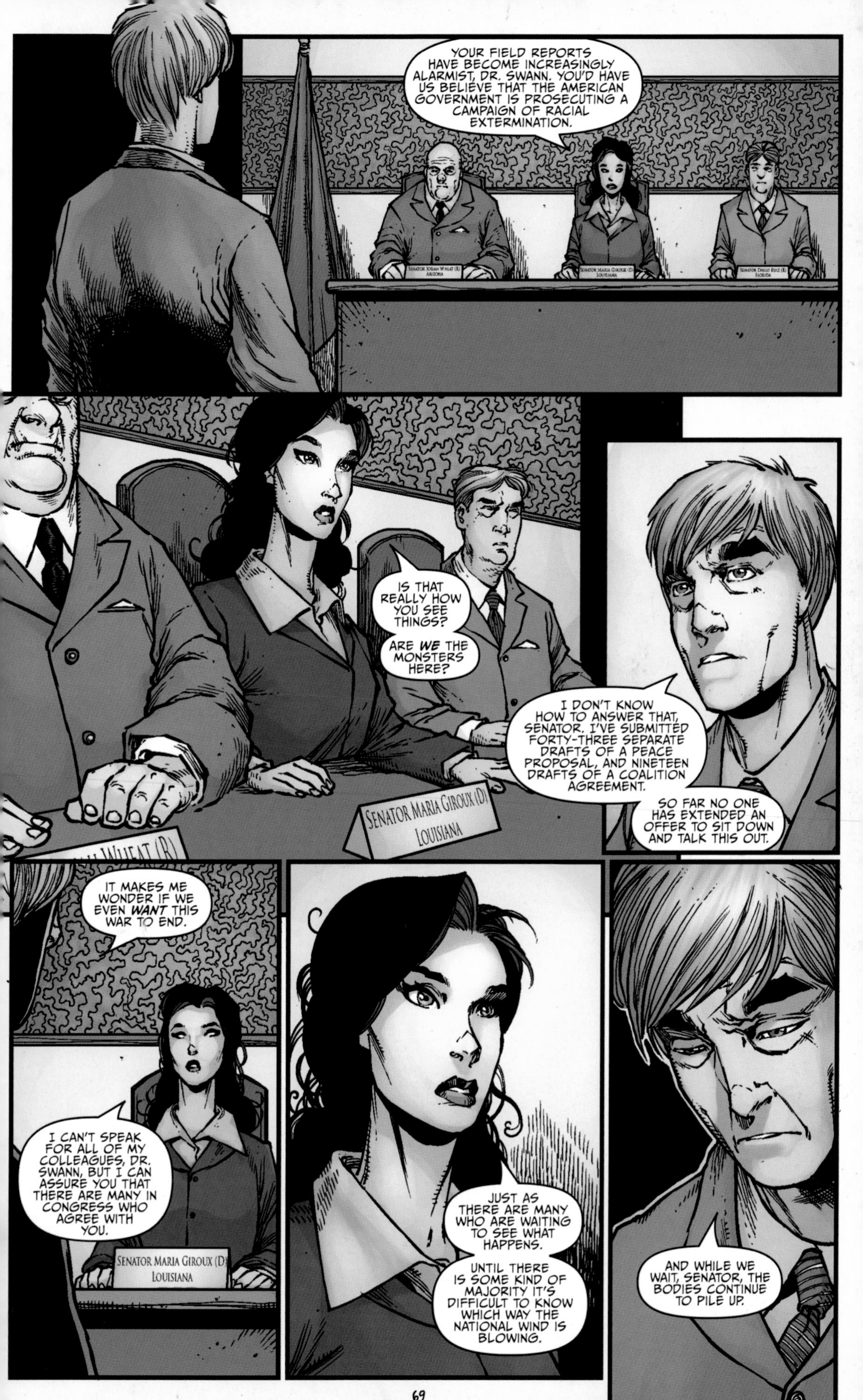
YOUR FIELD REPORTS HAVE BECOME INCREASINGLY ALARMIST, DR. SWANN. YOU'D HAVE US BELIEVE THAT THE AMERICAN GOVERNMENT IS PROSECUTING A CAMPAIGN OF RACIAL EXTERMINATION.
IS THAT REALLY HOW YOU SEE THINGS?
ARE *WE* THE MONSTERS HERE?
SENATOR MARIA GIROUX (D) LOUISIANA
I DON'T KNOW HOW TO ANSWER THAT, SENATOR. I'VE SUBMITTED FORTY-THREE SEPARATE DRAFTS OF A PEACE PROPOSAL, AND NINETEEN DRAFTS OF A COALITION AGREEMENT.
SO FAR NO ONE HAS EXTENDED AN OFFER TO SIT DOWN AND TALK THIS OUT.
IT MAKES ME WONDER IF WE EVEN *WANT* THIS WAR TO END.
I CAN'T SPEAK FOR ALL OF MY COLLEAGUES, DR. SWANN, BUT I CAN ASSURE YOU THAT THERE ARE MANY IN CONGRESS WHO AGREE WITH YOU.
SENATOR MARIA GIROUX (D) LOUISIANA
JUST AS THERE ARE MANY WHO ARE WAITING TO SEE WHAT HAPPENS.
UNTIL THERE IS SOME KIND OF MAJORITY IT'S DIFFICULT TO KNOW WHICH WAY THE NATIONAL WIND IS BLOWING.
AND WHILE WE WAIT, SENATOR, THE BODIES CONTINUE TO PILE UP.

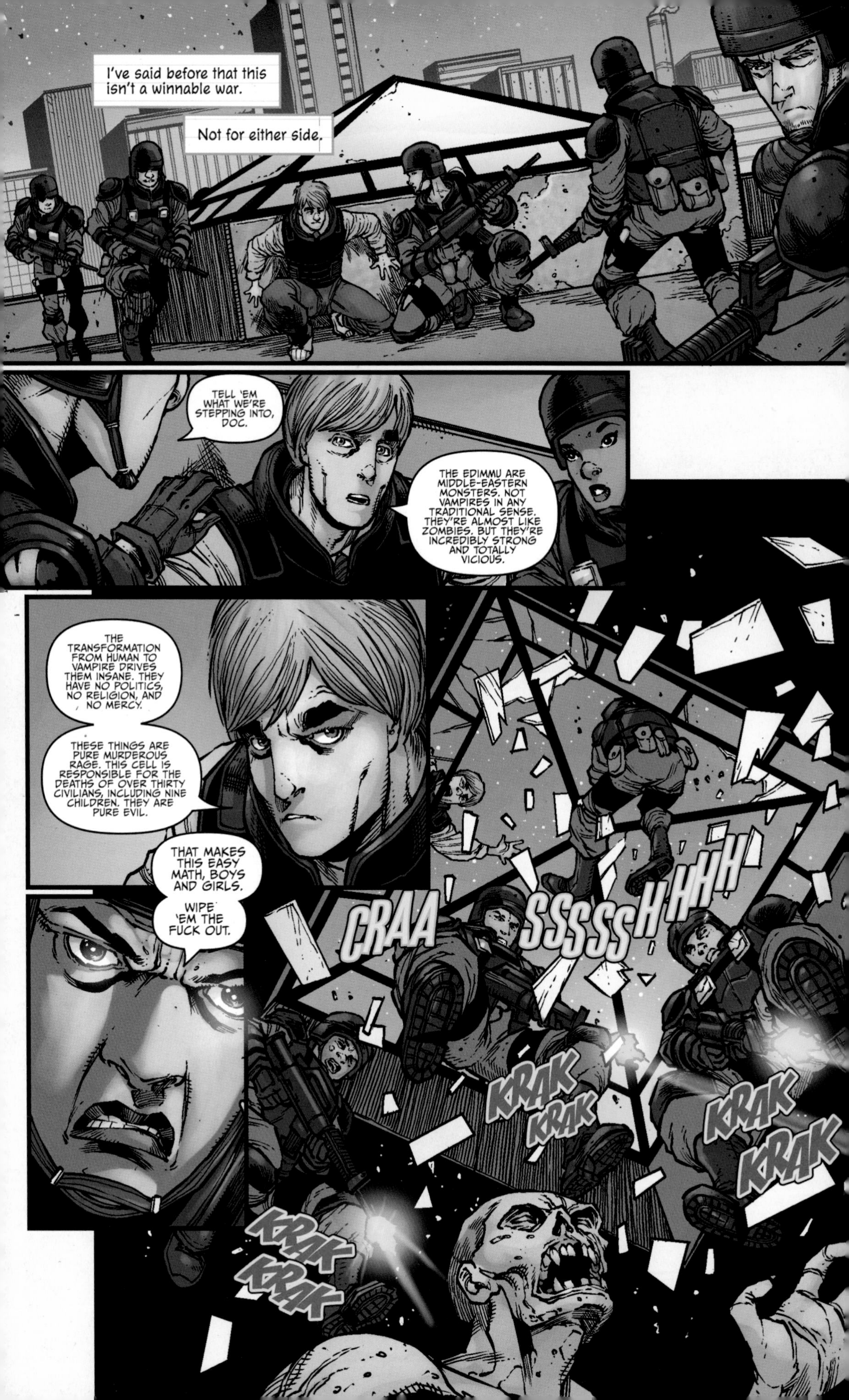
I've said before that this isn't a winnable war.
Not for either side.
TELL 'EM WHAT WE'RE STEPPING INTO, DOC.
THE EDIMMU ARE MIDDLE-EASTERN MONSTERS. NOT VAMPIRES IN ANY TRADITIONAL SENSE. THEY'RE ALMOST LIKE ZOMBIES. BUT THEY'RE INCREDIBLY STRONG AND TOTALLY VICIOUS.
THE TRANSFORMATION FROM HUMAN TO VAMPIRE DRIVES THEM INSANE. THEY HAVE NO POLITICS, NO RELIGION, AND NO MERCY.
THESE THINGS ARE PURE MURDEROUS RAGE. THIS CELL IS RESPONSIBLE FOR THE DEATHS OF OVER THIRTY CIVILIANS, INCLUDING NINE CHILDREN. THEY ARE PURE EVIL.
THAT MAKES THIS EASY MATH, BOYS AND GIRLS.
WIPE 'EM THE FUCK OUT.
CRAASSSSSHHHHH
KRAK KRAK
KRAK KRAK
KRAK KRAK

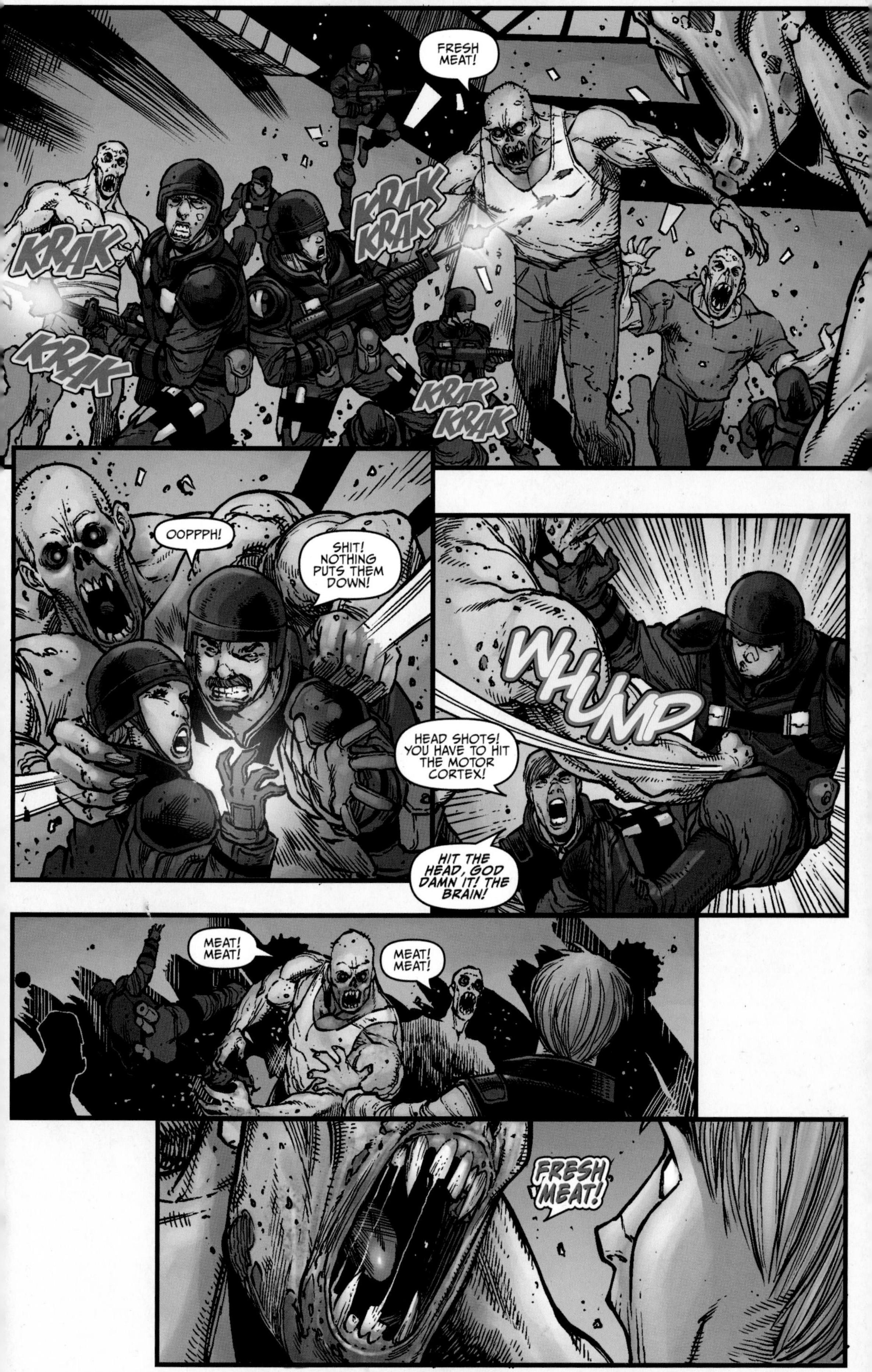

FRESH MEAT!
KRAK KRAK
KRAK
KRAK
KRAK KRAK
OOPPPH!
SHIT! NOTHING PUTS THEM DOWN!
WHUMP
HEAD SHOTS! YOU HAVE TO HIT THE MOTOR CORTEX!
HIT THE HEAD, GOD DAMN IT! THE BRAIN!
MEAT! MEAT!
MEAT! MEAT!
FRESH MEAT!

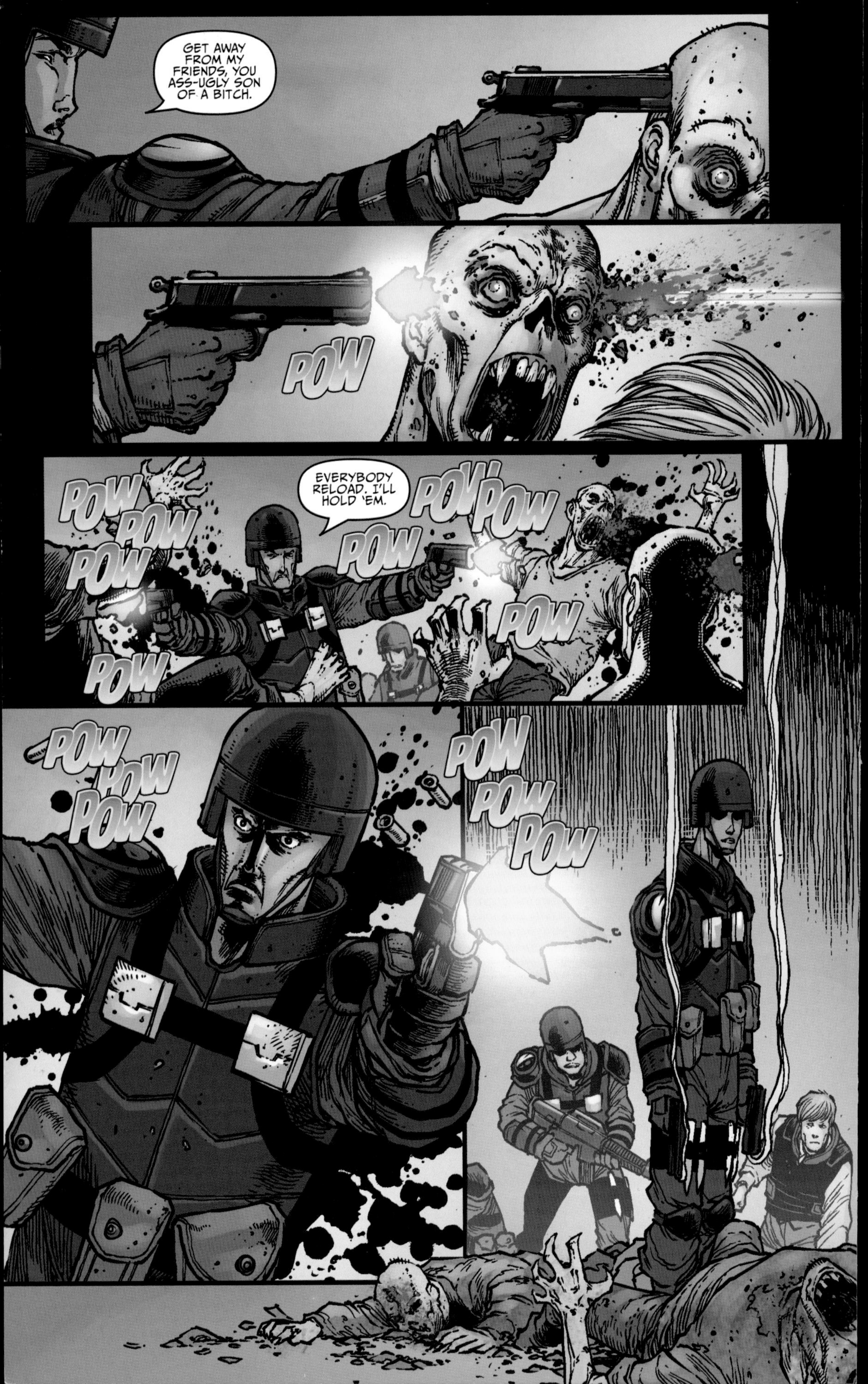
GET AWAY FROM MY FRIENDS, YOU ASS-UGLY SON OF A BITCH.
POW
POW
POW
POW
EVERYBODY RELOAD. I'LL HOLD 'EM.
POW
POW
POW
POW
POW
POW
POW
POW
POW
POW
POW

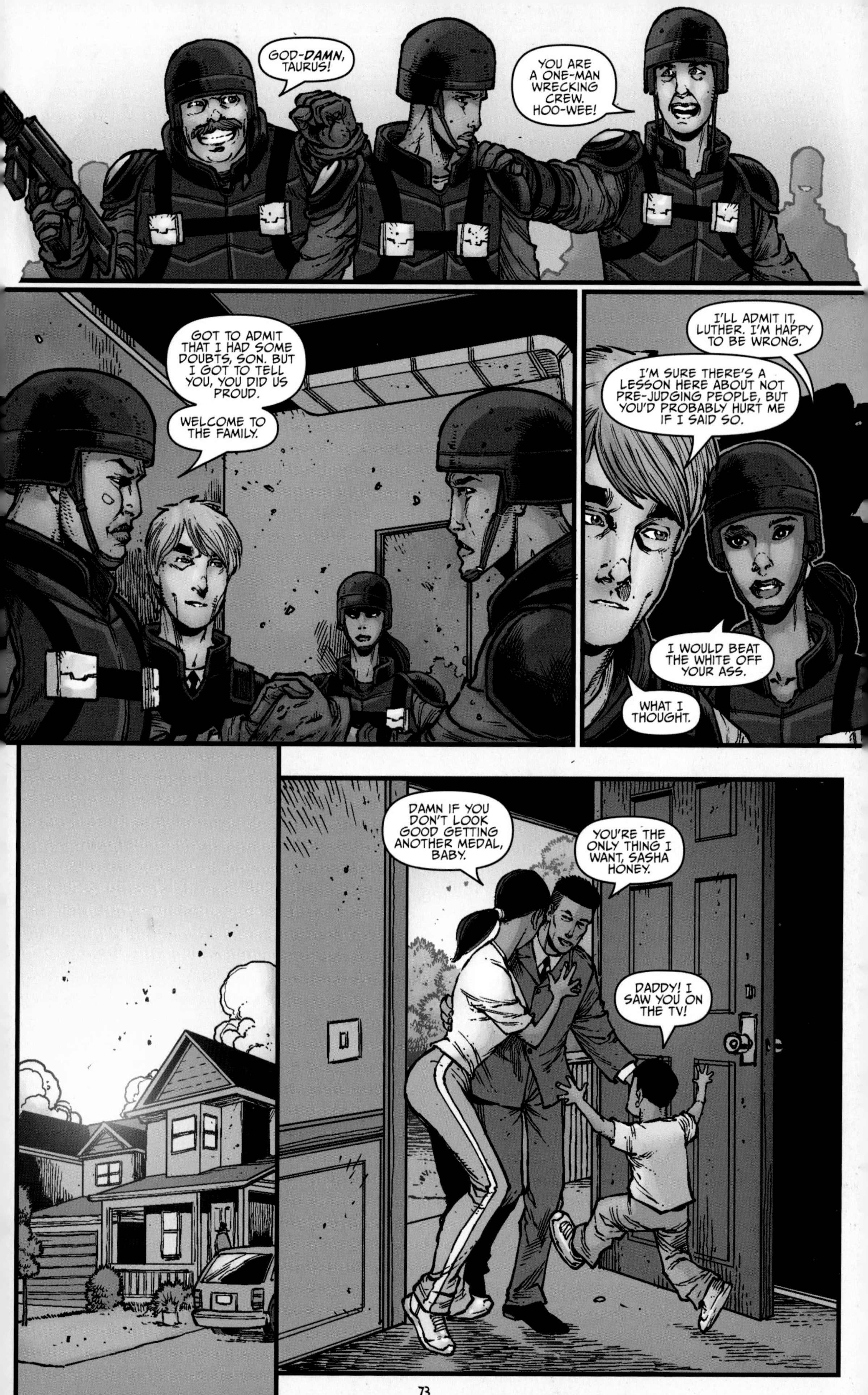
GOD-DAMN, TAURUS!
YOU ARE A ONE-MAN WRECKING CREW. HOO-WEE!
GOT TO ADMIT THAT I HAD SOME DOUBTS, SON. BUT I GOT TO TELL YOU, YOU DID US PROUD.
WELCOME TO THE FAMILY.
I'LL ADMIT IT, LUTHER. I'M HAPPY TO BE WRONG.
I'M SURE THERE'S A LESSON HERE ABOUT NOT PRE-JUDGING PEOPLE, BUT YOU'D PROBABLY HURT ME IF I SAID SO.
I WOULD BEAT THE WHITE OFF YOUR ASS.
WHAT I THOUGHT.
DAMN IF YOU DON'T LOOK GOOD GETTING ANOTHER MEDAL, BABY.
YOU'RE THE ONLY THING I WANT, SASHA HONEY.
DADDY! I SAW YOU ON THE TV!

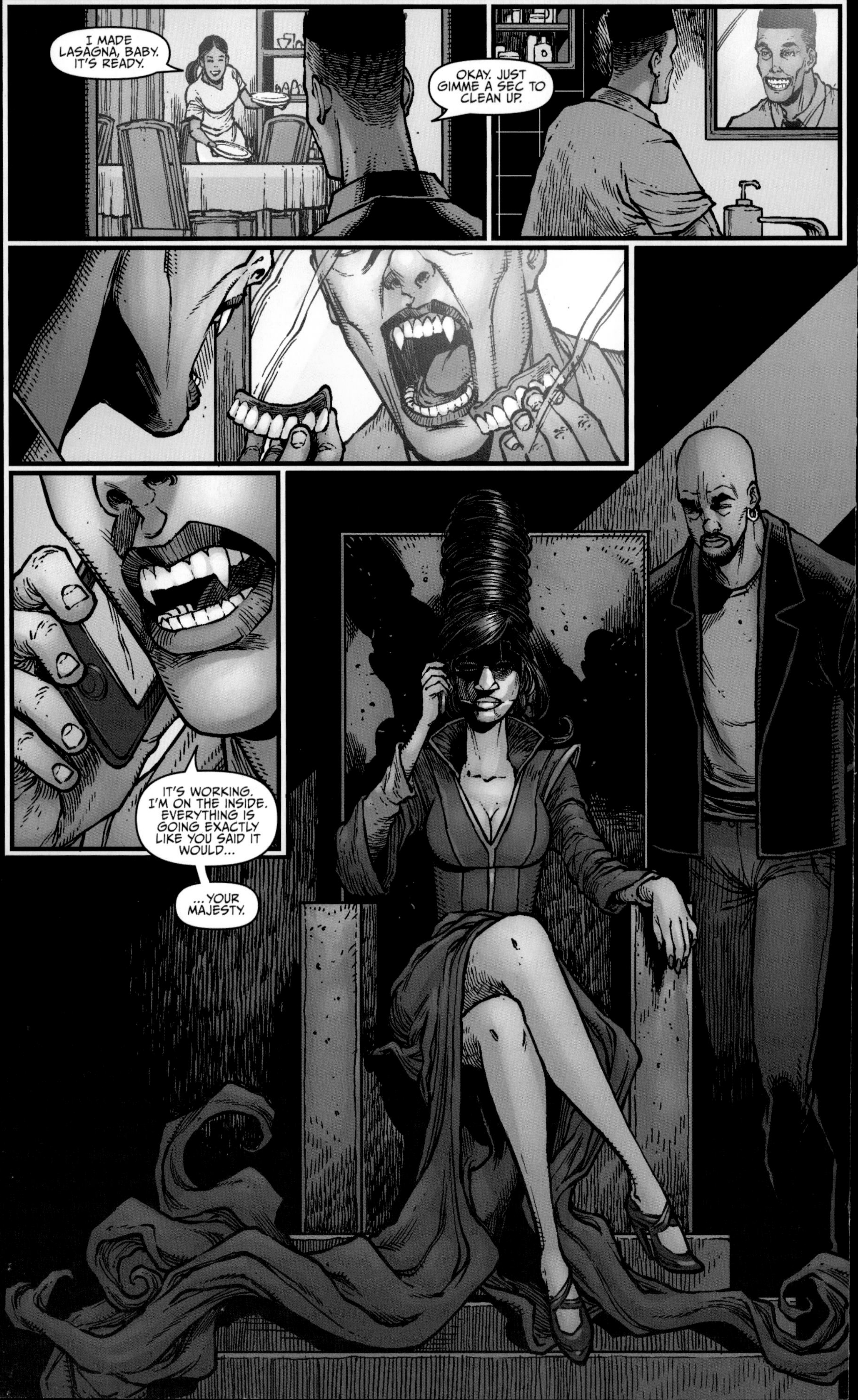
I MADE LASAGNA, BABY. IT'S READY.
OKAY. JUST GIMME A SEC TO CLEAN UP.
IT'S WORKING. I'M ON THE INSIDE. EVERYTHING IS GOING EXACTLY LIKE YOU SAID IT WOULD...
...YOUR MAJESTY.

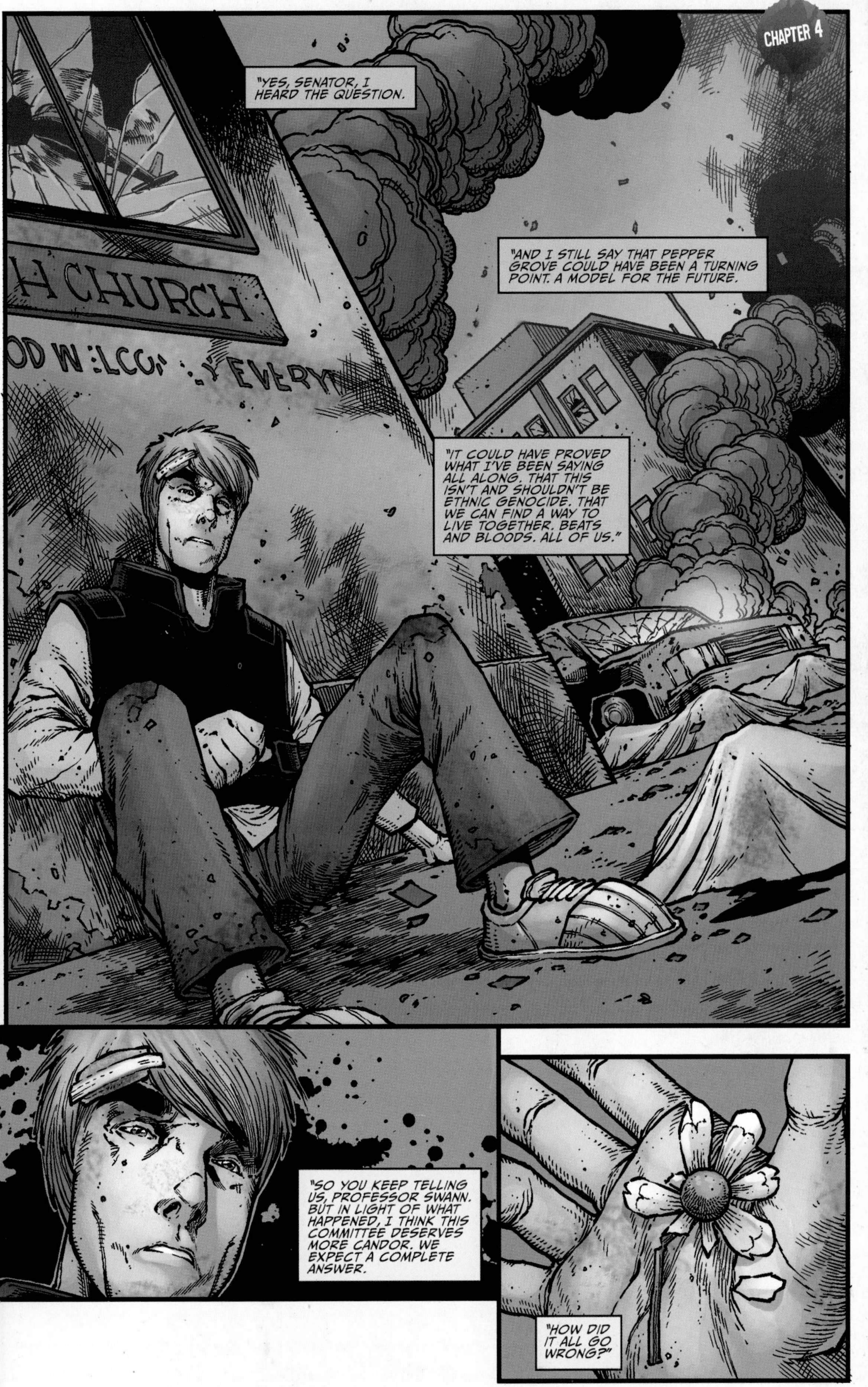
CHAPTER 4
"YES, SENATOR, I HEARD THE QUESTION.
"AND I STILL SAY THAT PEPPER GROVE COULD HAVE BEEN A TURNING POINT. A MODEL FOR THE FUTURE.
"IT COULD HAVE PROVED WHAT I'VE BEEN SAYING ALL ALONG. THAT THIS ISN'T AND SHOULDN'T BE ETHNIC GENOCIDE. THAT WE CAN FIND A WAY TO LIVE TOGETHER. BEATS AND BLOODS. ALL OF US."
"SO YOU KEEP TELLING US, PROFESSOR SWANN. BUT IN LIGHT OF WHAT HAPPENED, I THINK THIS COMMITTEE DESERVES MORE CANDOR. WE EXPECT A COMPLETE ANSWER.
"HOW DID IT ALL GO WRONG?"

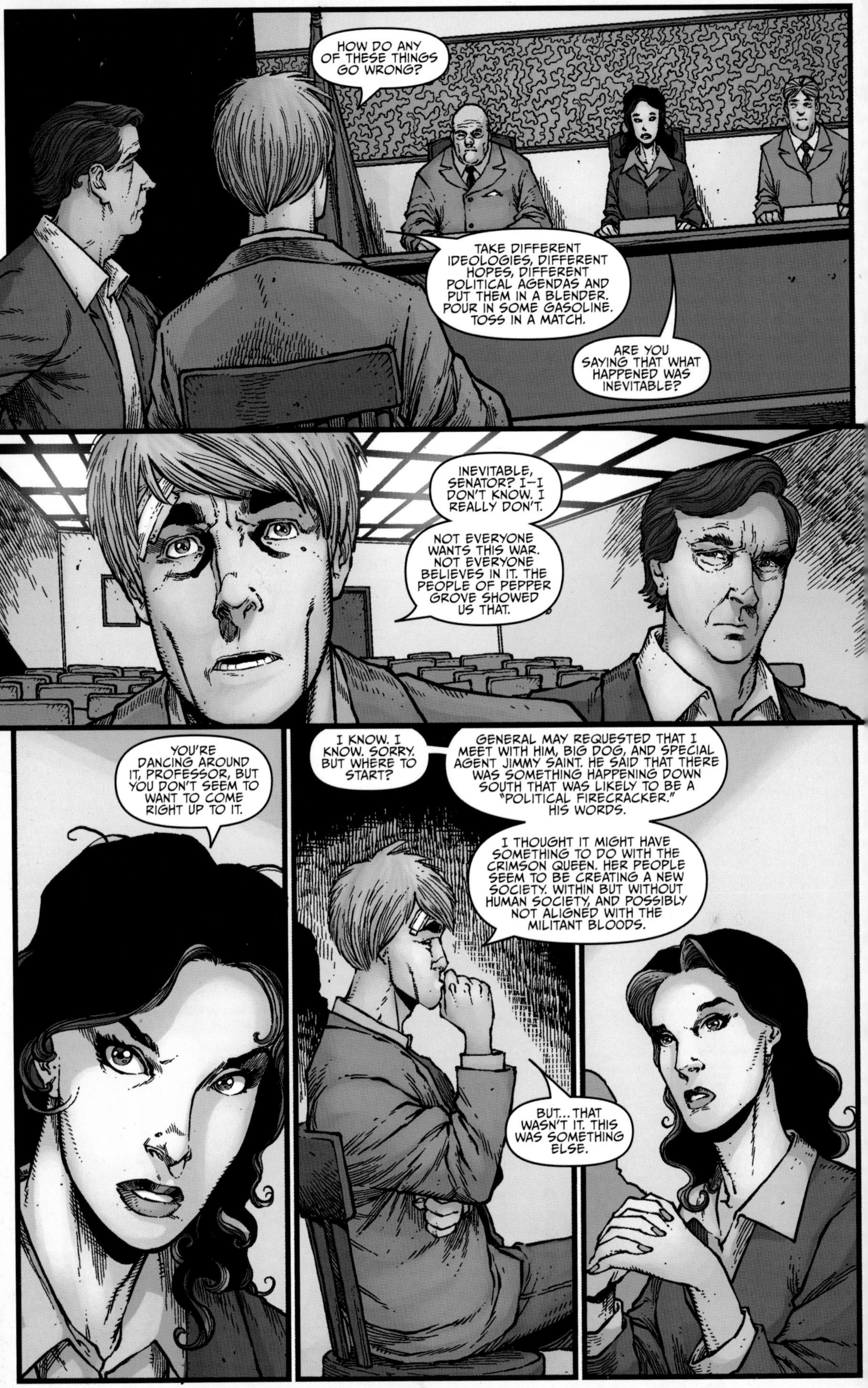
HOW DO ANY OF THESE THINGS GO WRONG?
TAKE DIFFERENT IDEOLOGIES, DIFFERENT HOPES, DIFFERENT POLITICAL AGENDAS AND PUT THEM IN A BLENDER. POUR IN SOME GASOLINE. TOSS IN A MATCH.
ARE YOU SAYING THAT WHAT HAPPENED WAS INEVITABLE?
INEVITABLE, SENATOR? I—I DON'T KNOW. I REALLY DON'T.
NOT EVERYONE WANTS THIS WAR. NOT EVERYONE BELIEVES IN IT. THE PEOPLE OF PEPPER GROVE SHOWED US THAT.
YOU'RE DANCING AROUND IT, PROFESSOR, BUT YOU DON'T SEEM TO WANT TO COME RIGHT UP TO IT.
I KNOW. I KNOW. SORRY. BUT WHERE TO START?
GENERAL MAY REQUESTED THAT I MEET WITH HIM, BIG DOG, AND SPECIAL AGENT JIMMY SAINT. HE SAID THAT THERE WAS SOMETHING HAPPENING DOWN SOUTH THAT WAS LIKELY TO BE A "POLITICAL FIRECRACKER." HIS WORDS.
I THOUGHT IT MIGHT HAVE SOMETHING TO DO WITH THE CRIMSON QUEEN. HER PEOPLE SEEM TO BE CREATING A NEW SOCIETY. WITHIN BUT WITHOUT HUMAN SOCIETY, AND POSSIBLY NOT ALIGNED WITH THE MILITANT BLOODS.
BUT... THAT WASN'T IT. THIS WAS SOMETHING ELSE.

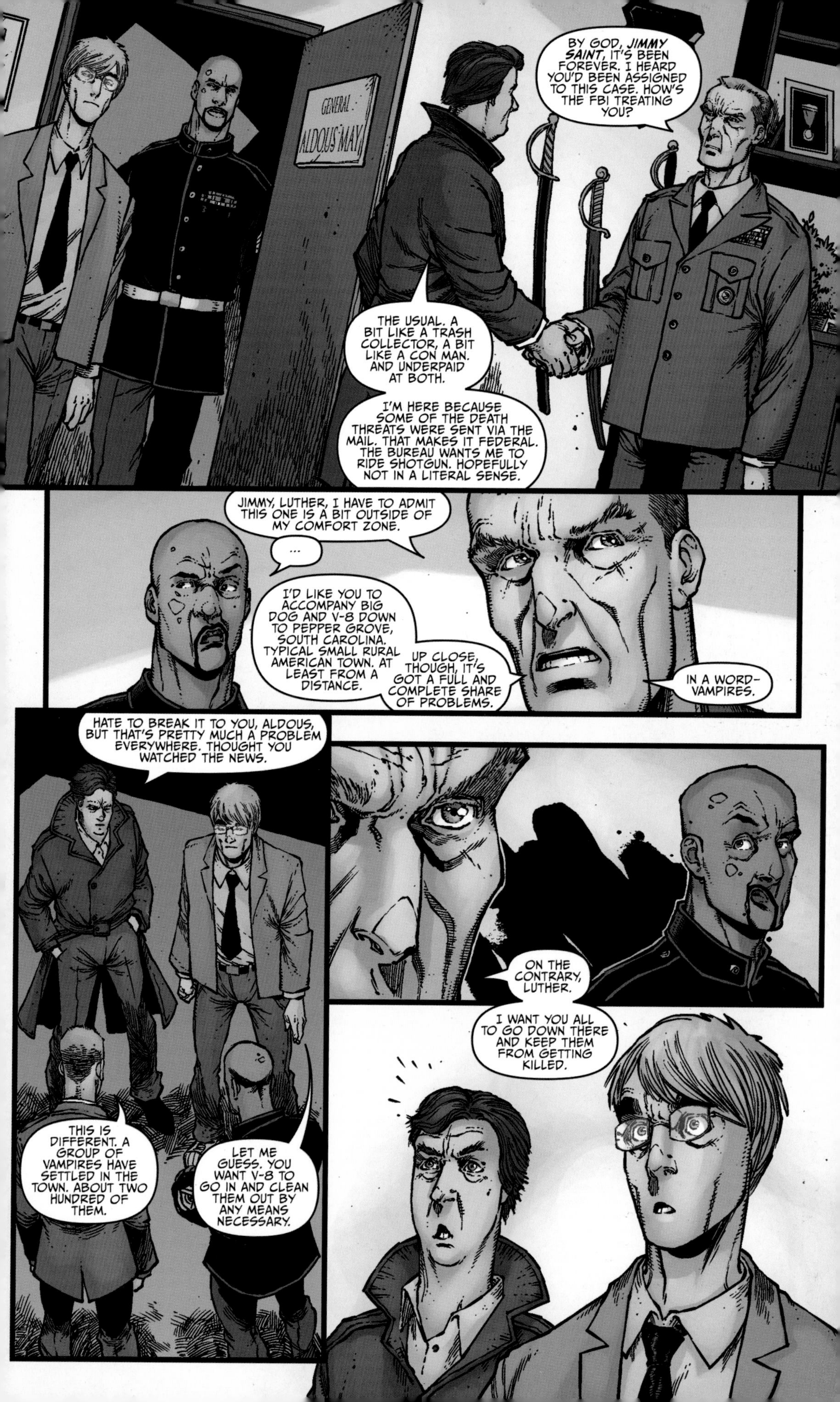
GENERAL ALDOUS MAY
BY GOD, JIMMY SAINT, IT'S BEEN FOREVER. I HEARD YOU'D BEEN ASSIGNED TO THIS CASE. HOW'S THE FBI TREATING YOU?
THE USUAL. A BIT LIKE A TRASH COLLECTOR, A BIT LIKE A CON MAN. AND UNDERPAID AT BOTH.
I'M HERE BECAUSE SOME OF THE DEATH THREATS WERE SENT VIA THE MAIL. THAT MAKES IT FEDERAL. THE BUREAU WANTS ME TO RIDE SHOTGUN. HOPEFULLY NOT IN A LITERAL SENSE.
JIMMY, LUTHER, I HAVE TO ADMIT THIS ONE IS A BIT OUTSIDE OF MY COMFORT ZONE.
...
I'D LIKE YOU TO ACCOMPANY BIG DOG AND V-8 DOWN TO PEPPER GROVE, SOUTH CAROLINA. TYPICAL SMALL RURAL AMERICAN TOWN. AT LEAST FROM A DISTANCE.
UP CLOSE, THOUGH, IT'S GOT A FULL AND COMPLETE SHARE OF PROBLEMS.
IN A WORD- VAMPIRES.
HATE TO BREAK IT TO YOU, ALDOUS, BUT THAT'S PRETTY MUCH A PROBLEM EVERYWHERE. THOUGHT YOU WATCHED THE NEWS.
THIS IS DIFFERENT. A GROUP OF VAMPIRES HAVE SETTLED IN THE TOWN. ABOUT TWO HUNDRED OF THEM.
LET ME GUESS. YOU WANT V-8 TO GO IN AND CLEAN THEM OUT BY ANY MEANS NECESSARY.
ON THE CONTRARY, LUTHER.
I WANT YOU ALL TO GO DOWN THERE AND KEEP THEM FROM GETTING KILLED.

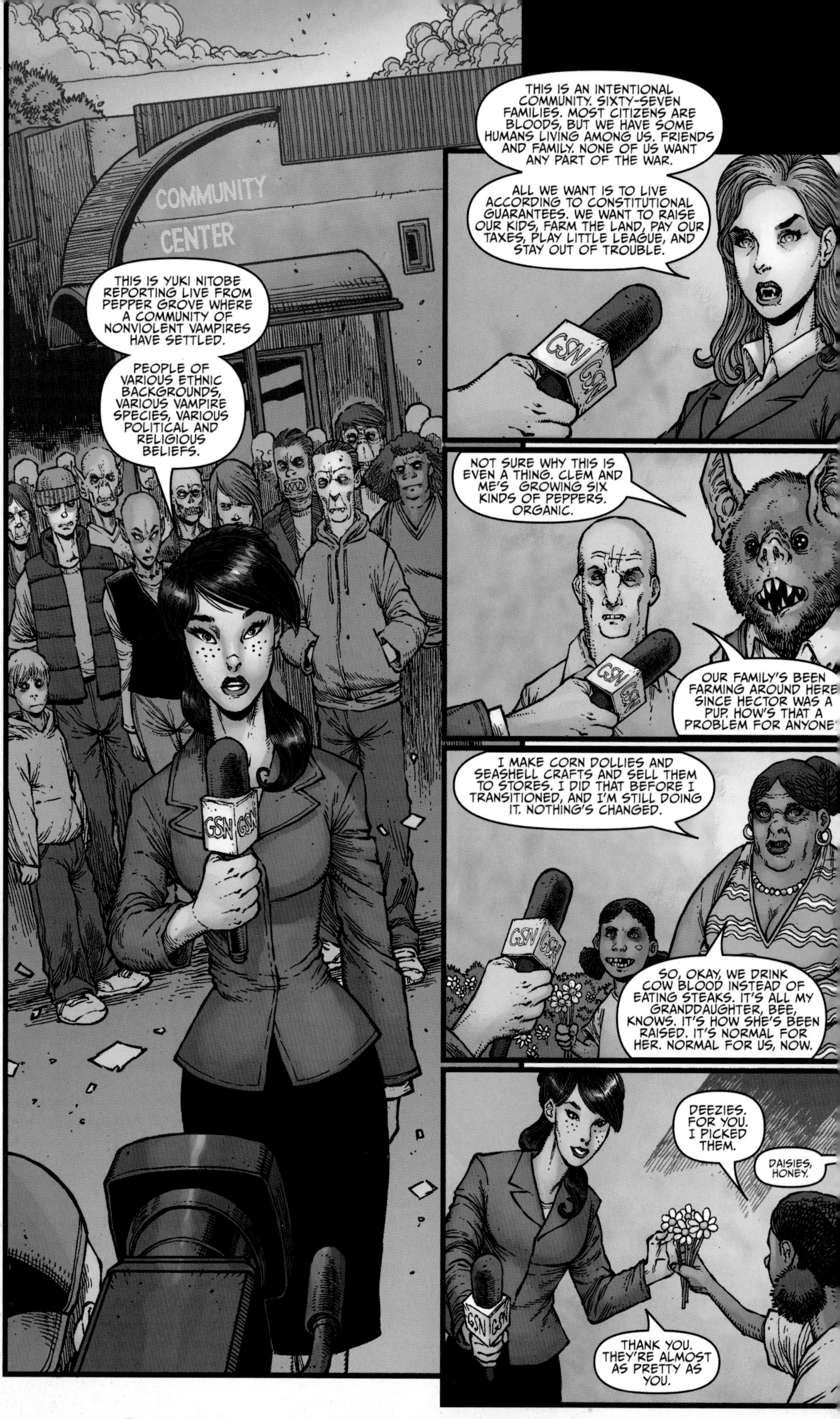
COMMUNITY CENTER
THIS IS YUKI NITOBE REPORTING LIVE FROM PEPPER GROVE WHERE A COMMUNITY OF NONVIOLENT VAMPIRES HAVE SETTLED.
PEOPLE OF VARIOUS ETHNIC BACKGROUNDS, VARIOUS VAMPIRE SPECIES, VARIOUS POLITICAL AND RELIGIOUS BELIEFS.
THIS IS AN INTENTIONAL COMMUNITY. SIXTY-SEVEN FAMILIES. MOST CITIZENS ARE BLOODS, BUT WE HAVE SOME HUMANS LIVING AMONG US. FRIENDS AND FAMILY. NONE OF US WANT ANY PART OF THE WAR.
ALL WE WANT IS TO LIVE ACCORDING TO CONSTITUTIONAL GUARANTEES. WE WANT TO RAISE OUR KIDS, FARM THE LAND, PAY OUR TAXES, PLAY LITTLE LEAGUE, AND STAY OUT OF TROUBLE.
GSN
NOT SURE WHY THIS IS EVEN A THING. CLEM AND ME'S GROWING SIX KINDS OF PEPPERS. ORGANIC.
OUR FAMILY'S BEEN FARMING AROUND HERE SINCE HECTOR WAS A PUP. HOW'S THAT A PROBLEM FOR ANYONE
I MAKE CORN DOLLIES AND SEASHELL CRAFTS AND SELL THEM TO STORES. I DID THAT BEFORE I TRANSITIONED, AND I'M STILL DOING IT. NOTHING'S CHANGED.
SO, OKAY, WE DRINK COW BLOOD INSTEAD OF EATING STEAKS. IT'S ALL MY GRANDDAUGHTER, BEE, KNOWS. IT'S HOW SHE'S BEEN RAISED. IT'S NORMAL FOR HER. NORMAL FOR US, NOW.
DEEZIES. FOR YOU. I PICKED THEM.
DAISIES, HONEY.
THANK YOU. THEY'RE ALMOST AS PRETTY AS YOU.

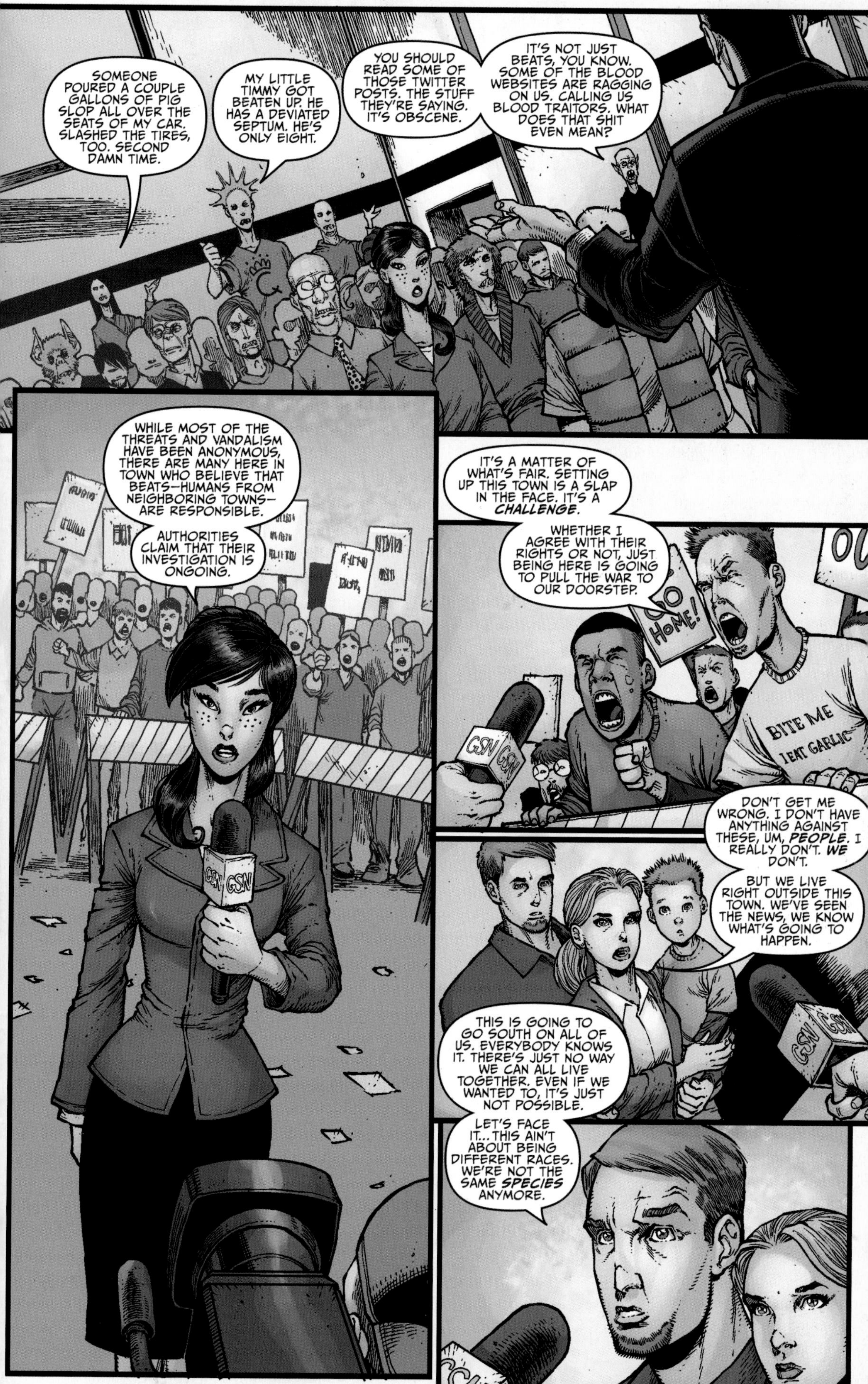
SOMEONE POURED A COUPLE GALLONS OF PIG SLOP ALL OVER THE SEATS OF MY CAR. SLASHED THE TIRES, TOO. SECOND DAMN TIME.
MY LITTLE TIMMY GOT BEATEN UP. HE HAS A DEVIATED SEPTUM. HE'S ONLY EIGHT.
YOU SHOULD READ SOME OF THOSE TWITTER POSTS. THE STUFF THEY'RE SAYING. IT'S OBSCENE.
IT'S NOT JUST BEATS, YOU KNOW. SOME OF THE BLOOD WEBSITES ARE RAGGING ON US. CALLING US BLOOD TRAITORS. WHAT DOES THAT SHIT EVEN MEAN?
WHILE MOST OF THE THREATS AND VANDALISM HAVE BEEN ANONYMOUS, THERE ARE MANY HERE IN TOWN WHO BELIEVE THAT BEATS—HUMANS FROM NEIGHBORING TOWNS—ARE RESPONSIBLE.
AUTHORITIES CLAIM THAT THEIR INVESTIGATION IS ONGOING.
GSN
IT'S A MATTER OF WHAT'S FAIR. SETTING UP THIS TOWN IS A SLAP IN THE FACE. IT'S A *CHALLENGE*.
WHETHER I AGREE WITH THEIR RIGHTS OR NOT, JUST BEING HERE IS GOING TO PULL THE WAR TO OUR DOORSTEP.
GO HOME!
BITE ME
I EAT GARLIC
GSN
DON'T GET ME WRONG. I DON'T HAVE ANYTHING AGAINST THESE, UM, *PEOPLE*. I REALLY DON'T. *WE* DON'T.
BUT WE LIVE RIGHT OUTSIDE THIS TOWN. WE'VE SEEN THE NEWS, WE KNOW WHAT'S GOING TO HAPPEN.
THIS IS GOING TO GO SOUTH ON ALL OF US. EVERYBODY KNOWS IT. THERE'S JUST NO WAY WE CAN ALL LIVE TOGETHER. EVEN IF WE WANTED TO, IT'S JUST NOT POSSIBLE.
GSN
LET'S FACE IT... THIS AIN'T ABOUT BEING DIFFERENT RACES. WE'RE NOT THE SAME *SPECIES* ANYMORE.

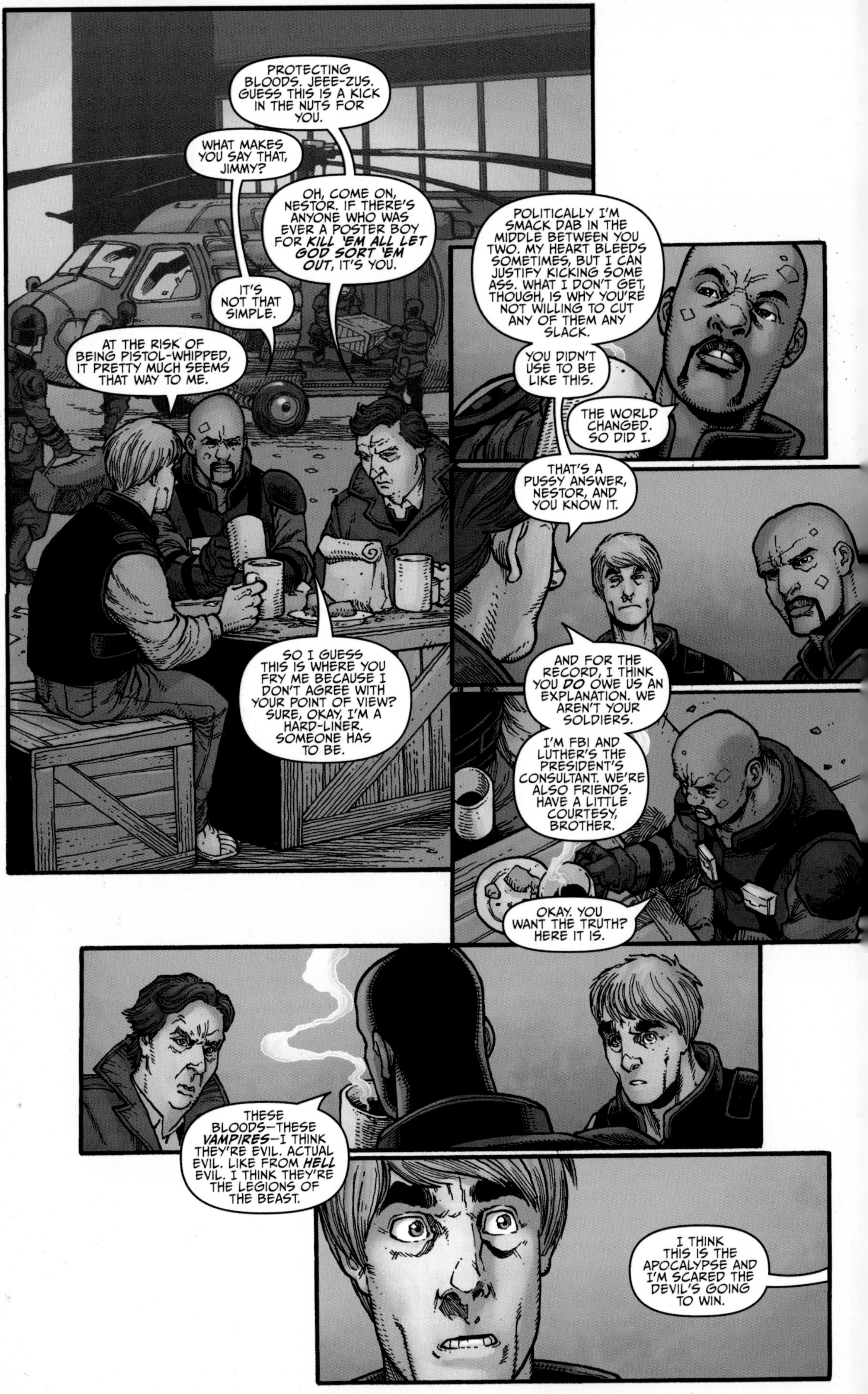
PROTECTING BLOODS. JEEE-ZUS. GUESS THIS IS A KICK IN THE NUTS FOR YOU.
WHAT MAKES YOU SAY THAT, JIMMY?
OH, COME ON, NESTOR. IF THERE'S ANYONE WHO WAS EVER A POSTER BOY FOR ***KILL 'EM ALL LET GOD SORT 'EM OUT***, IT'S YOU.
IT'S NOT THAT SIMPLE.
AT THE RISK OF BEING PISTOL-WHIPPED, IT PRETTY MUCH SEEMS THAT WAY TO ME.
SO I GUESS THIS IS WHERE YOU FRY ME BECAUSE I DON'T AGREE WITH YOUR POINT OF VIEW? SURE, OKAY, I'M A HARD-LINER. SOMEONE HAS TO BE.
POLITICALLY I'M SMACK DAB IN THE MIDDLE BETWEEN YOU TWO. MY HEART BLEEDS SOMETIMES, BUT I CAN JUSTIFY KICKING SOME ASS. WHAT I DON'T GET, THOUGH, IS WHY YOU'RE NOT WILLING TO CUT ANY OF THEM ANY SLACK.
YOU DIDN'T USE TO BE LIKE THIS.
THE WORLD CHANGED. SO DID I.
THAT'S A PUSSY ANSWER, NESTOR, AND YOU KNOW IT.
AND FOR THE RECORD, I THINK YOU ***DO*** OWE US AN EXPLANATION. WE AREN'T YOUR SOLDIERS.
I'M FBI AND LUTHER'S THE PRESIDENT'S CONSULTANT. WE'RE ALSO FRIENDS. HAVE A LITTLE COURTESY, BROTHER.
OKAY. YOU WANT THE TRUTH? HERE IT IS.
THESE BLOODS—THESE ***VAMPIRES***—I THINK THEY'RE EVIL. ACTUAL EVIL. LIKE FROM ***HELL*** EVIL. I THINK THEY'RE THE LEGIONS OF THE BEAST.
I THINK THIS IS THE APOCALYPSE AND I'M SCARED THE DEVIL'S GOING TO WIN.

WELL, HOLY FUCK.

NO WAY WE HAVE THIS CONVERSATION SOBER.

YOU SHOULD HAVE TOLD ME ABOUT THIS. WE COULD HAVE TALKED ABOUT IT.

WHY? SO YOU CAN TRASH MY RELIGIOUS BELIEFS THE WAY YOU PISS ALL OVER MY POLITICS?

I—

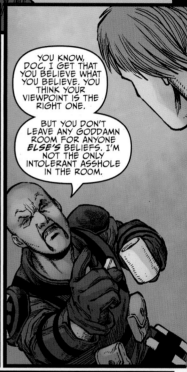

YOU KNOW, DOC, I GET THAT YOU BELIEVE WHAT YOU BELIEVE. YOU THINK YOUR VIEWPOINT IS THE RIGHT ONE.

BUT YOU DON'T LEAVE ANY GODDAMN ROOM FOR ANYONE ELSE'S BELIEFS. I'M NOT THE ONLY INTOLERANT ASSHOLE IN THE ROOM.

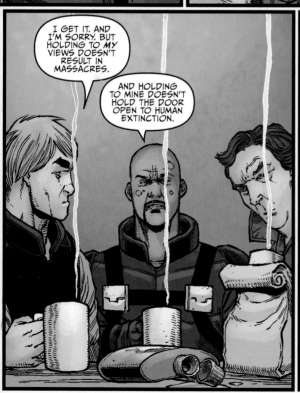

I GET IT. AND I'M SORRY. BUT HOLDING TO MY VIEWS DOESN'T RESULT IN MASSACRES.

AND HOLDING TO MINE DOESN'T HOLD THE DOOR OPEN TO HUMAN EXTINCTION.

SURE, GENERAL MAY, I'LL BE HAPPY TO JOIN THOSE GUYS DOWN IN PEPPER GROVE. SHOULD BE AN EASY GIG. NO PROBLEMS AT ALL.

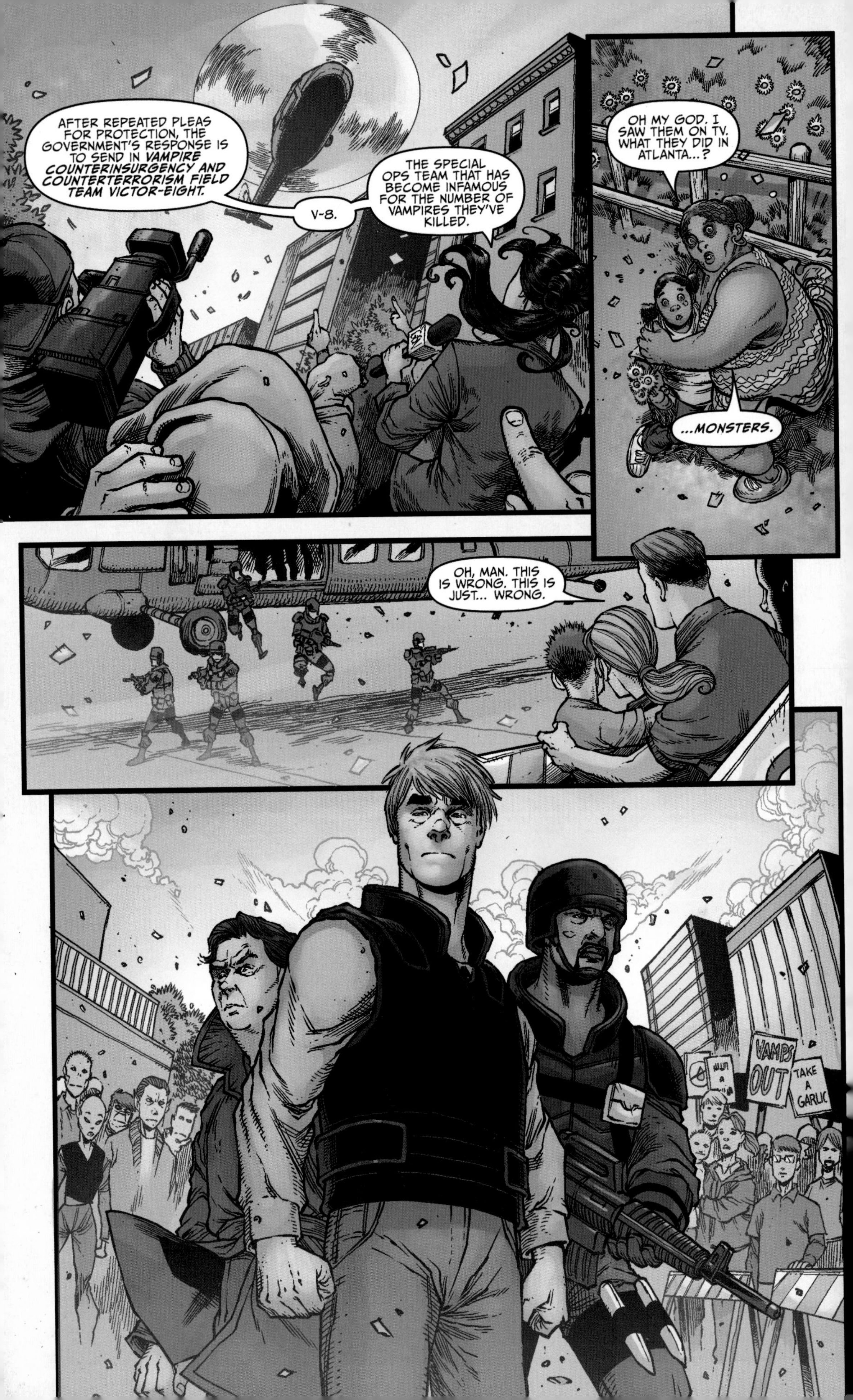
AFTER REPEATED PLEAS FOR PROTECTION, THE GOVERNMENT'S RESPONSE IS TO SEND IN VAMPIRE COUNTERINSURGENCY AND COUNTERTERRORISM FIELD TEAM VICTOR-EIGHT.
V-8.
THE SPECIAL OPS TEAM THAT HAS BECOME INFAMOUS FOR THE NUMBER OF VAMPIRES THEY'VE KILLED.
OH MY GOD. I SAW THEM ON TV. WHAT THEY DID IN ATLANTA...?
...MONSTERS.
OH, MAN. THIS IS WRONG. THIS IS JUST... WRONG.
VAMPS OUT
TAKE A GARLIC

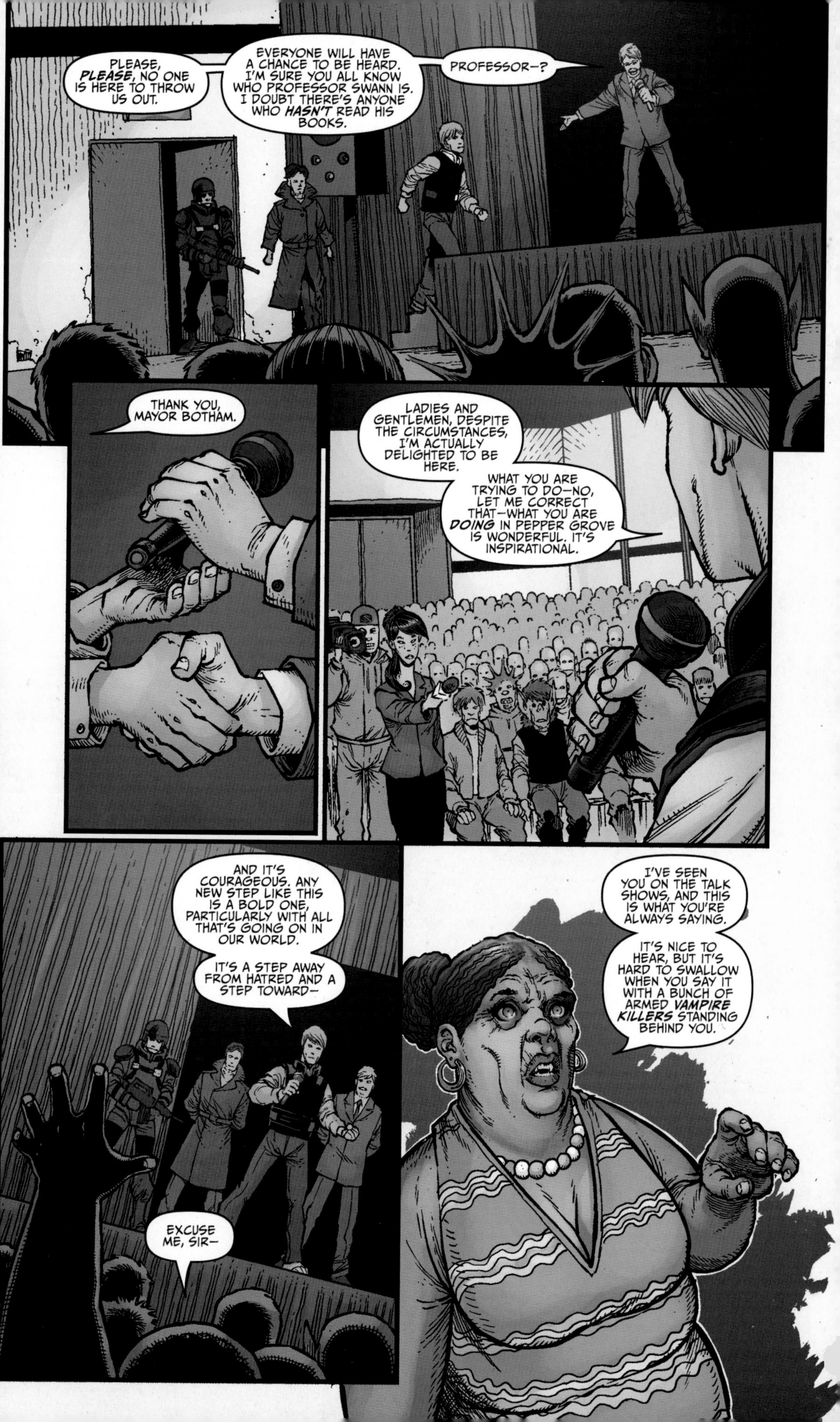
PLEASE, PLEASE, NO ONE IS HERE TO THROW US OUT.
EVERYONE WILL HAVE A CHANCE TO BE HEARD. I'M SURE YOU ALL KNOW WHO PROFESSOR SWANN IS. I DOUBT THERE'S ANYONE WHO HASN'T READ HIS BOOKS.
PROFESSOR—?
THANK YOU, MAYOR BOTHAM.
LADIES AND GENTLEMEN, DESPITE THE CIRCUMSTANCES, I'M ACTUALLY DELIGHTED TO BE HERE.
WHAT YOU ARE TRYING TO DO—NO, LET ME CORRECT THAT—WHAT YOU ARE DOING IN PEPPER GROVE IS WONDERFUL. IT'S INSPIRATIONAL.
AND IT'S COURAGEOUS. ANY NEW STEP LIKE THIS IS A BOLD ONE, PARTICULARLY WITH ALL THAT'S GOING ON IN OUR WORLD.
IT'S A STEP AWAY FROM HATRED AND A STEP TOWARD—
EXCUSE ME, SIR—
I'VE SEEN YOU ON THE TALK SHOWS, AND THIS IS WHAT YOU'RE ALWAYS SAYING.
IT'S NICE TO HEAR, BUT IT'S HARD TO SWALLOW WHEN YOU SAY IT WITH A BUNCH OF ARMED VAMPIRE KILLERS STANDING BEHIND YOU.

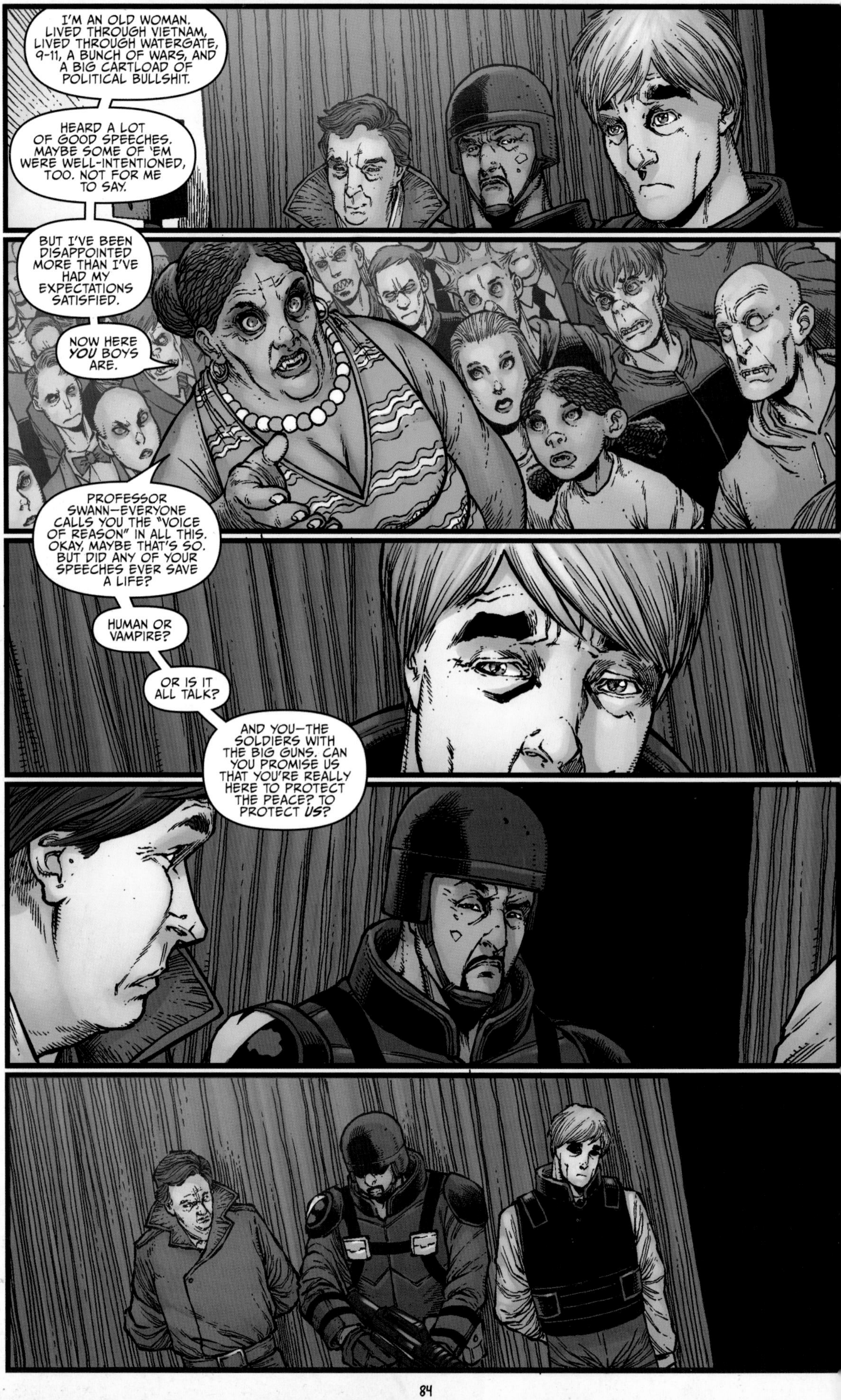

I'M AN OLD WOMAN. LIVED THROUGH VIETNAM, LIVED THROUGH WATERGATE, 9-11, A BUNCH OF WARS, AND A BIG CARTLOAD OF POLITICAL BULLSHIT.
HEARD A LOT OF GOOD SPEECHES. MAYBE SOME OF 'EM WERE WELL-INTENTIONED, TOO. NOT FOR ME TO SAY.
BUT I'VE BEEN DISAPPOINTED MORE THAN I'VE HAD MY EXPECTATIONS SATISFIED.
NOW HERE *YOU* BOYS ARE.
PROFESSOR SWANN—EVERYONE CALLS YOU THE "VOICE OF REASON" IN ALL THIS. OKAY, MAYBE THAT'S SO. BUT DID ANY OF YOUR SPEECHES EVER SAVE A LIFE?
HUMAN OR VAMPIRE?
OR IS IT ALL TALK?
AND YOU—THE SOLDIERS WITH THE BIG GUNS. CAN YOU PROMISE US THAT YOU'RE REALLY HERE TO PROTECT THE PEACE? TO PROTECT *US*?

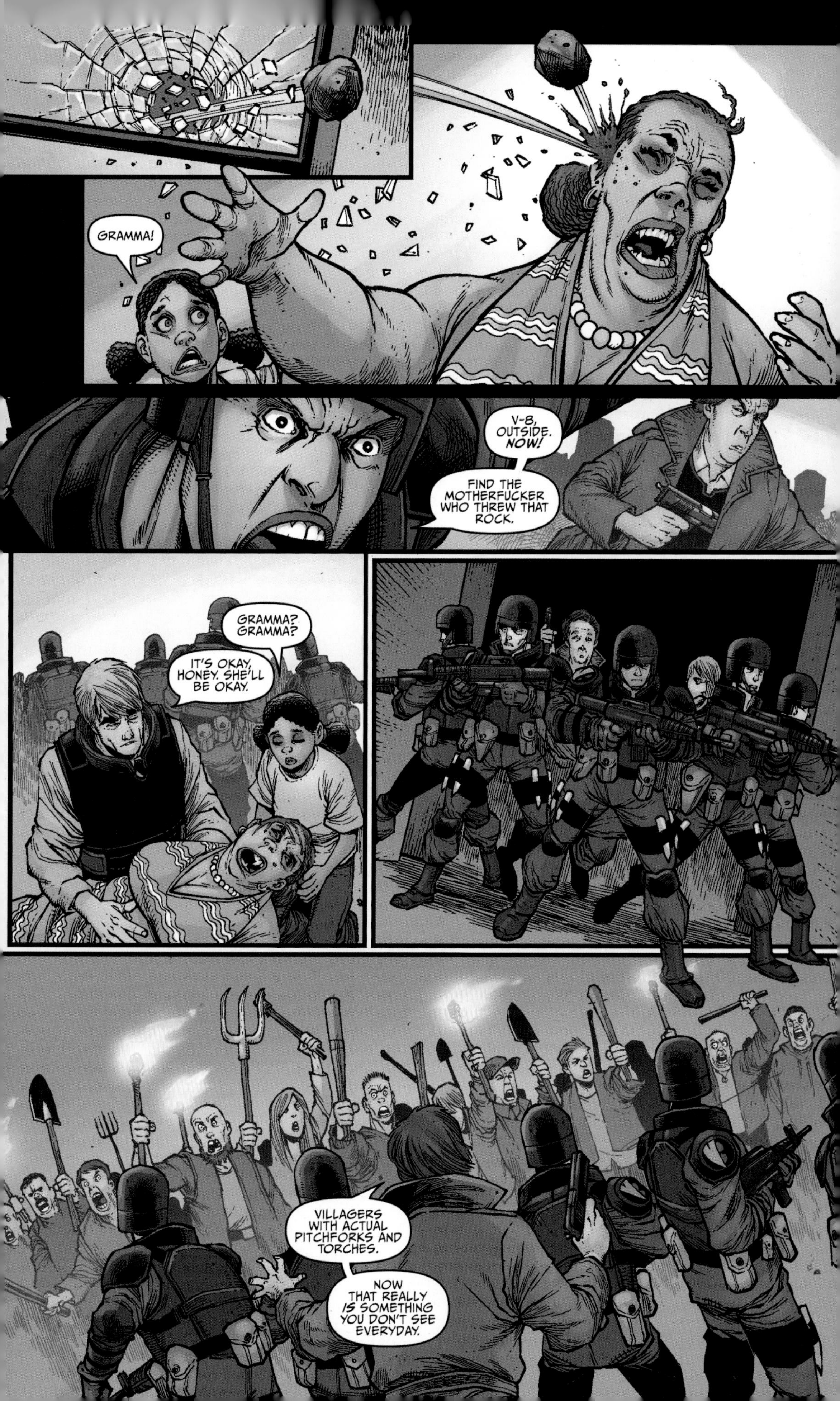
GRAMMA!
V-8, OUTSIDE. *NOW!*
FIND THE MOTHERFUCKER WHO THREW THAT ROCK.
GRAMMA? GRAMMA?
IT'S OKAY, HONEY. SHE'LL BE OKAY.
VILLAGERS WITH ACTUAL PITCHFORKS AND TORCHES.
NOW THAT REALLY *IS* SOMETHING YOU DON'T SEE EVERYDAY.

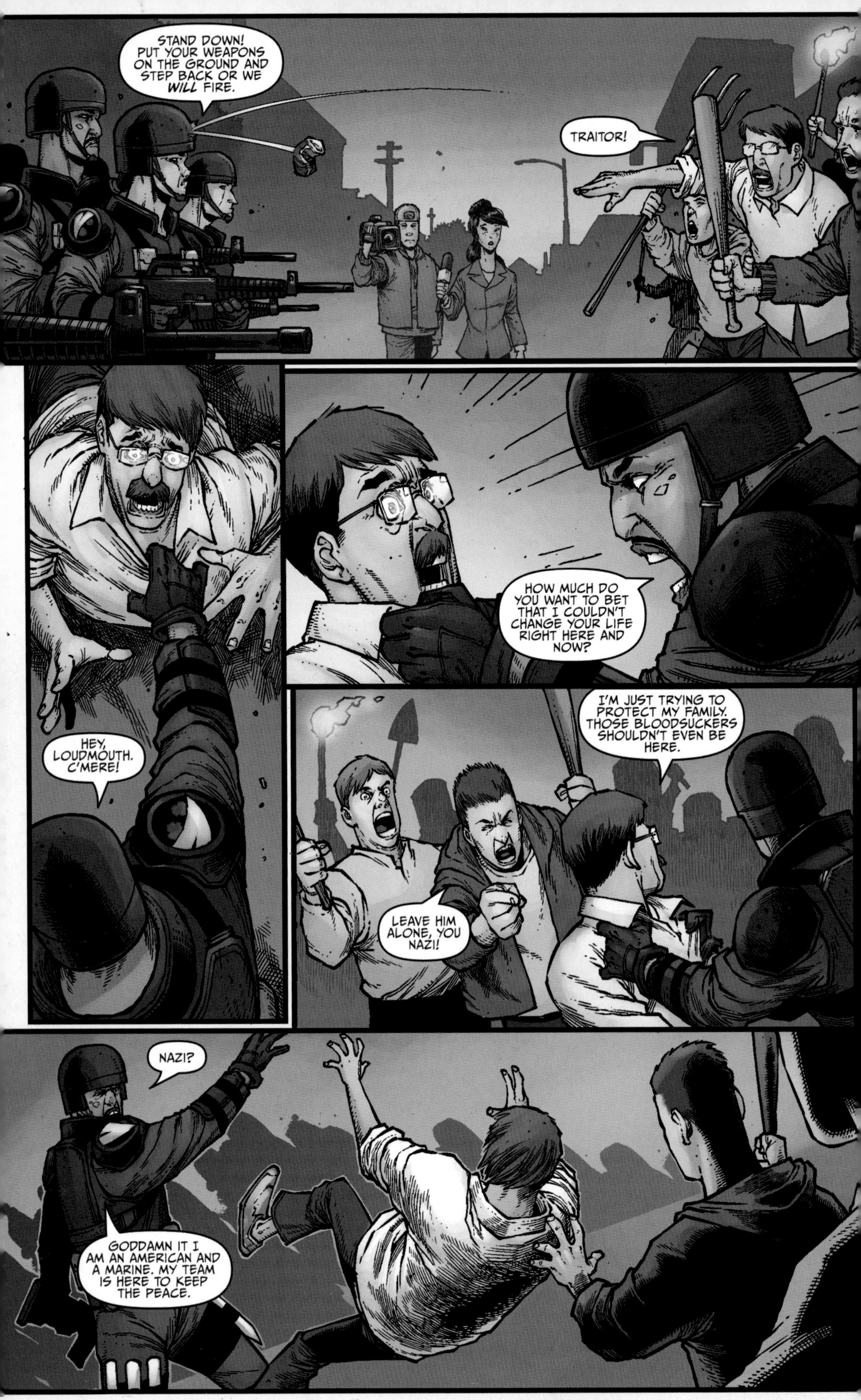
STAND DOWN! PUT YOUR WEAPONS ON THE GROUND AND STEP BACK OR WE WILL FIRE.
TRAITOR!
HEY, LOUDMOUTH. C'MERE!
HOW MUCH DO YOU WANT TO BET THAT I COULDN'T CHANGE YOUR LIFE RIGHT HERE AND NOW?
I'M JUST TRYING TO PROTECT MY FAMILY. THOSE BLOODSUCKERS SHOULDN'T EVEN BE HERE.
LEAVE HIM ALONE, YOU NAZI!
NAZI?
GODDAMN IT I AM AN AMERICAN AND A MARINE. MY TEAM IS HERE TO KEEP THE PEACE.

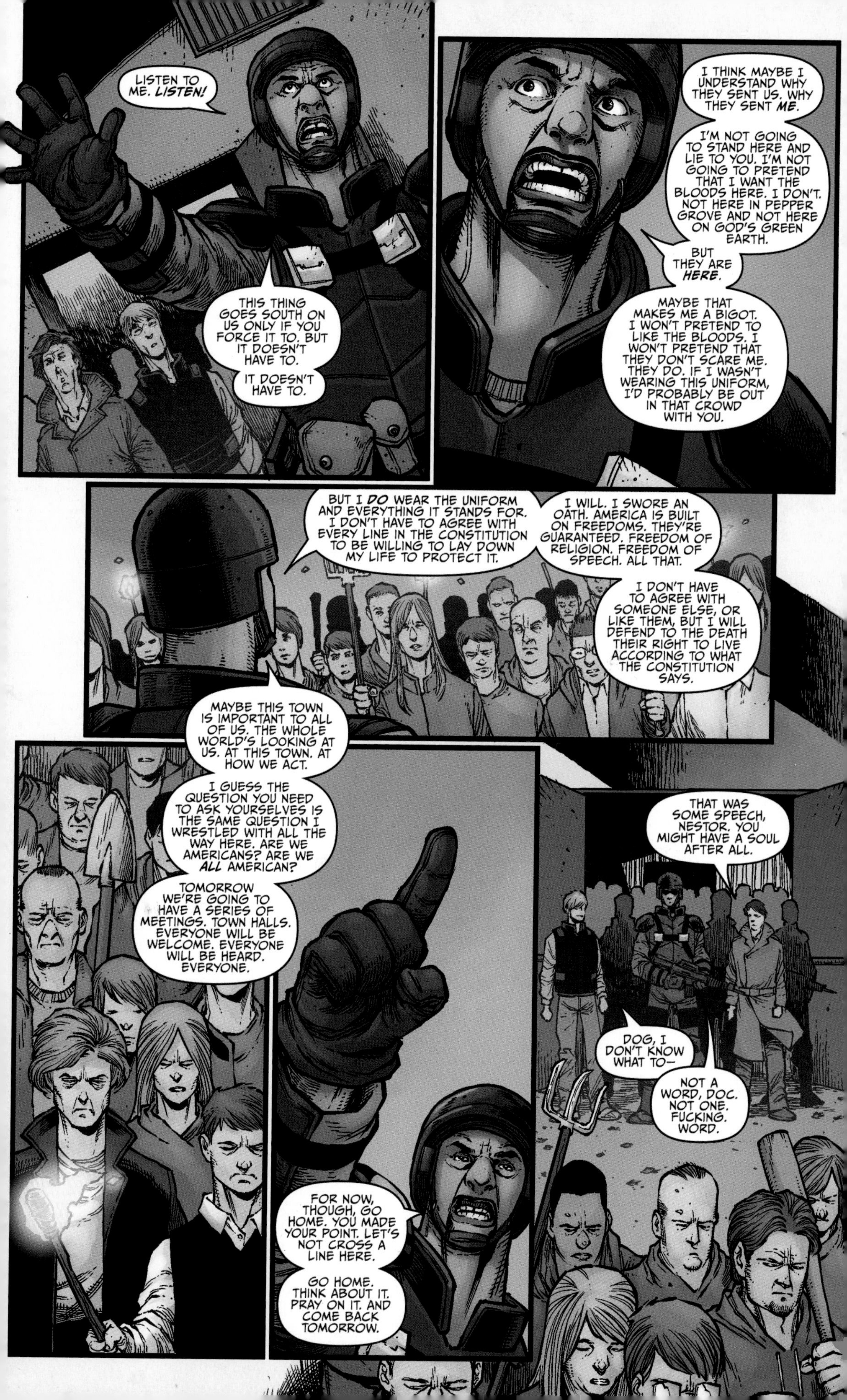
LISTEN TO ME. *LISTEN!*
THIS THING GOES SOUTH ON US ONLY IF YOU FORCE IT TO. BUT IT DOESN'T HAVE TO.
IT DOESN'T HAVE TO.
I THINK MAYBE I UNDERSTAND WHY THEY SENT US. WHY THEY SENT *ME*.
I'M NOT GOING TO STAND HERE AND LIE TO YOU. I'M NOT GOING TO PRETEND THAT I WANT THE BLOODS HERE. I DON'T. NOT HERE IN PEPPER GROVE AND NOT HERE ON GOD'S GREEN EARTH.
BUT THEY ARE *HERE*.
MAYBE THAT MAKES ME A BIGOT. I WON'T PRETEND TO LIKE THE BLOODS. I WON'T PRETEND THAT THEY DON'T SCARE ME. THEY DO. IF I WASN'T WEARING THIS UNIFORM, I'D PROBABLY BE OUT IN THAT CROWD WITH YOU.
BUT I *DO* WEAR THE UNIFORM AND EVERYTHING IT STANDS FOR. I DON'T HAVE TO AGREE WITH EVERY LINE IN THE CONSTITUTION TO BE WILLING TO LAY DOWN MY LIFE TO PROTECT IT.
I WILL. I SWORE AN OATH. AMERICA IS BUILT ON FREEDOMS. THEY'RE GUARANTEED. FREEDOM OF RELIGION. FREEDOM OF SPEECH. ALL THAT.
I DON'T HAVE TO AGREE WITH SOMEONE ELSE, OR LIKE THEM, BUT I WILL DEFEND TO THE DEATH THEIR RIGHT TO LIVE ACCORDING TO WHAT THE CONSTITUTION SAYS.
MAYBE THIS TOWN IS IMPORTANT TO ALL OF US. THE WHOLE WORLD'S LOOKING AT US. AT THIS TOWN. AT HOW WE ACT.
I GUESS THE QUESTION YOU NEED TO ASK YOURSELVES IS THE SAME QUESTION I WRESTLED WITH ALL THE WAY HERE. ARE WE AMERICANS? ARE WE *ALL* AMERICAN?
TOMORROW WE'RE GOING TO HAVE A SERIES OF MEETINGS. TOWN HALLS. EVERYONE WILL BE WELCOME. EVERYONE WILL BE HEARD. EVERYONE.
FOR NOW, THOUGH, GO HOME. YOU MADE YOUR POINT. LET'S NOT CROSS A LINE HERE.
GO HOME. THINK ABOUT IT. PRAY ON IT. AND COME BACK TOMORROW.
THAT WAS SOME SPEECH, NESTOR. YOU MIGHT HAVE A SOUL AFTER ALL.
DOG, I DON'T KNOW WHAT TO—
NOT A WORD, DOC. NOT ONE. FUCKING. WORD.

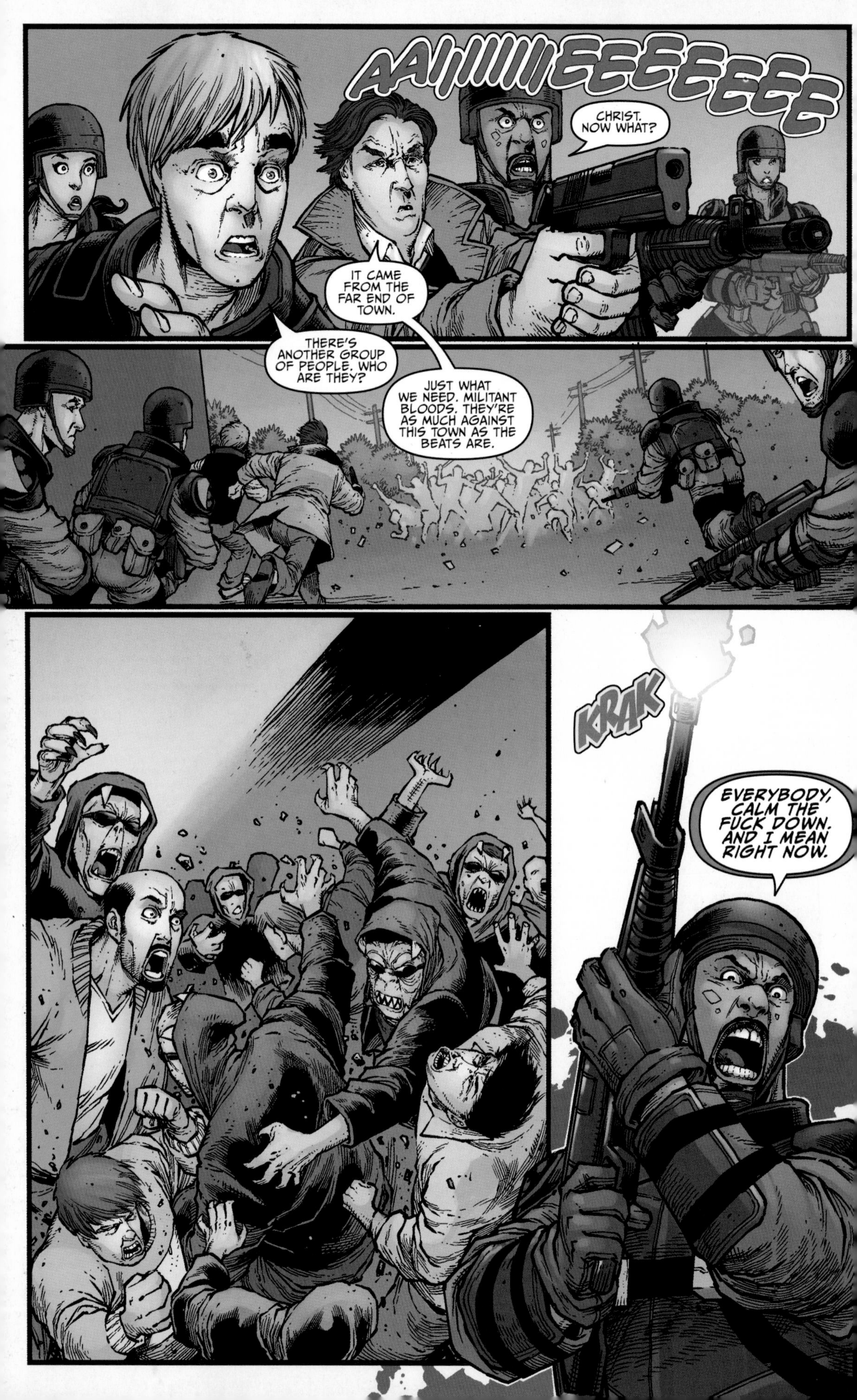
AAIIIIIIIEEEEEEEE
CHRIST. NOW WHAT?
IT CAME FROM THE FAR END OF TOWN.
THERE'S ANOTHER GROUP OF PEOPLE. WHO ARE THEY?
JUST WHAT WE NEED. MILITANT BLOODS. THEY'RE AS MUCH AGAINST THIS TOWN AS THE BEATS ARE.
KRAK
EVERYBODY, CALM THE FUCK DOWN. AND I MEAN RIGHT NOW.

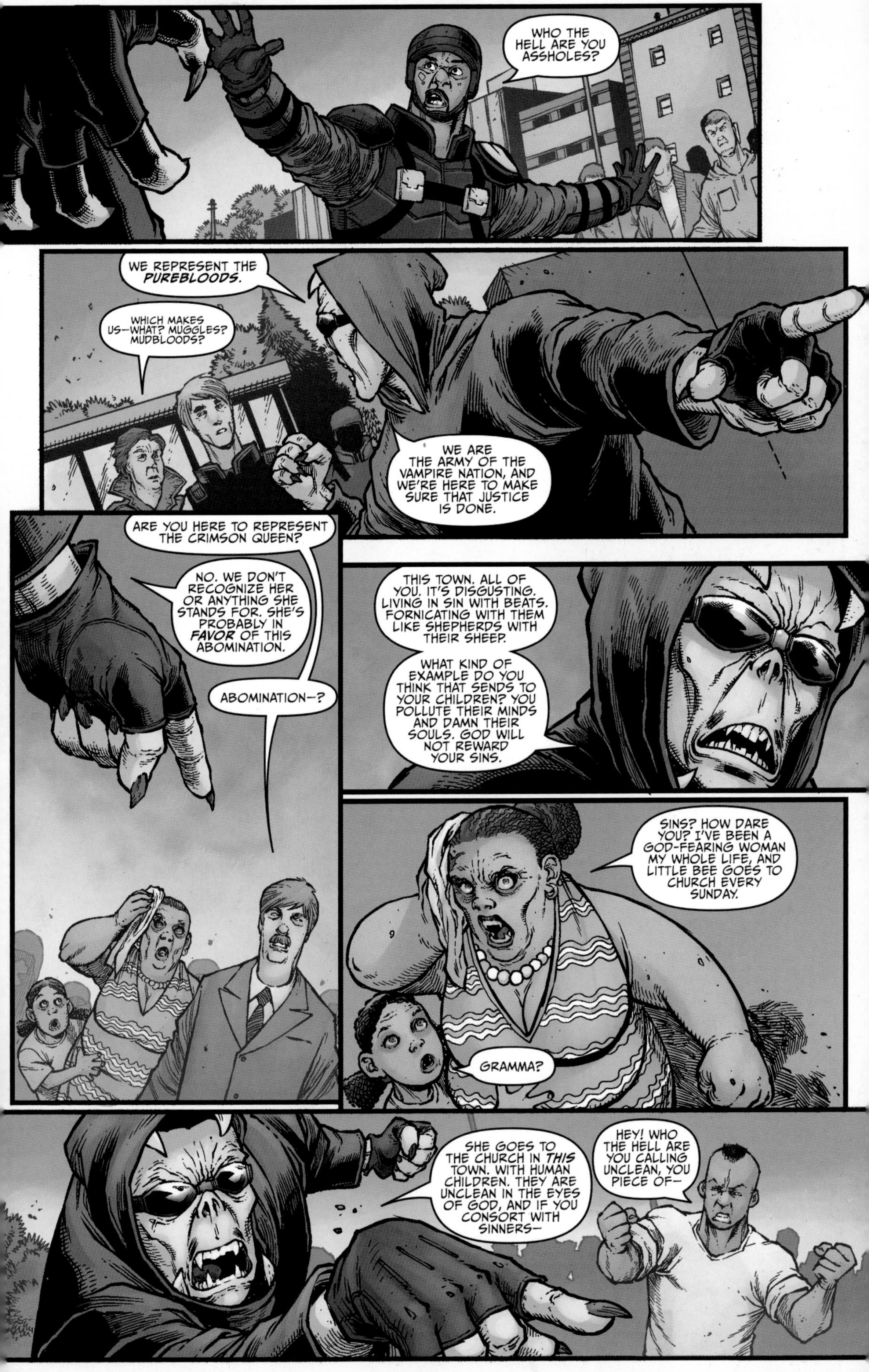
WHO THE HELL ARE YOU ASSHOLES?
WE REPRESENT THE *PUREBLOODS.*
WHICH MAKES US—WHAT? MUGGLES? MUDBLOODS?
WE ARE THE ARMY OF THE VAMPIRE NATION, AND WE'RE HERE TO MAKE SURE THAT JUSTICE IS DONE.
ARE YOU HERE TO REPRESENT THE CRIMSON QUEEN?
NO. WE DON'T RECOGNIZE HER OR ANYTHING SHE STANDS FOR. SHE'S PROBABLY IN *FAVOR* OF THIS ABOMINATION.
ABOMINATION—?
THIS TOWN. ALL OF YOU. IT'S DISGUSTING. LIVING IN SIN WITH BEATS. FORNICATING WITH THEM LIKE SHEPHERDS WITH THEIR SHEEP.
WHAT KIND OF EXAMPLE DO YOU THINK THAT SENDS TO YOUR CHILDREN? YOU POLLUTE THEIR MINDS AND DAMN THEIR SOULS. GOD WILL NOT REWARD YOUR SINS.
SINS? HOW DARE YOU? I'VE BEEN A GOD-FEARING WOMAN MY WHOLE LIFE, AND LITTLE BEE GOES TO CHURCH EVERY SUNDAY.
GRAMMA?
SHE GOES TO THE CHURCH IN *THIS* TOWN. WITH HUMAN CHILDREN. THEY ARE UNCLEAN IN THE EYES OF GOD, AND IF YOU CONSORT WITH SINNERS—
HEY! WHO THE HELL ARE YOU CALLING UNCLEAN, YOU PIECE OF—

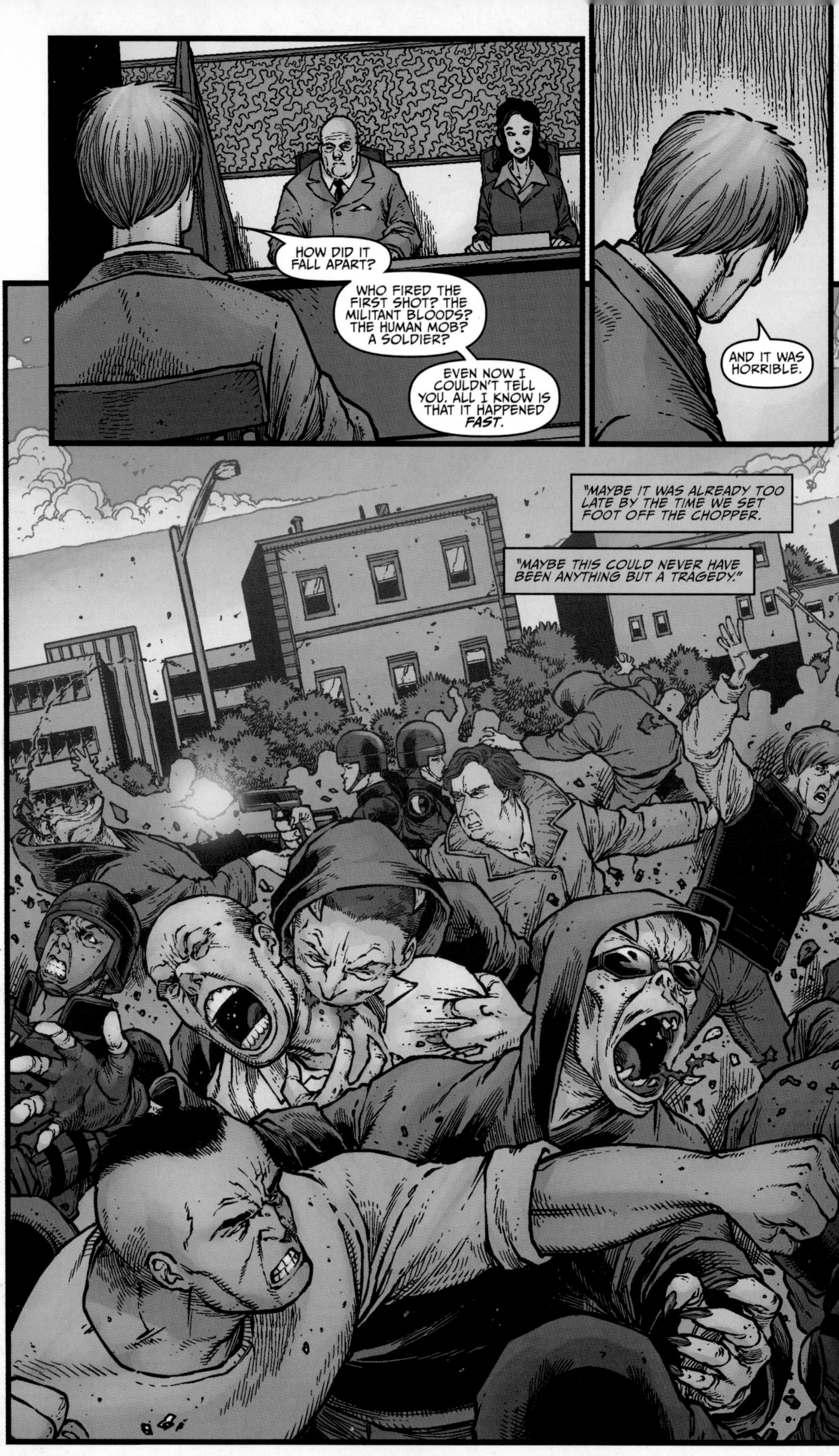
HOW DID IT FALL APART?
WHO FIRED THE FIRST SHOT? THE MILITANT BLOODS? THE HUMAN MOB? A SOLDIER?
EVEN NOW I COULDN'T TELL YOU. ALL I KNOW IS THAT IT HAPPENED *FAST*.
AND IT WAS HORRIBLE.
"MAYBE IT WAS ALREADY TOO LATE BY THE TIME WE SET FOOT OFF THE CHOPPER.
"MAYBE THIS COULD NEVER HAVE BEEN ANYTHING BUT A TRAGEDY."

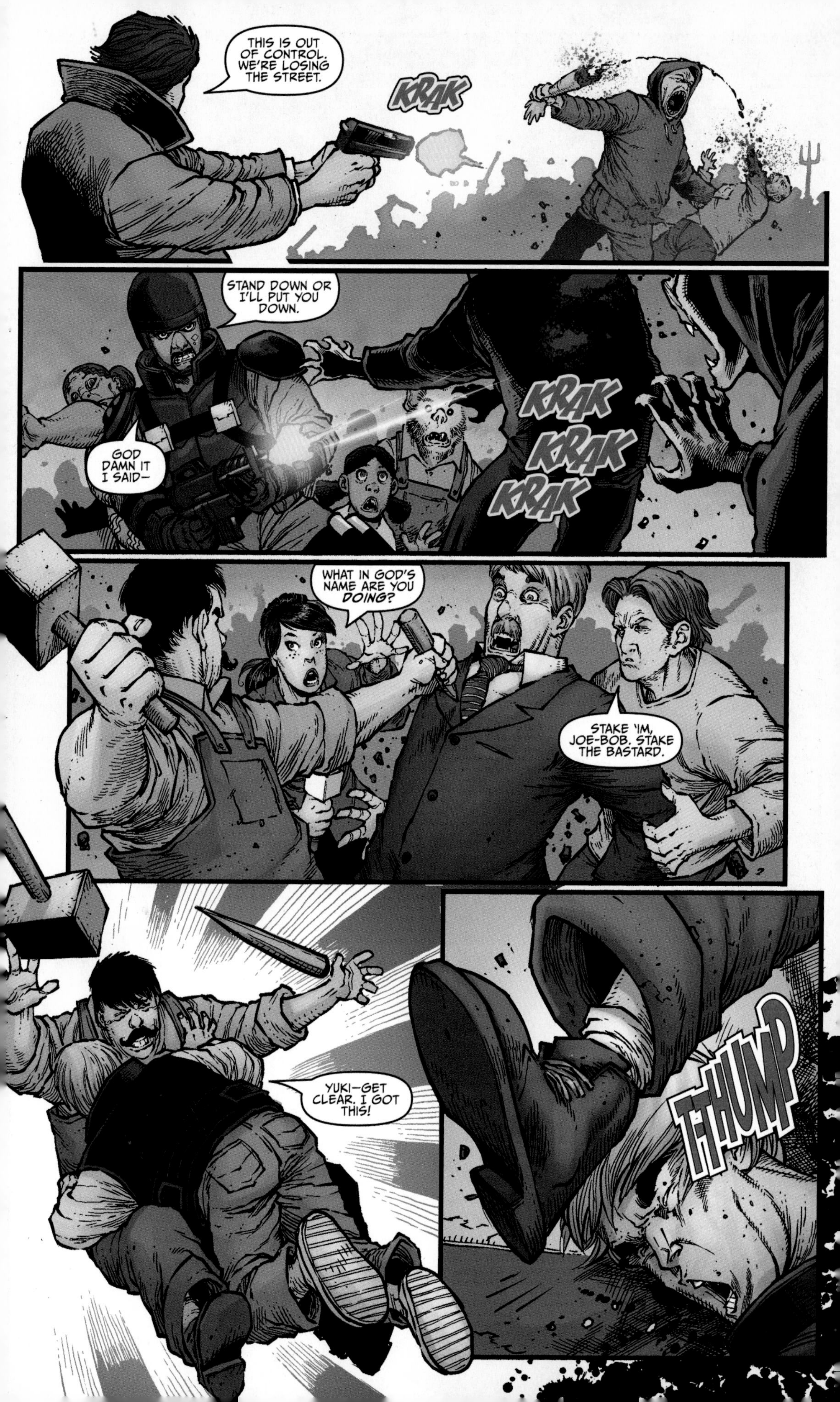

THIS IS OUT OF CONTROL. WE'RE LOSING THE STREET.
KRAK
STAND DOWN OR I'LL PUT YOU DOWN.
GOD DAMN IT I SAID—
KRAK
KRAK
KRAK
WHAT IN GOD'S NAME ARE YOU DOING?
STAKE 'IM, JOE-BOB. STAKE THE BASTARD.
YUKI—GET CLEAR. I GOT THIS!
T-THUMP

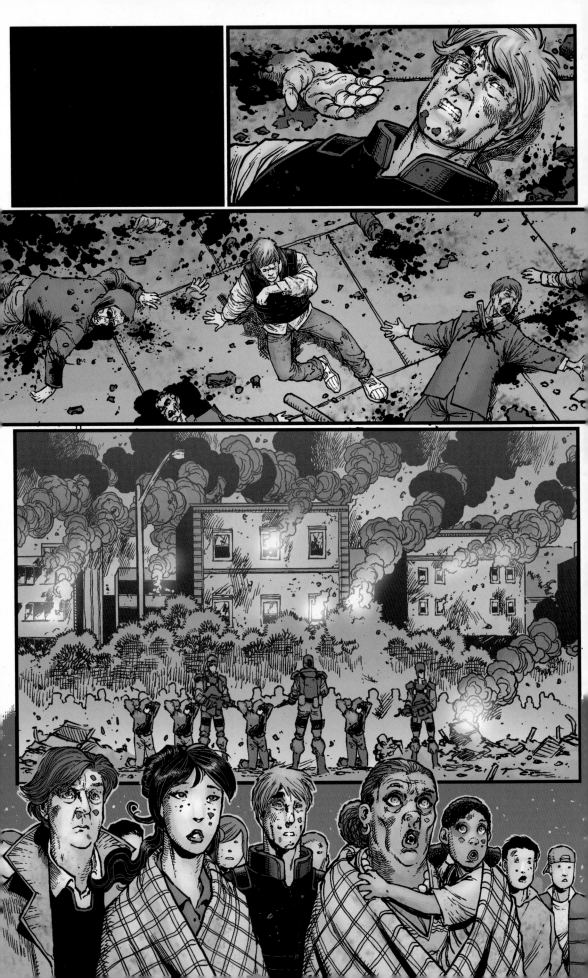

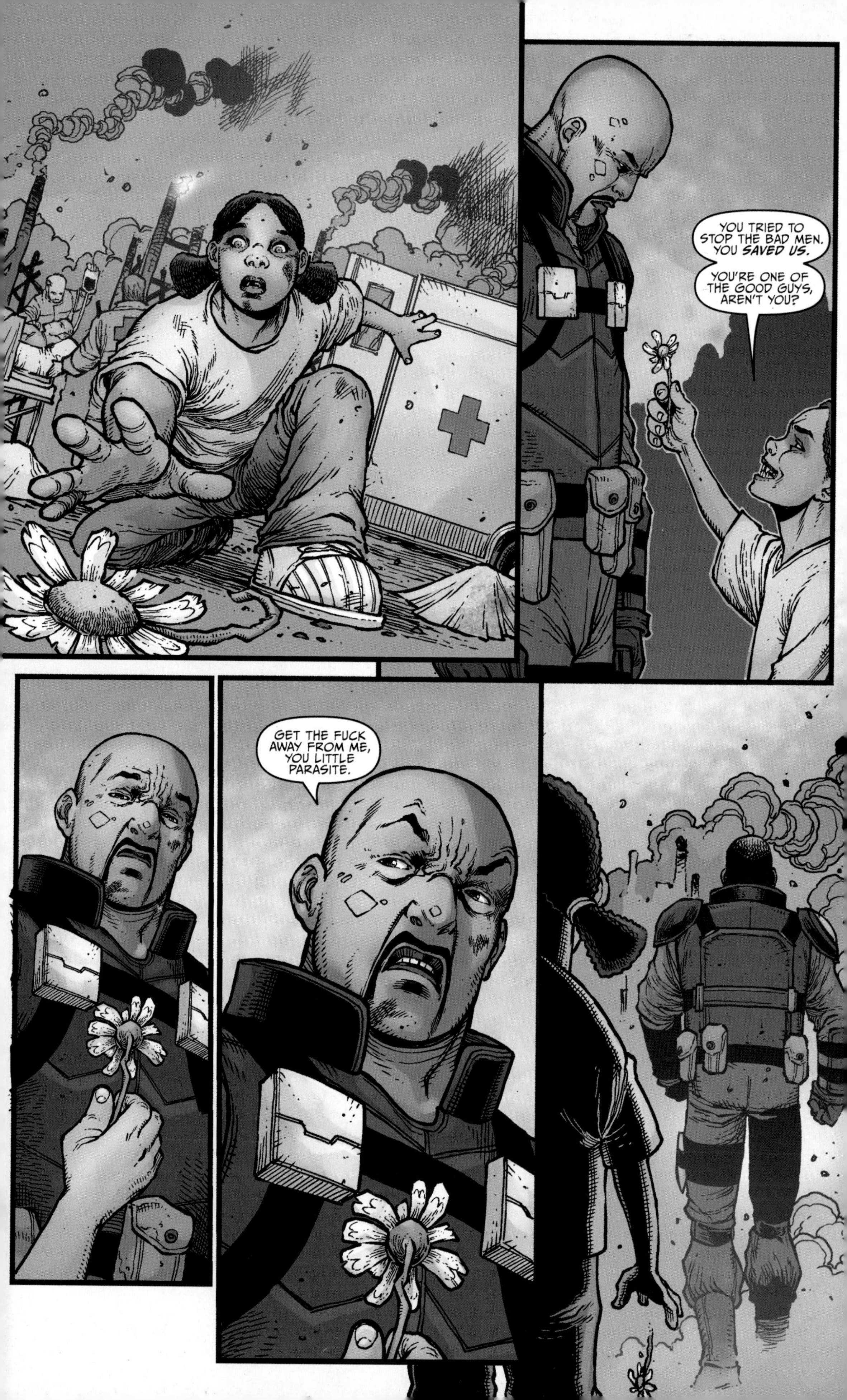
YOU TRIED TO STOP THE BAD MEN. YOU SAVED US.
YOU'RE ONE OF THE GOOD GUYS, AREN'T YOU?
GET THE FUCK AWAY FROM ME, YOU LITTLE PARASITE.

THIRTY-ONE PEOPLE DIED. MORE THAN TWO HUNDRED WERE INJURED. AND FOR WHAT? PEPPER GROVE HAS BEEN *ABANDONED*. WE LOST.

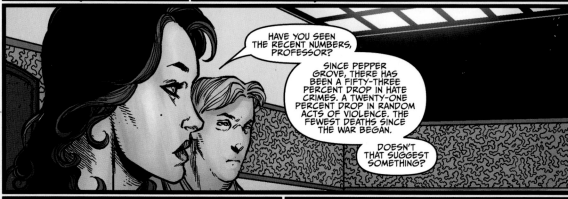

HAVE YOU SEEN THE RECENT NUMBERS, PROFESSOR?

SINCE PEPPER GROVE, THERE HAS BEEN A FIFTY-THREE PERCENT DROP IN HATE CRIMES. A TWENTY-ONE PERCENT DROP IN RANDOM ACTS OF VIOLENCE. THE FEWEST DEATHS SINCE THE WAR BEGAN.

DOESN'T THAT SUGGEST SOMETHING?

SURE. THAT COLLECTIVELY WE'RE CAPABLE OF SHAME. THAT MAYBE AFTER AN ACT SO HEINOUS, WE NEED TO TAKE A BREATH BEFORE TAKING ANOTHER SWING.

MAYBE.

OR MAYBE WE'RE LEARNING. SOMETIMES THERE'S A FINE LINE BETWEEN VICTIMS AND MARTYRS.

MAYBE THERE'S STILL SOME HOPE LEFT.

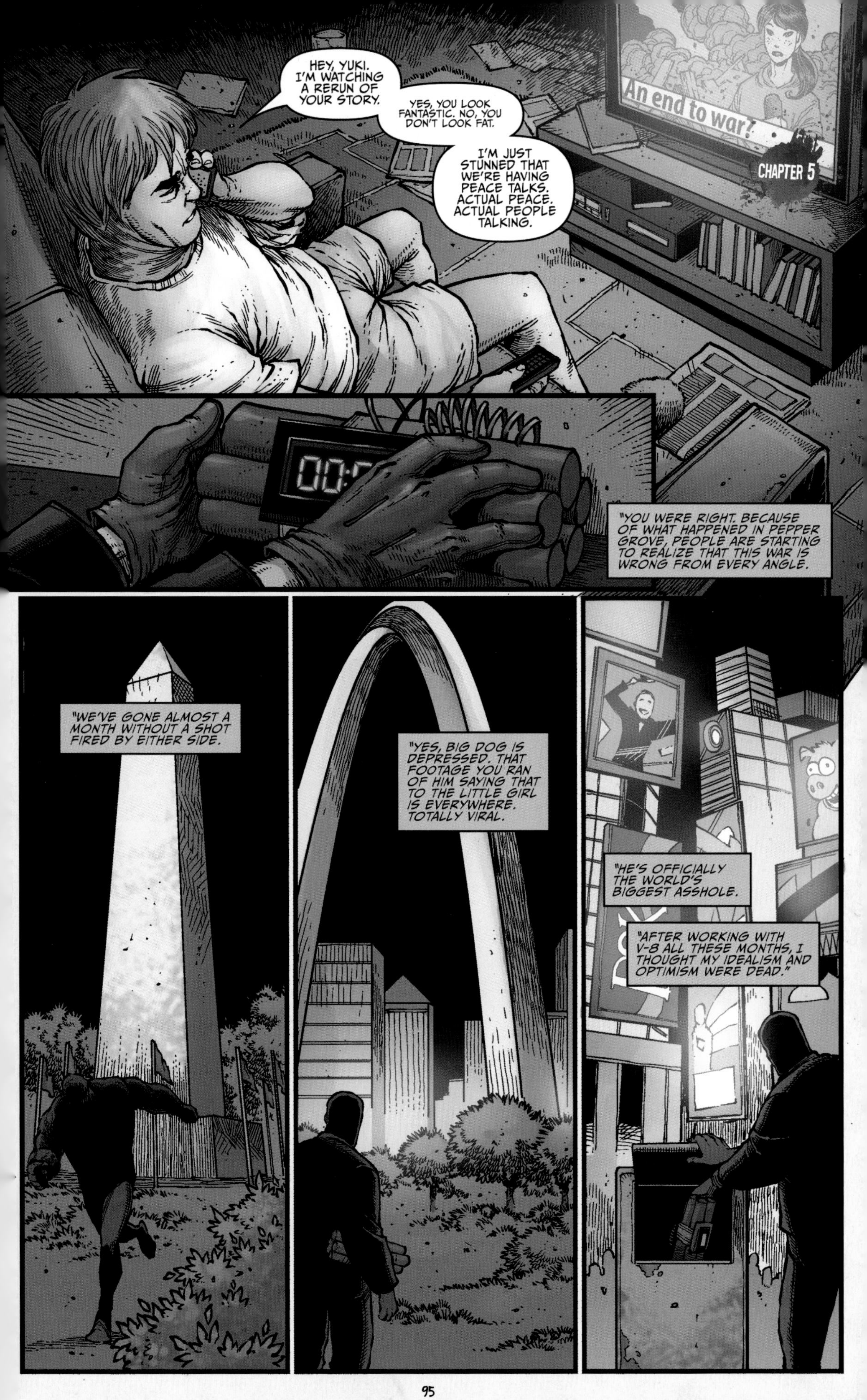
CHAPTER 5
An end to war?
HEY, YUKI. I'M WATCHING A RERUN OF YOUR STORY.
YES, YOU LOOK FANTASTIC. NO, YOU DON'T LOOK FAT.
I'M JUST STUNNED THAT WE'RE HAVING PEACE TALKS. ACTUAL PEACE. ACTUAL PEOPLE TALKING.
00:
"YOU WERE RIGHT. BECAUSE OF WHAT HAPPENED IN PEPPER GROVE, PEOPLE ARE STARTING TO REALIZE THAT THIS WAR IS WRONG FROM EVERY ANGLE.
"WE'VE GONE ALMOST A MONTH WITHOUT A SHOT FIRED BY EITHER SIDE.
"YES, BIG DOG IS DEPRESSED. THAT FOOTAGE YOU RAN OF HIM SAYING THAT TO THE LITTLE GIRL IS EVERYWHERE. TOTALLY VIRAL.
"HE'S OFFICIALLY THE WORLD'S BIGGEST ASSHOLE.
"AFTER WORKING WITH V-8 ALL THESE MONTHS, I THOUGHT MY IDEALISM AND OPTIMISM WERE DEAD."

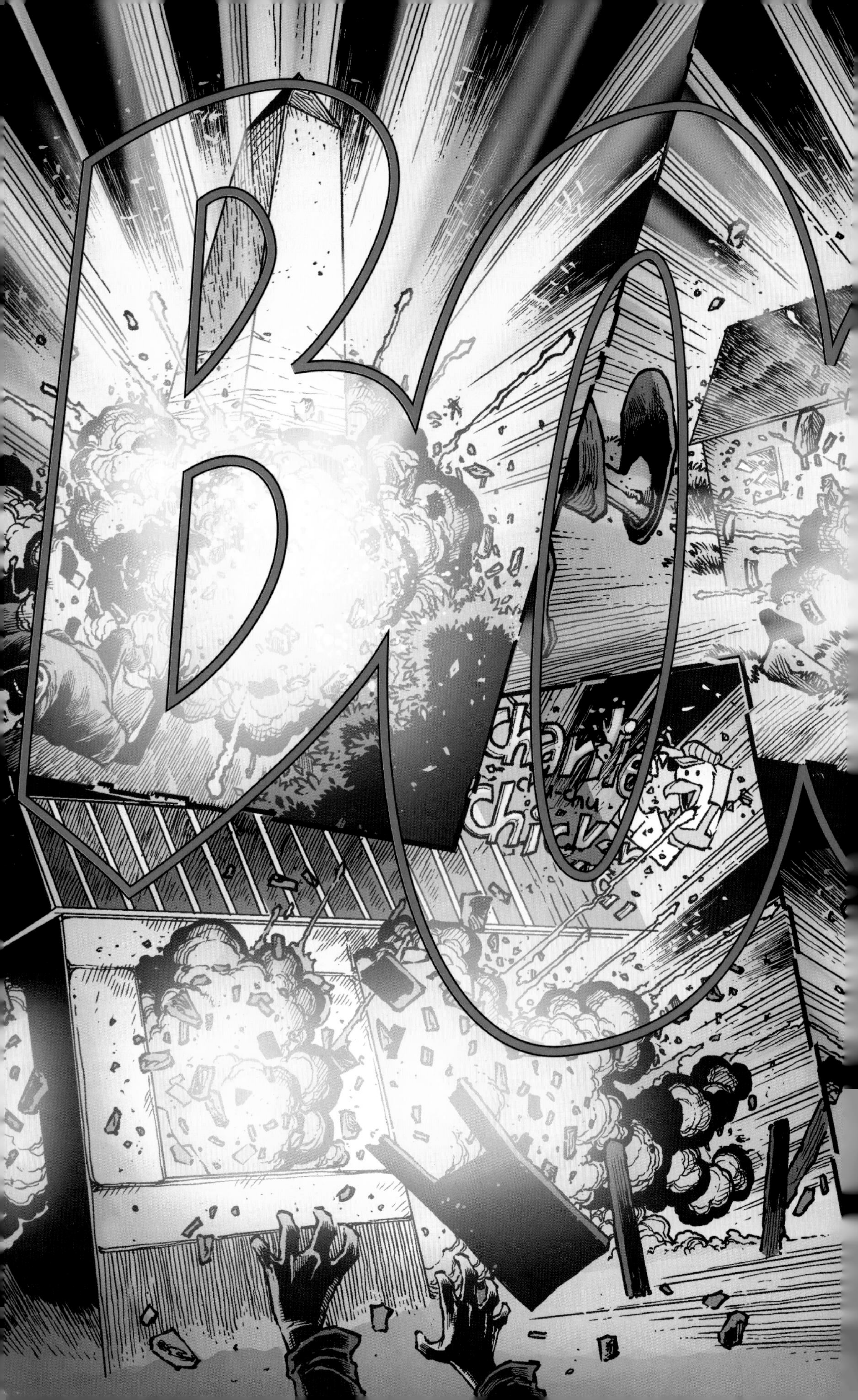
BO
Charlie
chu-chu

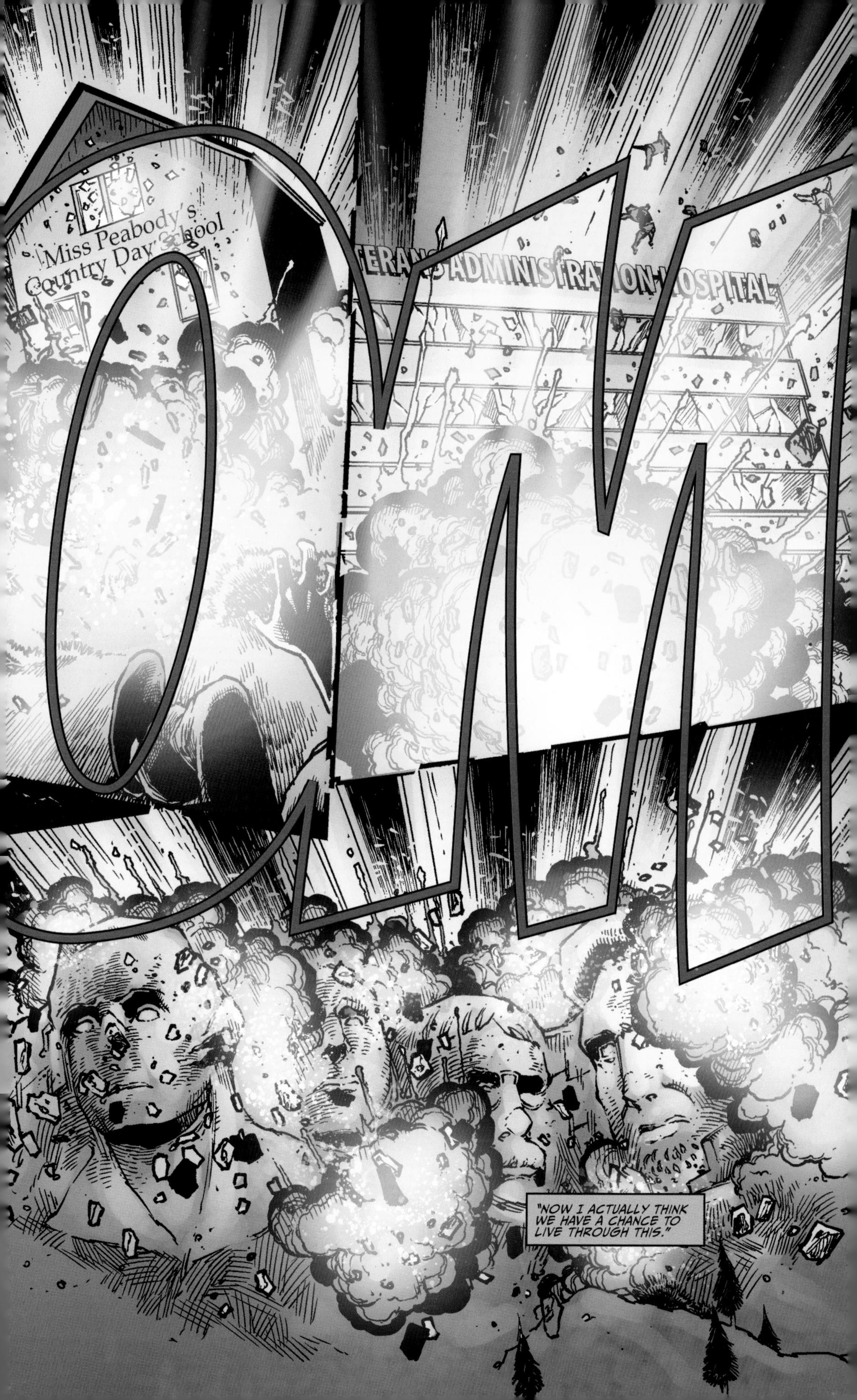
OMM
Miss Peabody's Country Day School
ADMINISTRATION
"NOW I ACTUALLY THINK WE HAVE A CHANCE TO LIVE THROUGH THIS."

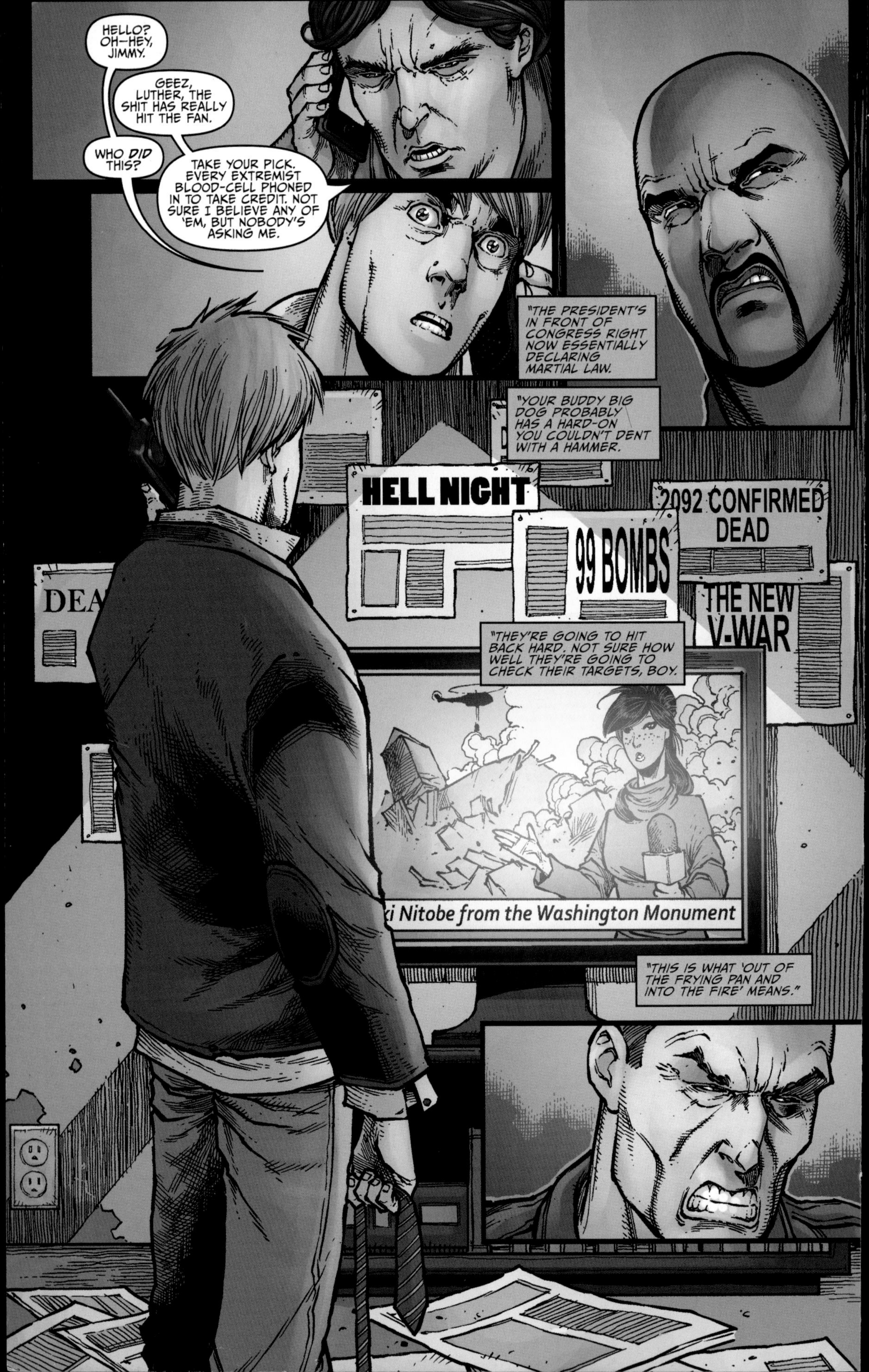
HELLO? OH—HEY, JIMMY.
GEEZ, LUTHER, THE SHIT HAS REALLY HIT THE FAN.
WHO DID THIS?
TAKE YOUR PICK. EVERY EXTREMIST BLOOD-CELL PHONED IN TO TAKE CREDIT. NOT SURE I BELIEVE ANY OF 'EM, BUT NOBODY'S ASKING ME.
"THE PRESIDENT'S IN FRONT OF CONGRESS RIGHT NOW ESSENTIALLY DECLARING MARTIAL LAW.
"YOUR BUDDY BIG DOG PROBABLY HAS A HARD-ON YOU COULDN'T DENT WITH A HAMMER.
HELL NIGHT
99 BOMBS
2092 CONFIRMED DEAD
THE NEW V-WAR
"THEY'RE GOING TO HIT BACK HARD. NOT SURE HOW WELL THEY'RE GOING TO CHECK THEIR TARGETS, BOY.
ki Nitobe from the Washington Monument
"THIS IS WHAT 'OUT OF THE FRYING PAN AND INTO THE FIRE' MEANS."

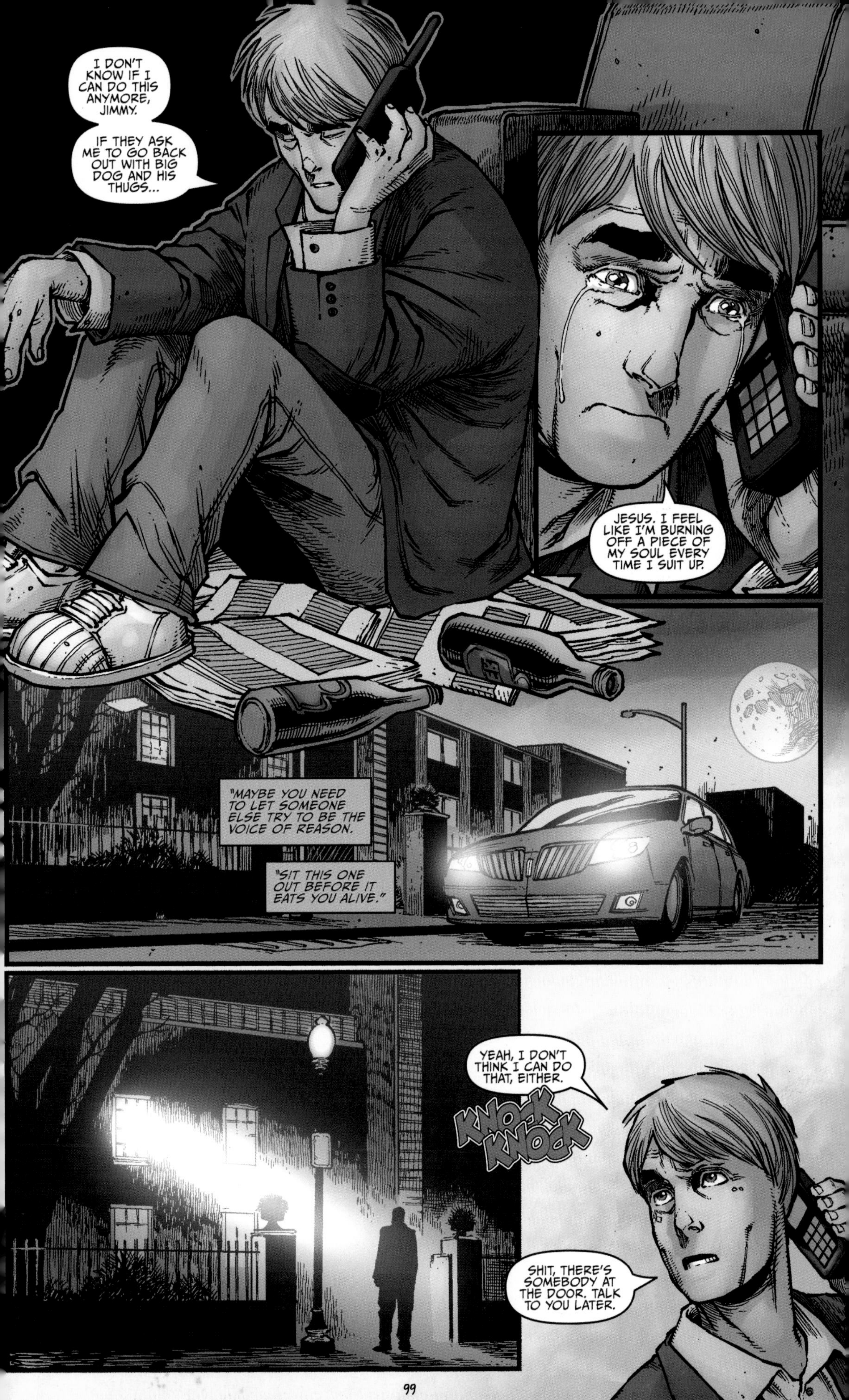
I DON'T KNOW IF I CAN DO THIS ANYMORE, JIMMY.
IF THEY ASK ME TO GO BACK OUT WITH BIG DOG AND HIS THUGS...
JESUS. I FEEL LIKE I'M BURNING OFF A PIECE OF MY SOUL EVERY TIME I SUIT UP.
"MAYBE YOU NEED TO LET SOMEONE ELSE TRY TO BE THE VOICE OF REASON.
"SIT THIS ONE OUT BEFORE IT EATS YOU ALIVE."
YEAH, I DON'T THINK I CAN DO THAT, EITHER.
KNOCK KNOCK
SHIT, THERE'S SOMEBODY AT THE DOOR. TALK TO YOU LATER.

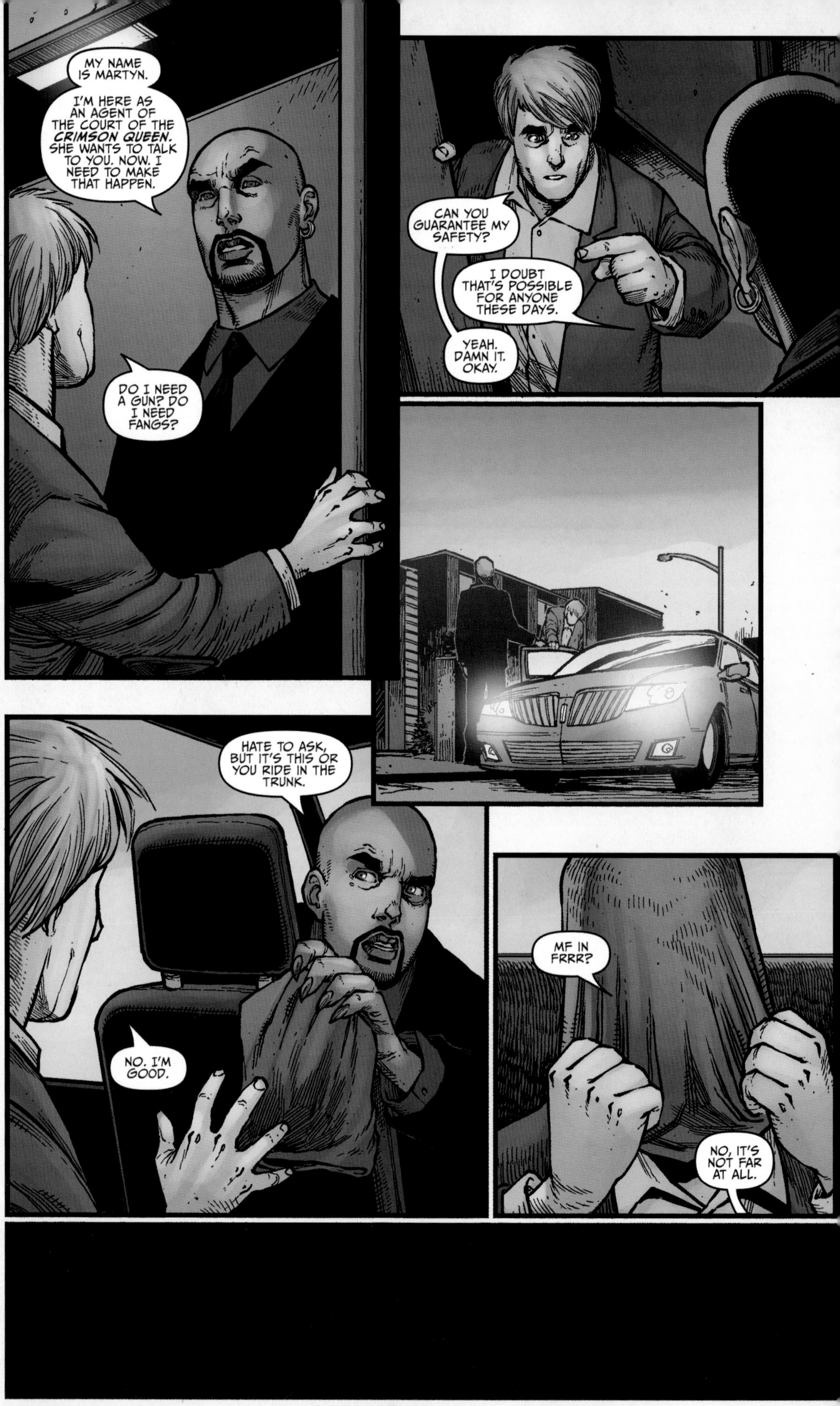
MY NAME IS MARTYN.
I'M HERE AS AN AGENT OF THE COURT OF THE ***CRIMSON QUEEN***. SHE WANTS TO TALK TO YOU. NOW. I NEED TO MAKE THAT HAPPEN.
DO I NEED A GUN? DO I NEED FANGS?
CAN YOU GUARANTEE MY SAFETY?
I DOUBT THAT'S POSSIBLE FOR ANYONE THESE DAYS.
YEAH. DAMN IT. OKAY.
HATE TO ASK, BUT IT'S THIS OR YOU RIDE IN THE TRUNK.
NO. I'M GOOD.
MF IN FRRR?
NO, IT'S NOT FAR AT ALL.

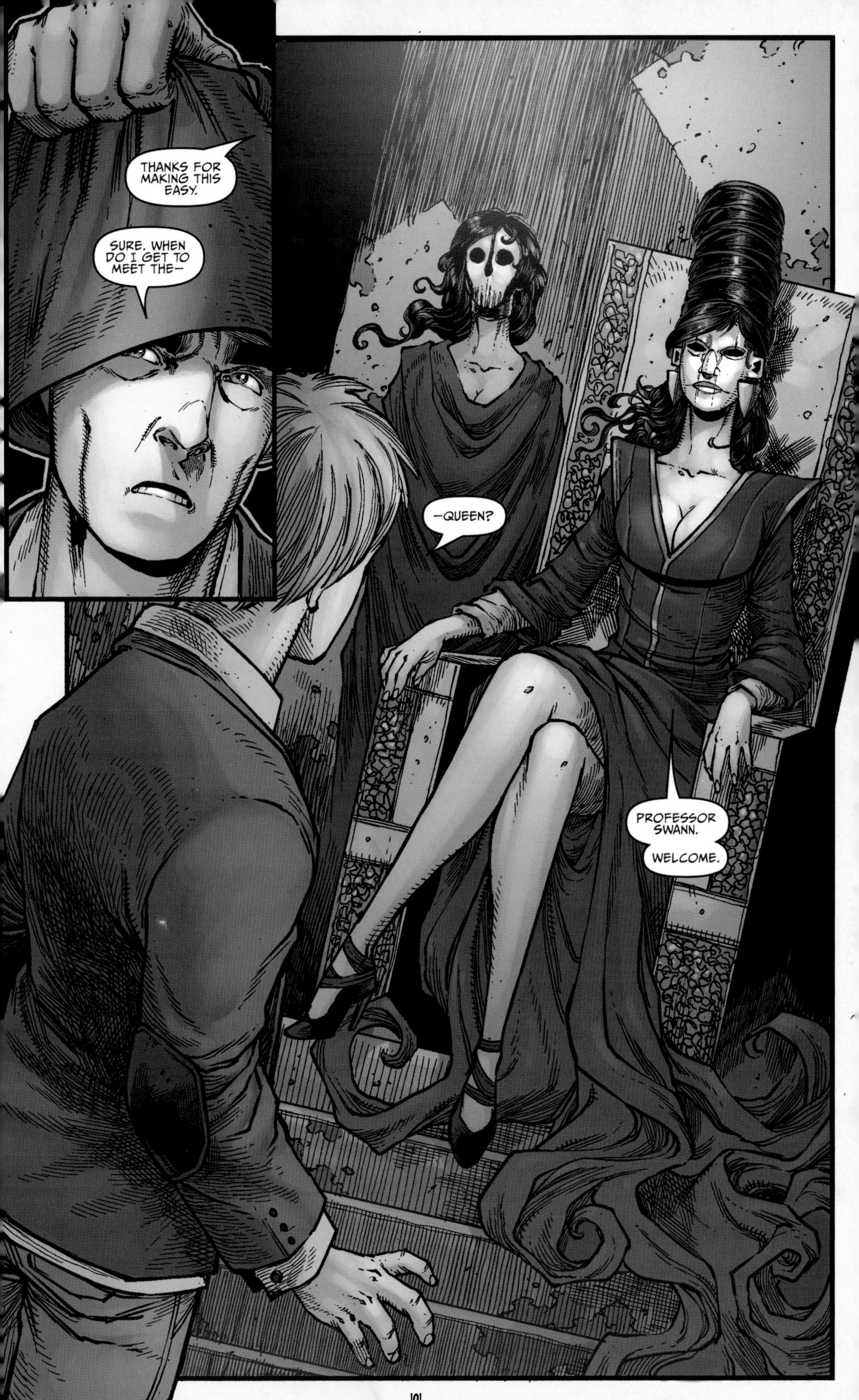
THANKS FOR MAKING THIS EASY.
SURE. WHEN DO I GET TO MEET THE—
—QUEEN?
PROFESSOR SWANN.
WELCOME.

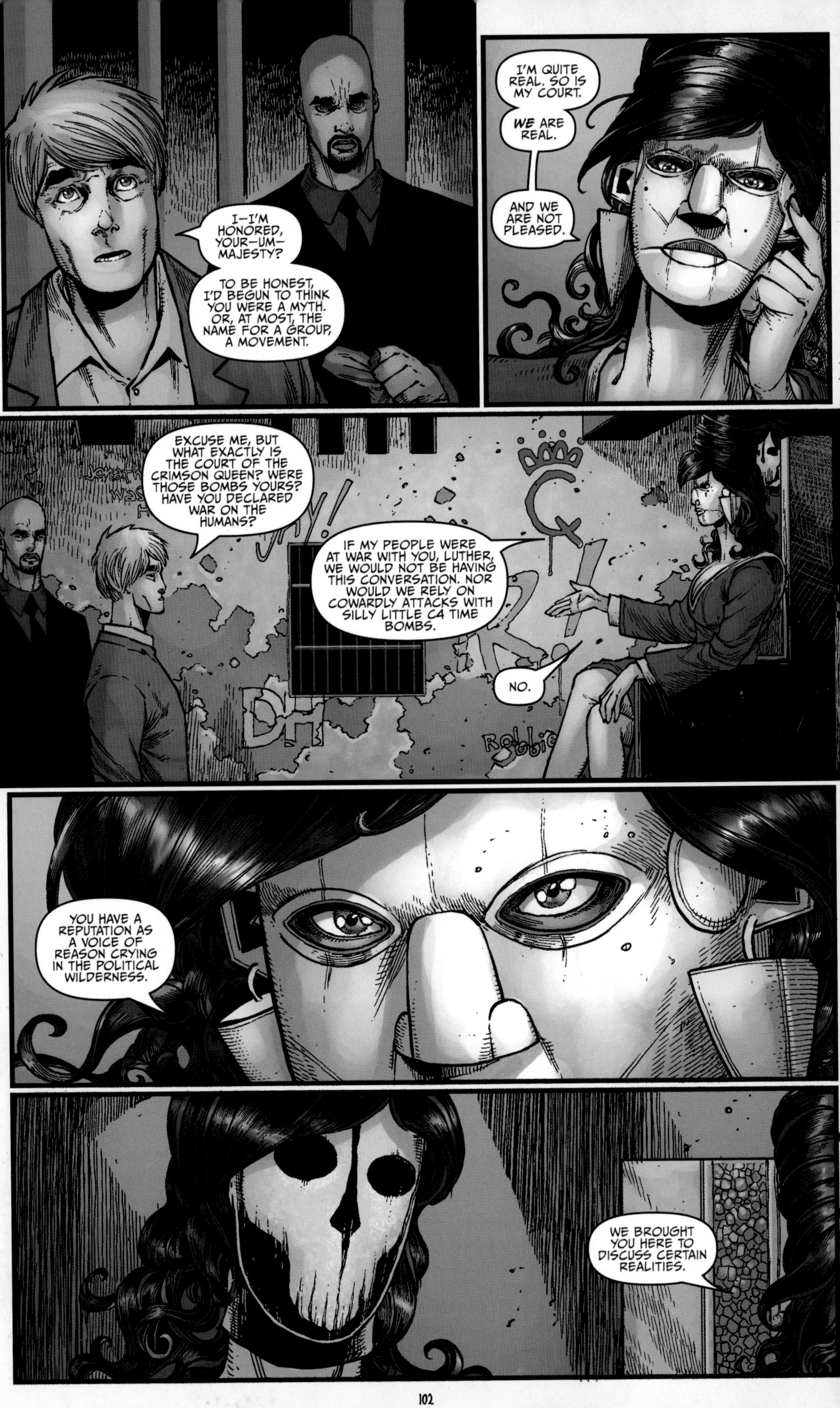
I—I'M HONORED, YOUR—UM—MAJESTY?
TO BE HONEST, I'D BEGUN TO THINK YOU WERE A MYTH. OR, AT MOST, THE NAME FOR A GROUP, A MOVEMENT.
I'M QUITE REAL. SO IS MY COURT.
WE ARE REAL.
AND WE ARE NOT PLEASED.
EXCUSE ME, BUT WHAT EXACTLY IS THE COURT OF THE CRIMSON QUEEN? WERE THOSE BOMBS YOURS? HAVE YOU DECLARED WAR ON THE HUMANS?
IF MY PEOPLE WERE AT WAR WITH YOU, LUTHER, WE WOULD NOT BE HAVING THIS CONVERSATION. NOR WOULD WE RELY ON COWARDLY ATTACKS WITH SILLY LITTLE C4 TIME BOMBS.
NO.
YOU HAVE A REPUTATION AS A VOICE OF REASON CRYING IN THE POLITICAL WILDERNESS.
WE BROUGHT YOU HERE TO DISCUSS CERTAIN REALITIES.

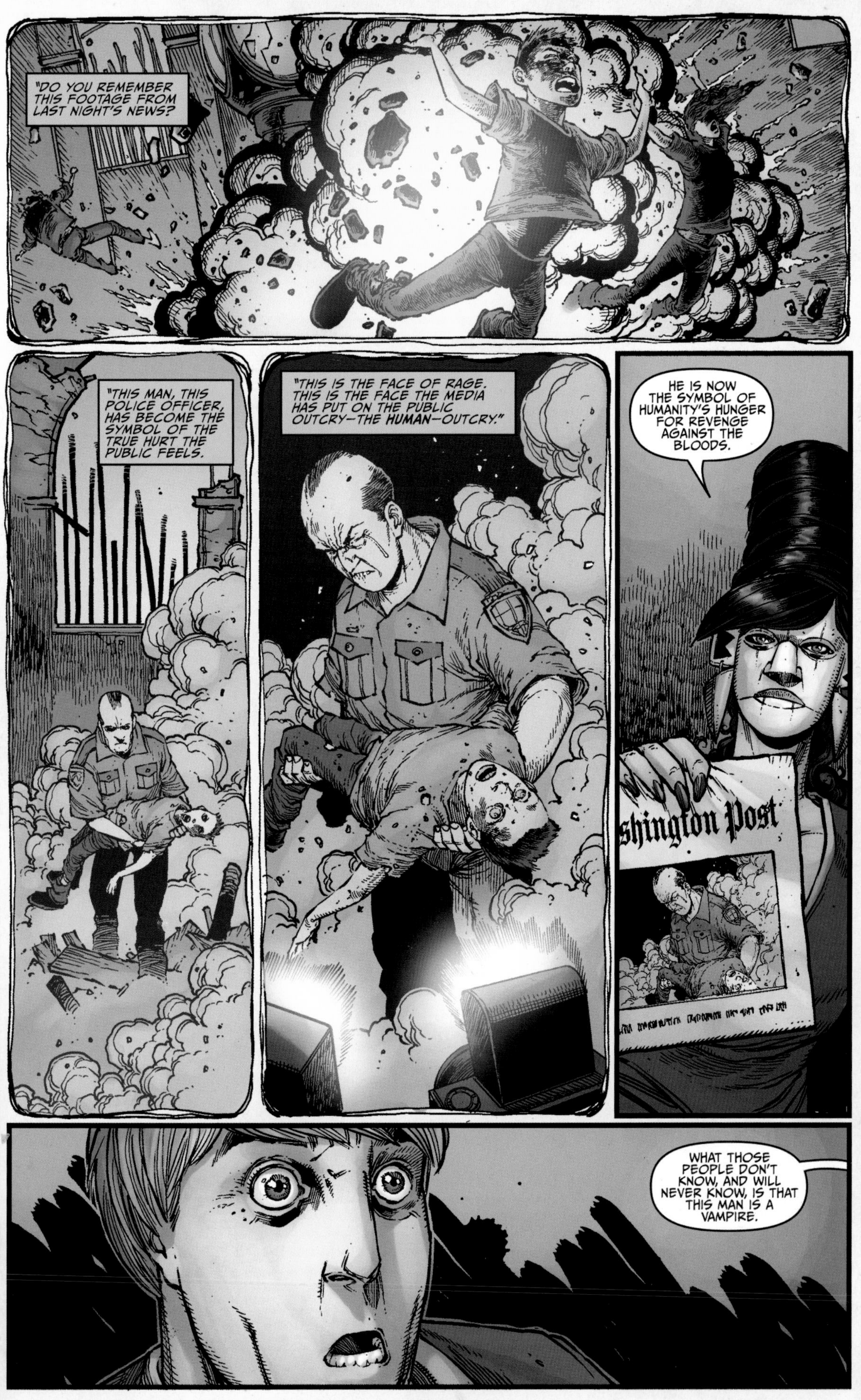
"DO YOU REMEMBER THIS FOOTAGE FROM LAST NIGHT'S NEWS?
"THIS MAN, THIS POLICE OFFICER, HAS BECOME THE SYMBOL OF THE TRUE HURT THE PUBLIC FEELS.
"THIS IS THE FACE OF RAGE. THIS IS THE FACE THE MEDIA HAS PUT ON THE PUBLIC OUTCRY—THE HUMAN—OUTCRY."
HE IS NOW THE SYMBOL OF HUMANITY'S HUNGER FOR REVENGE AGAINST THE BLOODS.
shington Post
WHAT THOSE PEOPLE DON'T KNOW, AND WILL NEVER KNOW, IS THAT THIS MAN IS A VAMPIRE.

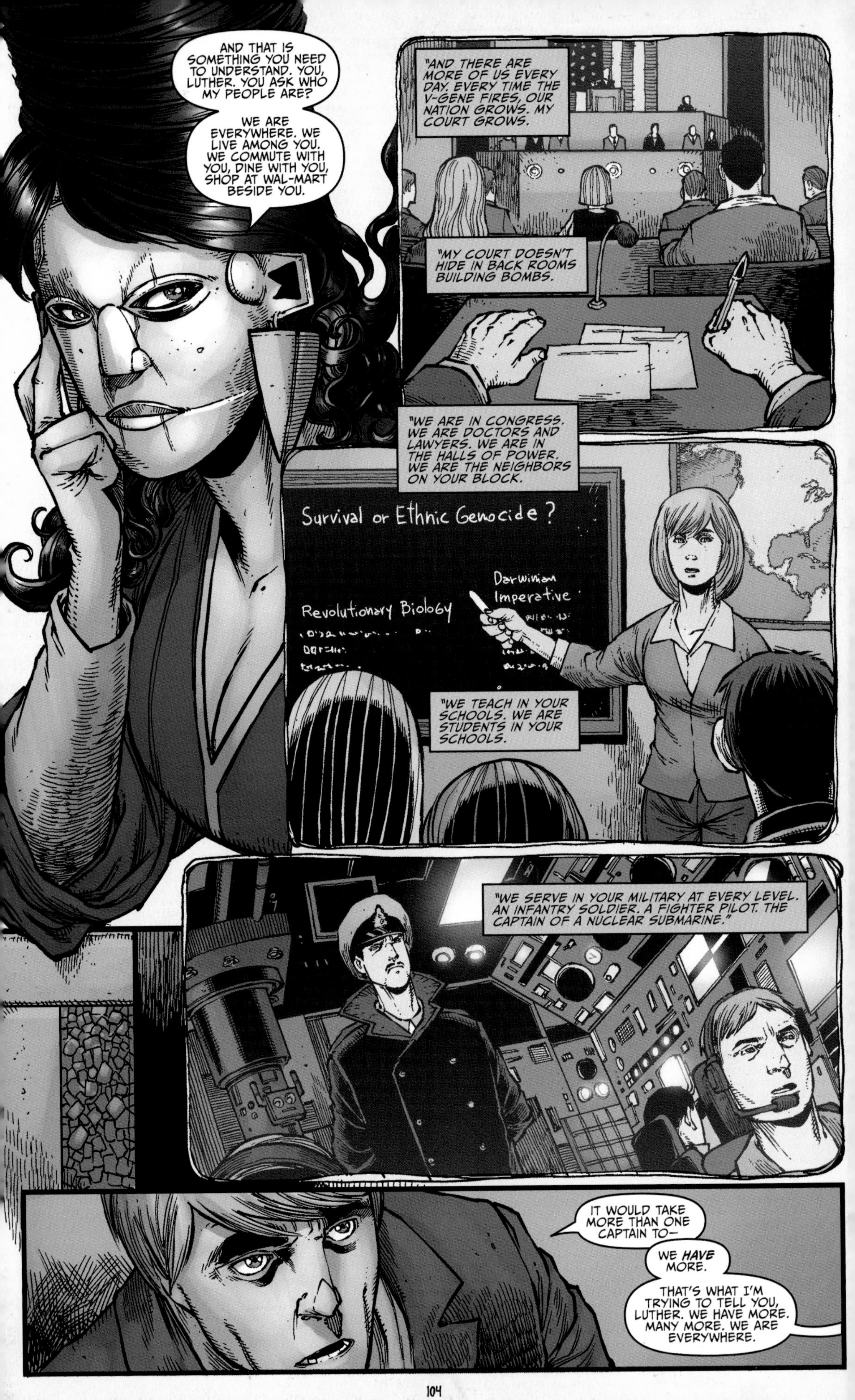
AND THAT IS SOMETHING YOU NEED TO UNDERSTAND. YOU, LUTHER. YOU ASK WHO MY PEOPLE ARE?
WE ARE EVERYWHERE. WE LIVE AMONG YOU. WE COMMUTE WITH YOU, DINE WITH YOU, SHOP AT WAL-MART BESIDE YOU.
"AND THERE ARE MORE OF US EVERY DAY. EVERY TIME THE V-GENE FIRES, OUR NATION GROWS. MY COURT GROWS.
"MY COURT DOESN'T HIDE IN BACK ROOMS BUILDING BOMBS.
"WE ARE IN CONGRESS. WE ARE DOCTORS AND LAWYERS. WE ARE IN THE HALLS OF POWER. WE ARE THE NEIGHBORS ON YOUR BLOCK.
Survival or Ethnic Genocide?
Darwinian Imperative
Revolutionary Biology
"WE TEACH IN YOUR SCHOOLS. WE ARE STUDENTS IN YOUR SCHOOLS.
"WE SERVE IN YOUR MILITARY AT EVERY LEVEL. AN INFANTRY SOLDIER. A FIGHTER PILOT. THE CAPTAIN OF A NUCLEAR SUBMARINE."
IT WOULD TAKE MORE THAN ONE CAPTAIN TO—
WE *HAVE* MORE.
THAT'S WHAT I'M TRYING TO TELL YOU, LUTHER. WE HAVE MORE. MANY MORE. WE ARE EVERYWHERE.

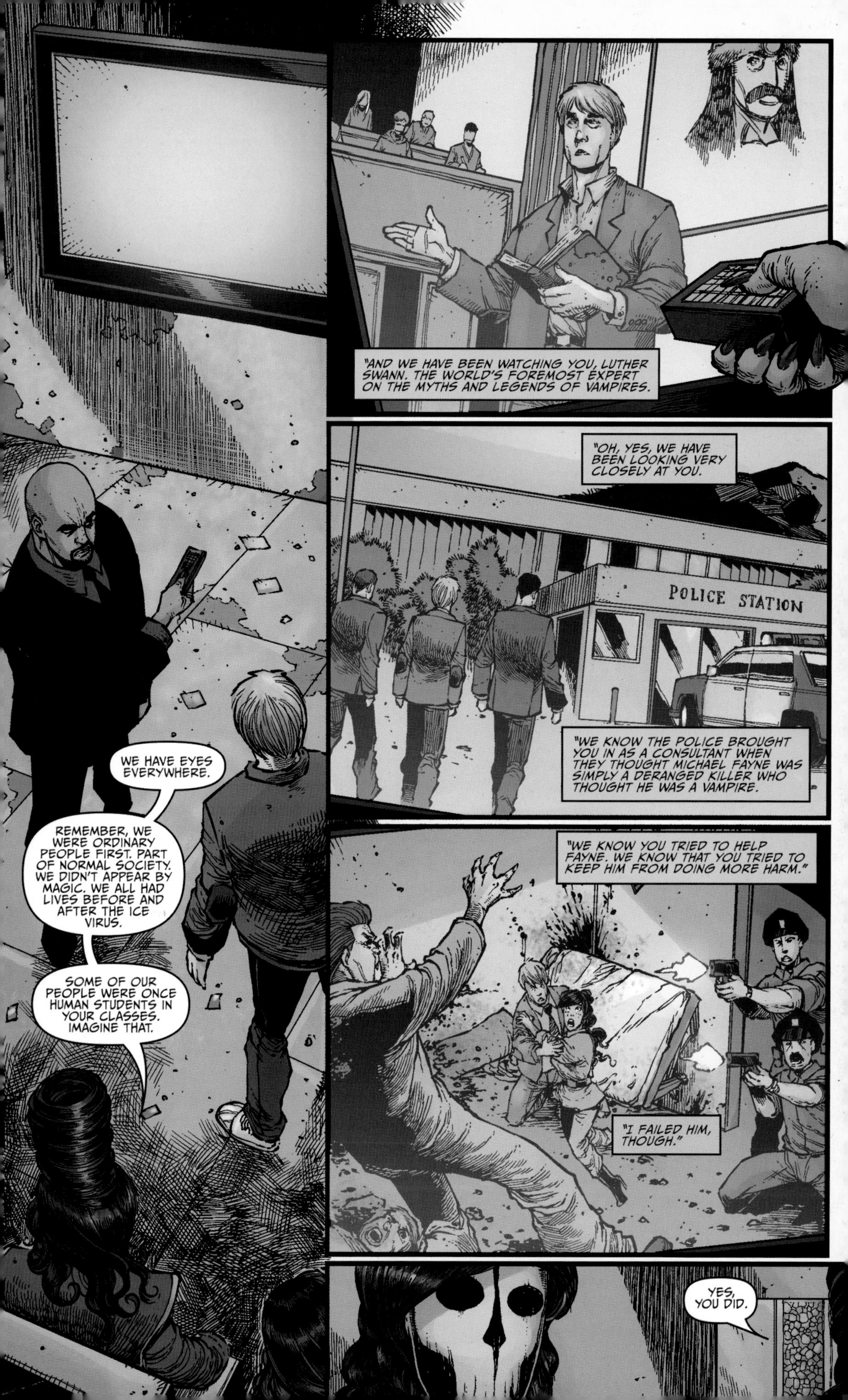
"AND WE HAVE BEEN WATCHING YOU, LUTHER SWANN. THE WORLD'S FOREMOST EXPERT ON THE MYTHS AND LEGENDS OF VAMPIRES.
"OH, YES, WE HAVE BEEN LOOKING VERY CLOSELY AT YOU.
POLICE STATION
"WE KNOW THE POLICE BROUGHT YOU IN AS A CONSULTANT WHEN THEY THOUGHT MICHAEL FAYNE WAS SIMPLY A DERANGED KILLER WHO THOUGHT HE WAS A VAMPIRE.
WE HAVE EYES EVERYWHERE.
REMEMBER, WE WERE ORDINARY PEOPLE FIRST. PART OF NORMAL SOCIETY. WE DIDN'T APPEAR BY MAGIC. WE ALL HAD LIVES BEFORE AND AFTER THE ICE VIRUS.
SOME OF OUR PEOPLE WERE ONCE HUMAN STUDENTS IN YOUR CLASSES. IMAGINE THAT.
"WE KNOW YOU TRIED TO HELP FAYNE. WE KNOW THAT YOU TRIED TO KEEP HIM FROM DOING MORE HARM."
"I FAILED HIM, THOUGH."
YES, YOU DID.

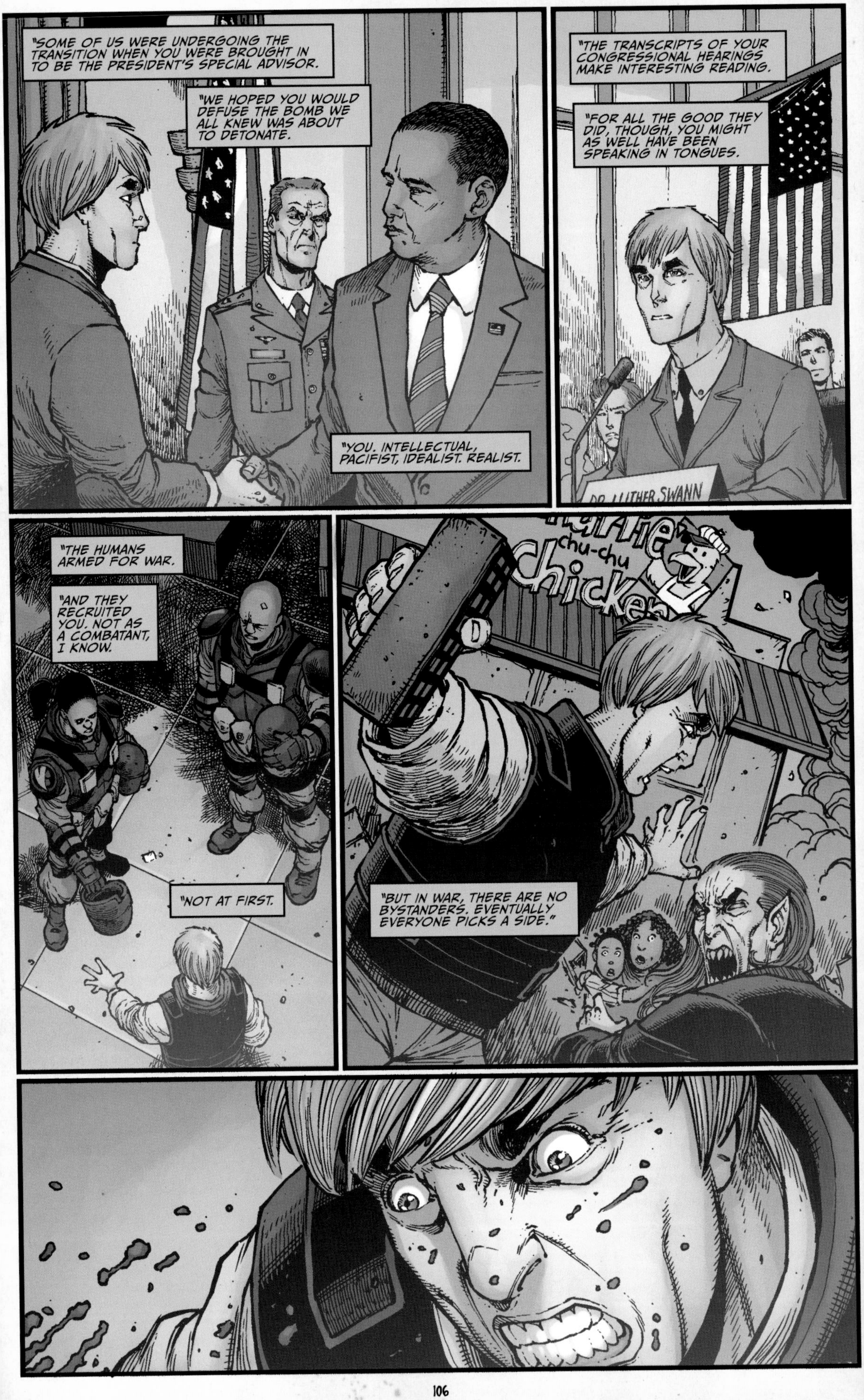
"SOME OF US WERE UNDERGOING THE TRANSITION WHEN YOU WERE BROUGHT IN TO BE THE PRESIDENT'S SPECIAL ADVISOR.
"WE HOPED YOU WOULD DEFUSE THE BOMB WE ALL KNEW WAS ABOUT TO DETONATE.
"YOU. INTELLECTUAL, PACIFIST, IDEALIST. REALIST.
"THE TRANSCRIPTS OF YOUR CONGRESSIONAL HEARINGS MAKE INTERESTING READING.
"FOR ALL THE GOOD THEY DID, THOUGH, YOU MIGHT AS WELL HAVE BEEN SPEAKING IN TONGUES.
DR. LUTHER SWANN
"THE HUMANS ARMED FOR WAR.
"AND THEY RECRUITED YOU. NOT AS A COMBATANT, I KNOW.
"NOT AT FIRST.
chu-chu
Chicken
"BUT IN WAR, THERE ARE NO BYSTANDERS. EVENTUALLY EVERYONE PICKS A SIDE."

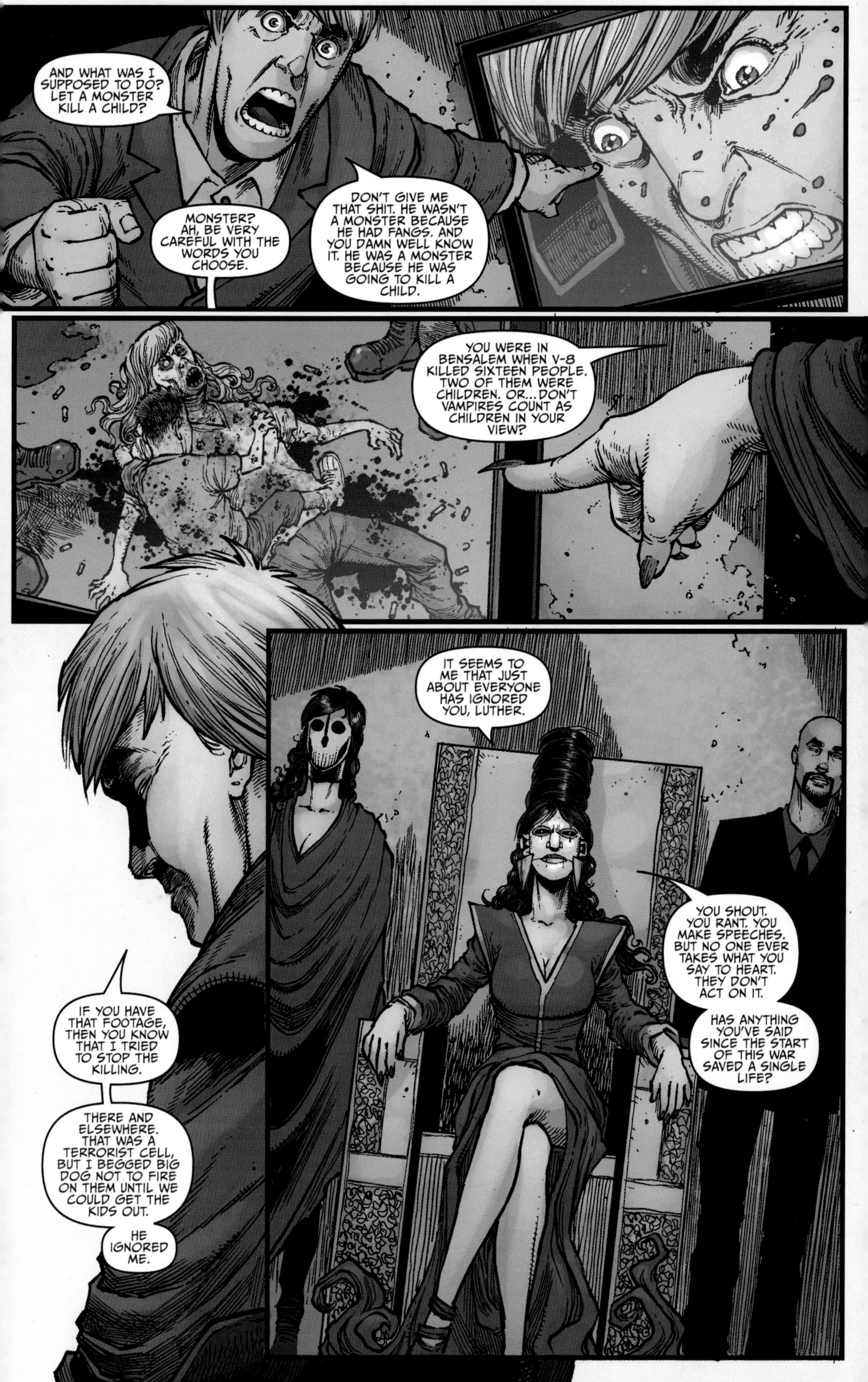
AND WHAT WAS I SUPPOSED TO DO? LET A MONSTER KILL A CHILD?
MONSTER? AH, BE VERY CAREFUL WITH THE WORDS YOU CHOOSE.
DON'T GIVE ME THAT SHIT. HE WASN'T A MONSTER BECAUSE HE HAD FANGS. AND YOU DAMN WELL KNOW IT. HE WAS A MONSTER BECAUSE HE WAS GOING TO KILL A CHILD.
YOU WERE IN BENSALEM WHEN V-8 KILLED SIXTEEN PEOPLE. TWO OF THEM WERE CHILDREN. OR...DON'T VAMPIRES COUNT AS CHILDREN IN YOUR VIEW?
IF YOU HAVE THAT FOOTAGE, THEN YOU KNOW THAT I TRIED TO STOP THE KILLING.
THERE AND ELSEWHERE. THAT WAS A TERRORIST CELL, BUT I BEGGED BIG DOG NOT TO FIRE ON THEM UNTIL WE COULD GET THE KIDS OUT.
HE IGNORED ME.
IT SEEMS TO ME THAT JUST ABOUT EVERYONE HAS IGNORED YOU, LUTHER.
YOU SHOUT. YOU RANT. YOU MAKE SPEECHES. BUT NO ONE EVER TAKES WHAT YOU SAY TO HEART. THEY DON'T ACT ON IT.
HAS ANYTHING YOU'VE SAID SINCE THE START OF THIS WAR SAVED A SINGLE LIFE?

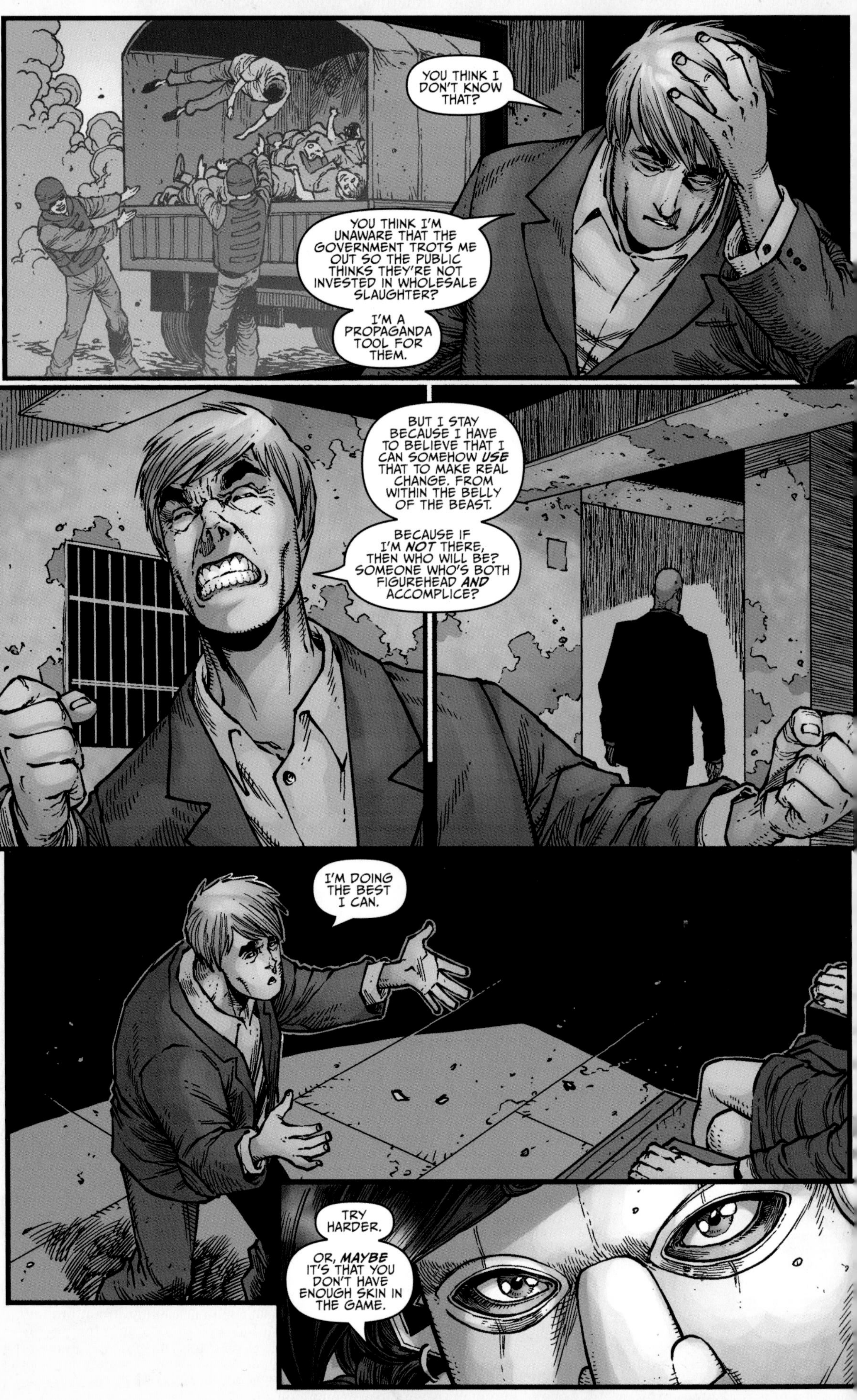
YOU THINK I DON'T KNOW THAT?
YOU THINK I'M UNAWARE THAT THE GOVERNMENT TROTS ME OUT SO THE PUBLIC THINKS THEY'RE NOT INVESTED IN WHOLESALE SLAUGHTER?
I'M A PROPAGANDA TOOL FOR THEM.
BUT I STAY BECAUSE I HAVE TO BELIEVE THAT I CAN SOMEHOW USE THAT TO MAKE REAL CHANGE. FROM WITHIN THE BELLY OF THE BEAST.
BECAUSE IF I'M NOT THERE, THEN WHO WILL BE? SOMEONE WHO'S BOTH FIGUREHEAD AND ACCOMPLICE?
I'M DOING THE BEST I CAN.
TRY HARDER.
OR, MAYBE IT'S THAT YOU DON'T HAVE ENOUGH SKIN IN THE GAME.

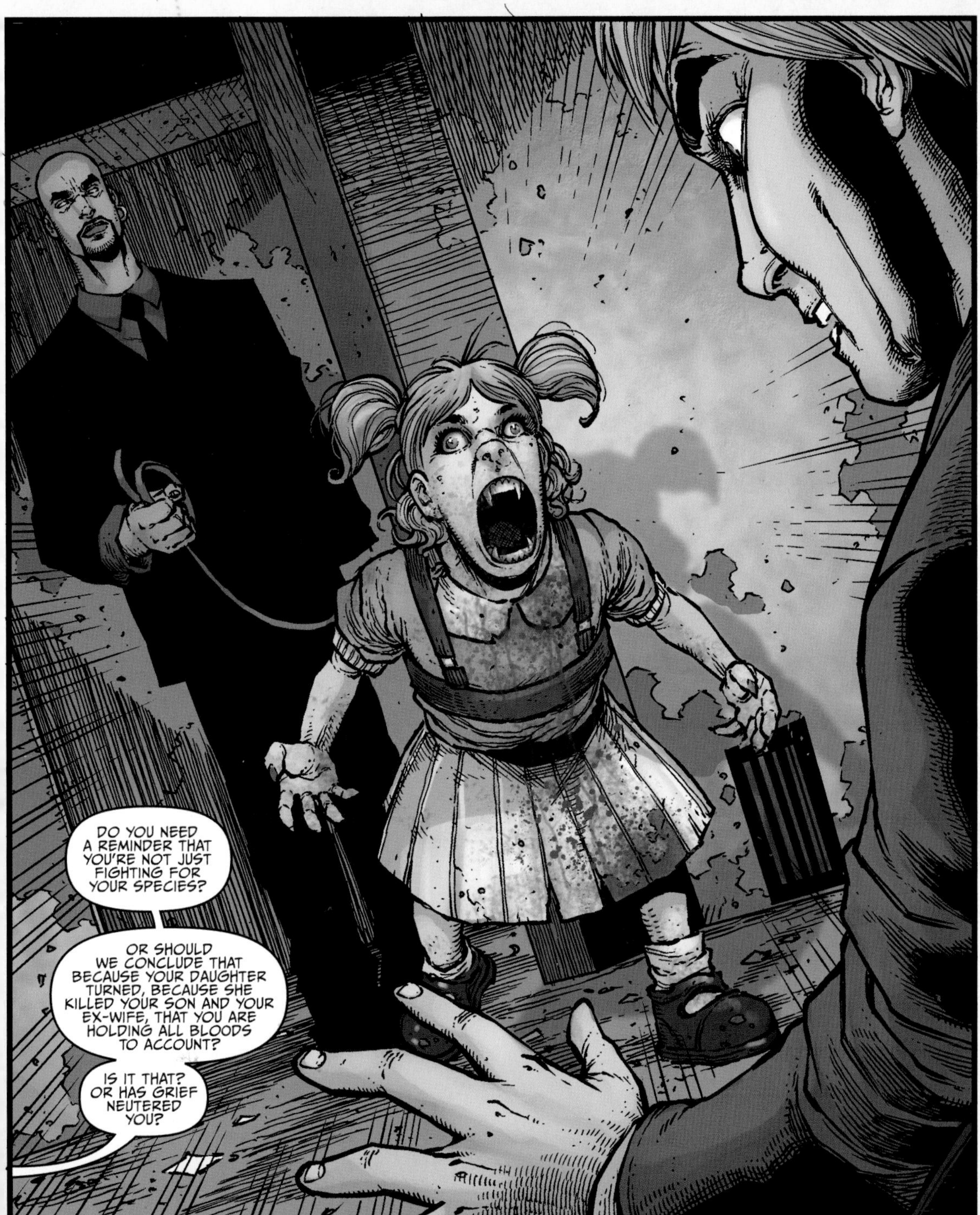
DO YOU NEED A REMINDER THAT YOU'RE NOT JUST FIGHTING FOR YOUR SPECIES?
OR SHOULD WE CONCLUDE THAT BECAUSE YOUR DAUGHTER TURNED, BECAUSE SHE KILLED YOUR SON AND YOUR EX-WIFE, THAT YOU ARE HOLDING ALL BLOODS TO ACCOUNT?
IS IT THAT? OR HAS GRIEF NEUTERED YOU?

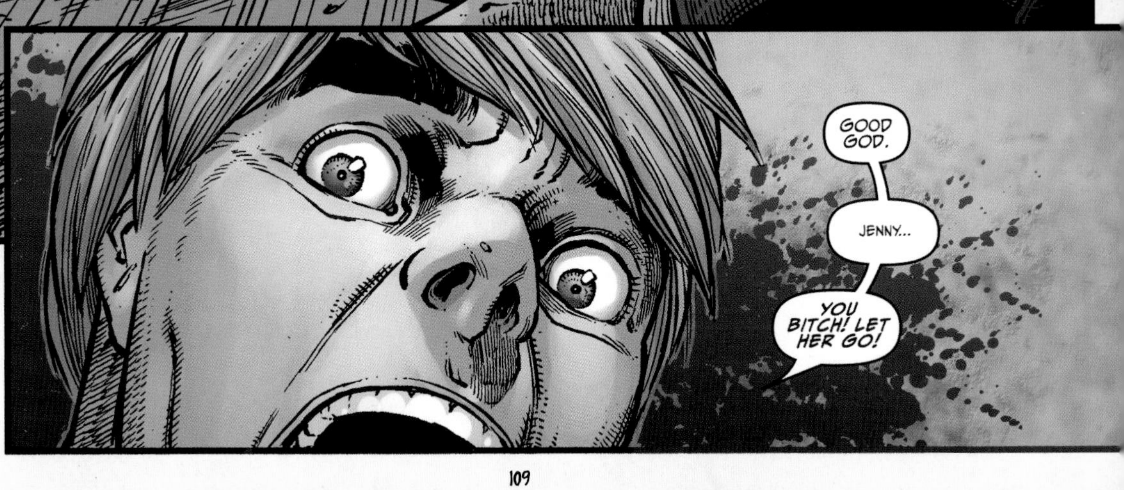
GOOD GOD.
JENNY...
YOU BITCH! LET HER GO!

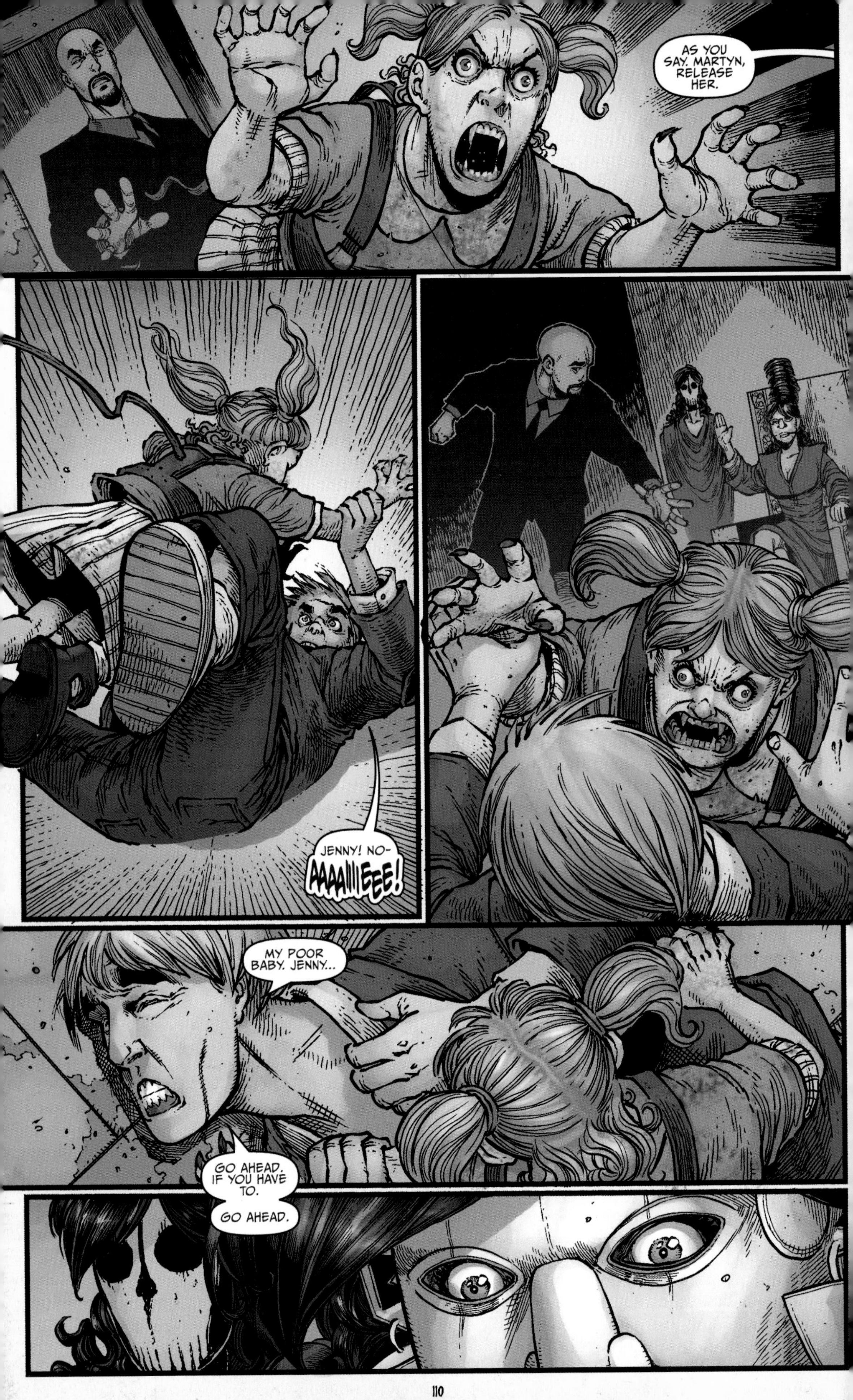
AS YOU SAY. MARTYN, RELEASE HER.
JENNY! NO-
AAAAIIIIIEEE!
MY POOR BABY. JENNY...
GO AHEAD. IF YOU HAVE TO.
GO AHEAD.

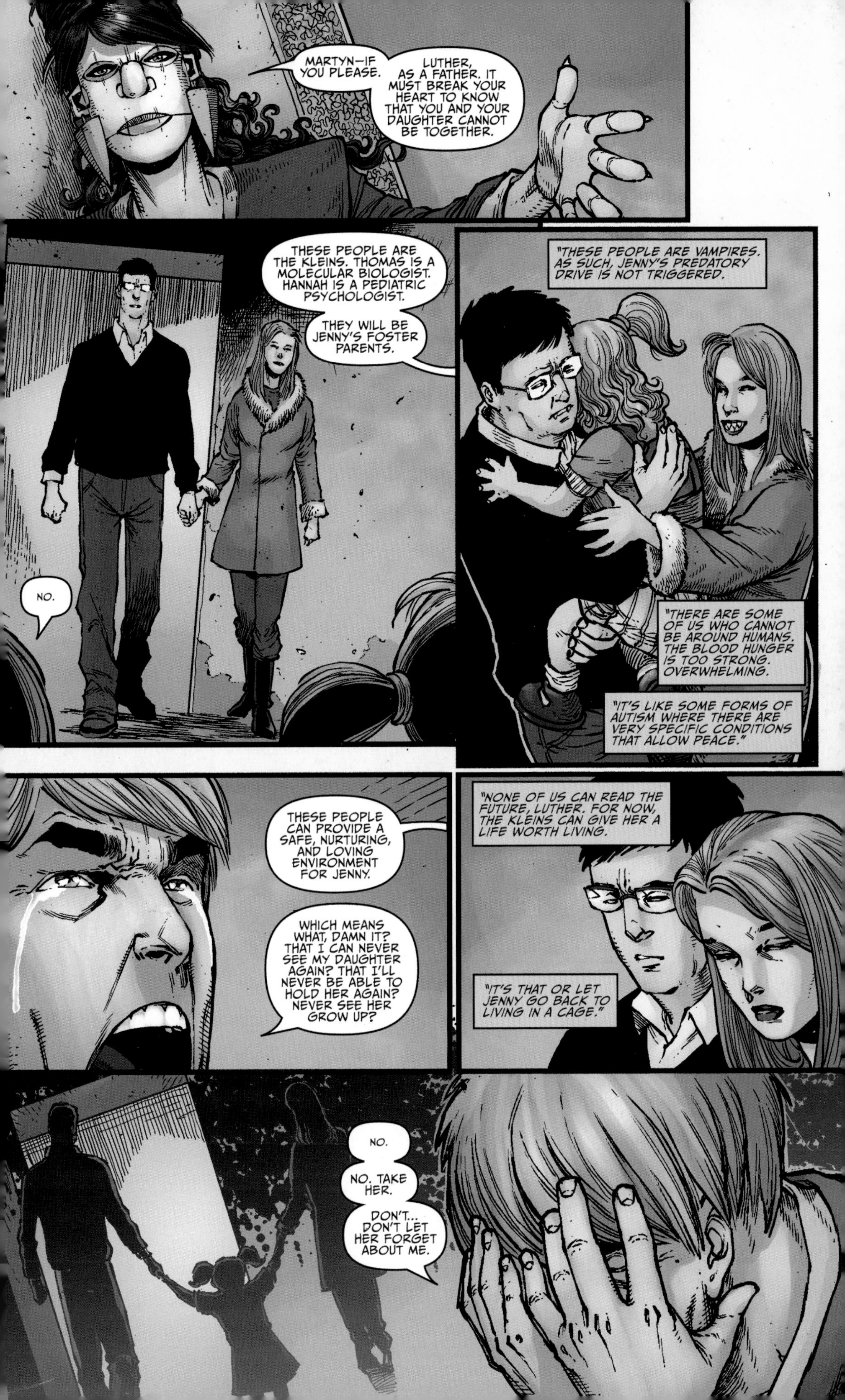
MARTYN—IF YOU PLEASE.
LUTHER, AS A FATHER, IT MUST BREAK YOUR HEART TO KNOW THAT YOU AND YOUR DAUGHTER CANNOT BE TOGETHER.
THESE PEOPLE ARE THE KLEINS. THOMAS IS A MOLECULAR BIOLOGIST. HANNAH IS A PEDIATRIC PSYCHOLOGIST.
THEY WILL BE JENNY'S FOSTER PARENTS.
NO.
"THESE PEOPLE ARE VAMPIRES. AS SUCH, JENNY'S PREDATORY DRIVE IS NOT TRIGGERED.
"THERE ARE SOME OF US WHO CANNOT BE AROUND HUMANS. THE BLOOD HUNGER IS TOO STRONG. OVERWHELMING.
"IT'S LIKE SOME FORMS OF AUTISM WHERE THERE ARE VERY SPECIFIC CONDITIONS THAT ALLOW PEACE."
THESE PEOPLE CAN PROVIDE A SAFE, NURTURING, AND LOVING ENVIRONMENT FOR JENNY.
WHICH MEANS WHAT, DAMN IT? THAT I CAN NEVER SEE MY DAUGHTER AGAIN? THAT I'LL NEVER BE ABLE TO HOLD HER AGAIN? NEVER SEE HER GROW UP?
"NONE OF US CAN READ THE FUTURE, LUTHER. FOR NOW, THE KLEINS CAN GIVE HER A LIFE WORTH LIVING.
"IT'S THAT OR LET JENNY GO BACK TO LIVING IN A CAGE."
NO.
NO. TAKE HER.
DON'T... DON'T LET HER FORGET ABOUT ME.

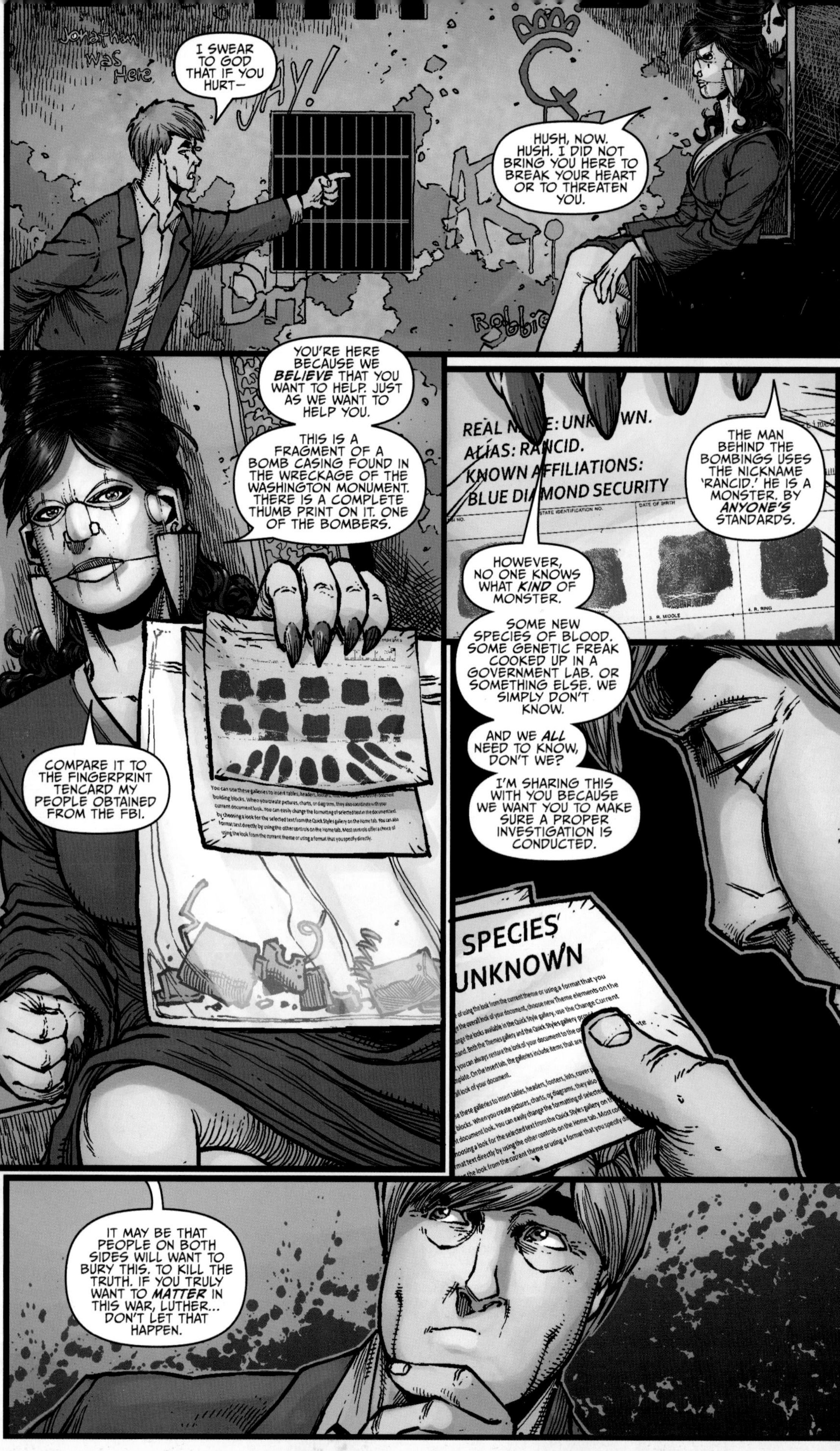
Jonathan Was Here
I SWEAR TO GOD THAT IF YOU HURT—
HUSH, NOW. HUSH. I DID NOT BRING YOU HERE TO BREAK YOUR HEART OR TO THREATEN YOU.
Robbie
YOU'RE HERE BECAUSE WE *BELIEVE* THAT YOU WANT TO HELP. JUST AS WE WANT TO HELP YOU.
THIS IS A FRAGMENT OF A BOMB CASING FOUND IN THE WRECKAGE OF THE WASHINGTON MONUMENT. THERE IS A COMPLETE THUMB PRINT ON IT. ONE OF THE BOMBERS.
COMPARE IT TO THE FINGERPRINT TENCARD MY PEOPLE OBTAINED FROM THE FBI.
ALIAS: RANCID.
KNOWN AFFILIATIONS:
BLUE DIAMOND SECURITY
THE MAN BEHIND THE BOMBINGS USES THE NICKNAME 'RANCID.' HE IS A MONSTER. BY *ANYONE'S* STANDARDS.
HOWEVER, NO ONE KNOWS WHAT *KIND* OF MONSTER.
SOME NEW SPECIES OF BLOOD. SOME GENETIC FREAK COOKED UP IN A GOVERNMENT LAB. OR SOMETHING ELSE. WE SIMPLY DON'T KNOW.
AND WE *ALL* NEED TO KNOW, DON'T WE?
I'M SHARING THIS WITH YOU BECAUSE WE WANT YOU TO MAKE SURE A PROPER INVESTIGATION IS CONDUCTED.
SPECIES UNKNOWN
IT MAY BE THAT PEOPLE ON BOTH SIDES WILL WANT TO BURY THIS. TO KILL THE TRUTH. IF YOU TRULY WANT TO *MATTER* IN THIS WAR, LUTHER... DON'T LET THAT HAPPEN.

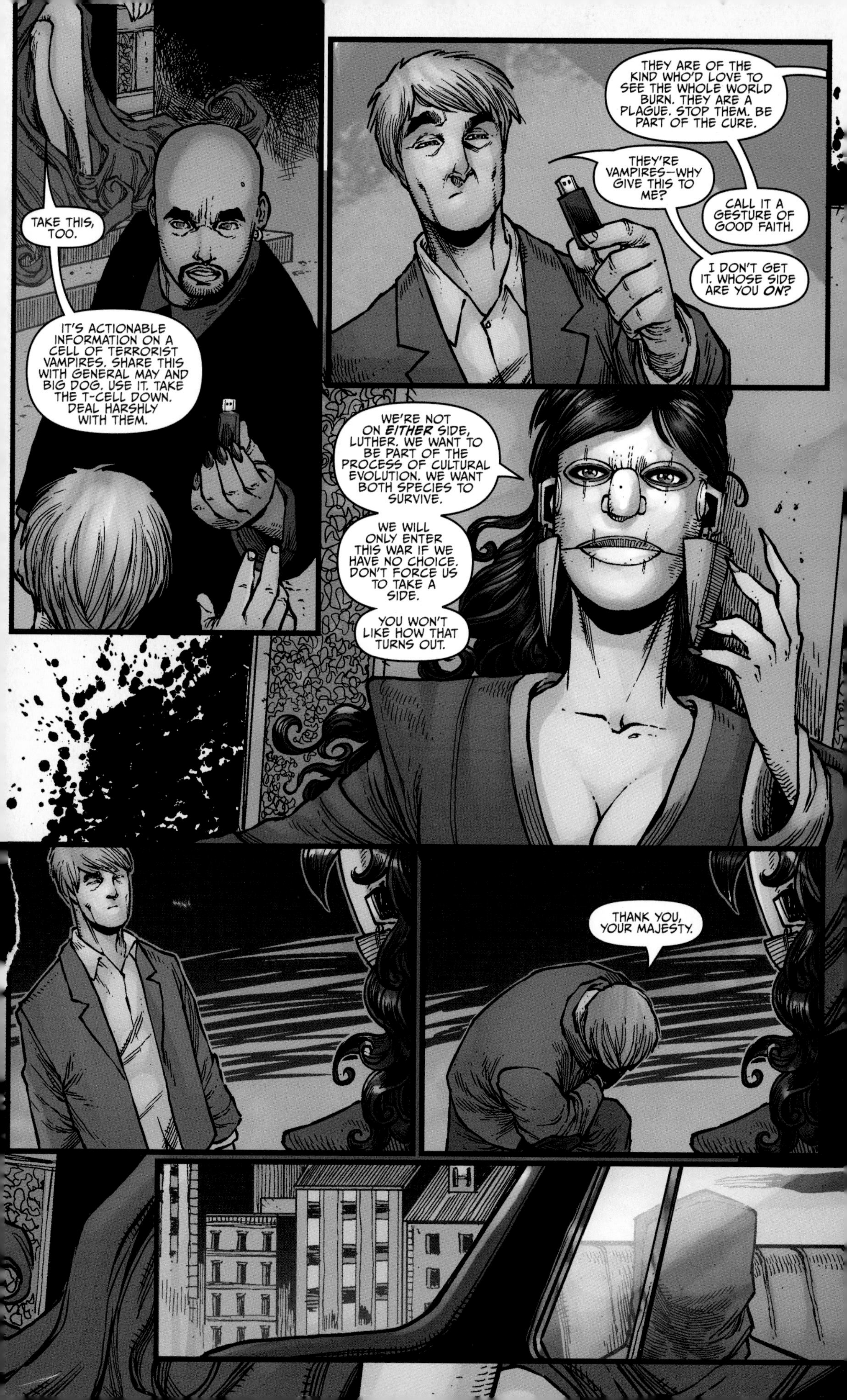
TAKE THIS, TOO.
IT'S ACTIONABLE INFORMATION ON A CELL OF TERRORIST VAMPIRES. SHARE THIS WITH GENERAL MAY AND BIG DOG. USE IT. TAKE THE T-CELL DOWN. DEAL HARSHLY WITH THEM.
THEY ARE OF THE KIND WHO'D LOVE TO SEE THE WHOLE WORLD BURN. THEY ARE A PLAGUE. STOP THEM. BE PART OF THE CURE.
THEY'RE VAMPIRES—WHY GIVE THIS TO ME?
CALL IT A GESTURE OF GOOD FAITH.
I DON'T GET IT. WHOSE SIDE ARE YOU *ON*?
WE'RE NOT ON ***EITHER*** SIDE, LUTHER. WE WANT TO BE PART OF THE PROCESS OF CULTURAL EVOLUTION. WE WANT BOTH SPECIES TO SURVIVE.
WE WILL ONLY ENTER THIS WAR IF WE HAVE NO CHOICE. DON'T FORCE US TO TAKE A SIDE.
YOU WON'T LIKE HOW THAT TURNS OUT.
THANK YOU, YOUR MAJESTY.

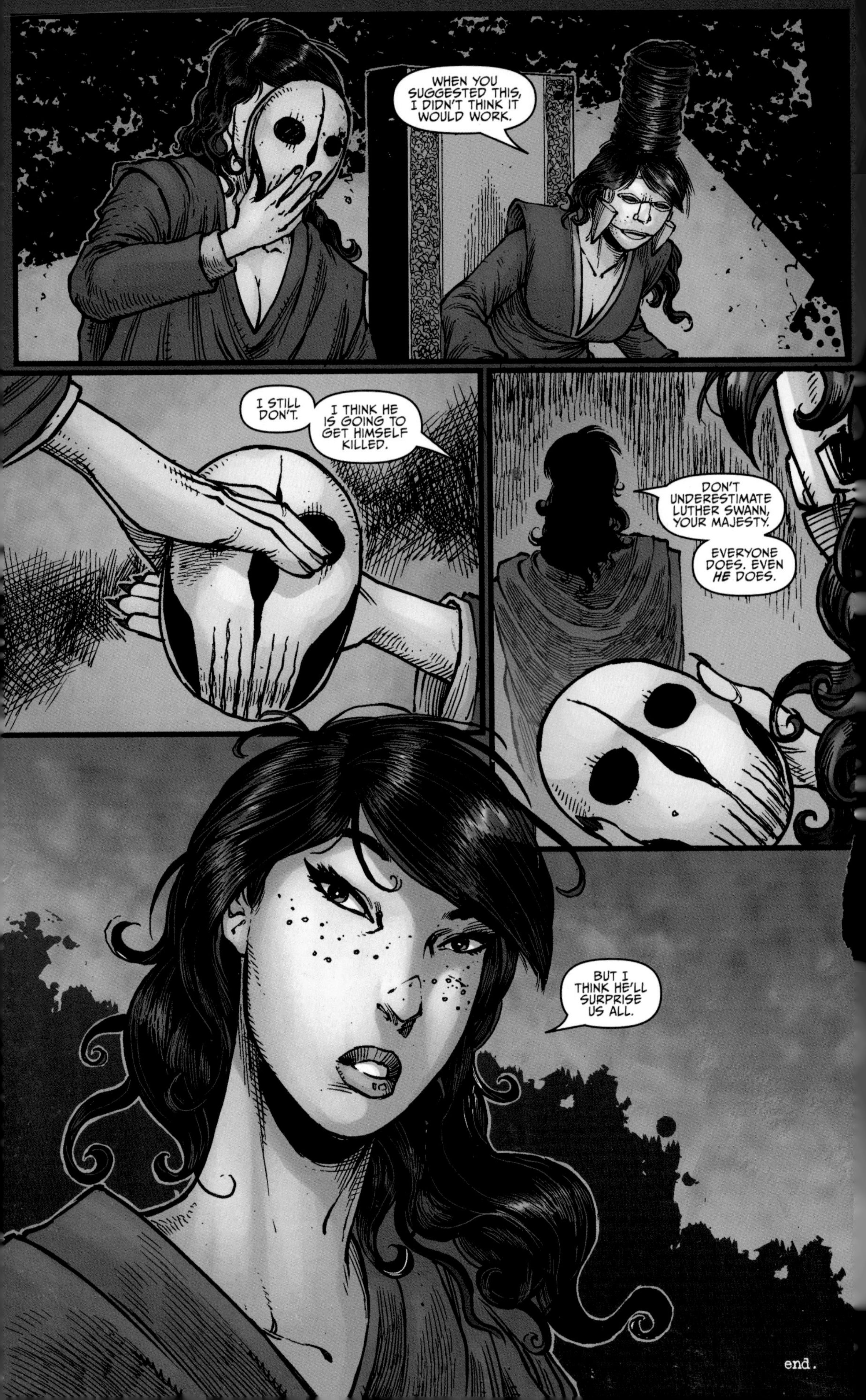
WHEN YOU SUGGESTED THIS, I DIDN'T THINK IT WOULD WORK.
I STILL DON'T.
I THINK HE IS GOING TO GET HIMSELF KILLED.
DON'T UNDERESTIMATE LUTHER SWANN, YOUR MAJESTY.
EVERYONE DOES. EVEN HE DOES.
BUT I THINK HE'LL SURPRISE US ALL.
end.